WRECKING CREW

DEMOLISHING THE CASE AGAINST STEVEN AVERY

JOHN FERAK

WILDBLUE
PRESS

WildBluePress.com

WRECKING CREW published by:

WILDBLUE PRESS
P.O. Box 102440
Denver, Colorado 80250

Publisher Disclaimer: Any opinions, statements of fact or fiction, descriptions, dialogue, and citations found in this book were provided by the author, and are solely those of the author. The publisher makes no claim as to their veracity or accuracy, and assumes no liability for the content.

Copyright 2018 by John Ferak

All rights reserved. No part of this book may be reproduced in any form or by any means without the prior written consent of the Publisher, excepting brief quotes used in reviews.

WILDBLUE PRESS is registered at the U.S. Patent and Trademark Offices.

ISBN 978-1-947290-98-3   Trade Paperback
ISBN 978-1-947290-97-6   eBook

Interior Formatting/Book Cover Design by Elijah Toten
www.totencreative.com

WRECKING CREW

OTHER WILDBLUE PRESS BOOKS BY JOHN FERAK

FAILURE OF JUSTICE: *A Brutal Murder, An Obsessed Cop, Six Wrongful Convictions*
http://wbp.bz/foja

DIXIE'S LAST STAND: *Was It Murder Or Self-Defense?*
http://wbp.bz/dixiea

BODY OF PROOF: *Tainted Evidence In The Murder Of Jessica O'Grady*
http://wbp.bz/bopa

TABLE OF CONTENTS

INTRODUCTION

When a Midwest farm girl named Teresa Halbach went off to college in Green Bay, Wisconsin, she found her calling holding the camera. A short distance from Lambeau Field, she started making money as a part-time photographer at Green Bay's west side shopping mall.

To her family, Teresa Halbach was the happy-go-lucky aspiring photographer. She took photographs at weddings and also snapped children's photos.

But after graduating college, Teresa started dabbling in more risky, provocative photography. She had a wild and crazy side. Future employment prospects with X-rated magazines such as Hustler and Penthouse were not out of the question.

"I gave my permission to Miss Halbach on a number of occasions to use my photography studio for nude portraits of her clients. In fact, a portion of my own business was taking nude photographs of my clients," reflected Tom Pearce, owner of Pearce Photography.(1)

During Teresa's last year of life, she was sucked into some of the darkest corners of the web. Her business, "Photography by Teresa," was out hustling for new sexually explicit photography clients, people who needed someone to capture them in more daring and provocative poses.

"Photography by Teresa is Adult Entertainment Products and Services, Photography, Portrait Photography, Professional Photography, Special Occasion Photography,

---

1. Affidavit of Thomas E. Pearce; April 21, 2017. All quotes from Pearce in this book are from affidavit.

Visual Arts Company. Get in touch with Photography by Teresa with contact details …" (2)

Many years after his understudy's untimely and gruesome death, Pearce was asked to review Teresa's business profile advertising her adult-oriented photography services.

"Based upon my personal knowledge of Ms. Halbach's business (that) is an accurate depiction of the services offered by Ms. Halbach in the regular course of her business," Pearce said.

Besides her nude photography business, Halbach also hit the backroads for Auto Trader Magazine. She snapped photos of cars, trucks, and vans that people desired to sell. This work was concentrated around the Green Bay area, including Sheboygan and Manitowoc Counties to the south. With Auto Trader, a number of the men she encountered found she had sex appeal. They were attracted to her small frame and wanted to experience her wild side.

"In March 2005, Ms. Halbach told me that a male Auto Trader client made sexual advances toward her and invited her into his residence," Pearce recalls. "Teresa told me that this advance made her feel uncomfortable. After this incident, Ms. Halbach did not mention any problems with Auto Trader clients. Specifically Ms. Halbach never expressed concern about going to the Avery property."

Yet before she disappeared, on Halloween 2005, Halbach had reason to be apprehensive.

Her life was in grave danger.

"I was aware that Ms. Halbach was getting phone calls from someone who was harassing her," Pearce said.

At the same time, a messy divorce case at the Brown County Courthouse in downtown Green Bay was also preoccupying her time.

A husband and wife who lived near Green Bay had used her nude photography services at her Green Bay studio on

---

2. Exhibit from Affidavit with Pearce

Western Avenue. But when the couple's rocky marriage crumbled, Teresa began a romantic relationship with the man, who was almost a decade older than her. He ran a wedding disc jockey service and worked for a Green Bay television station.

"Teresa had taken nude photographs of Bradley and his wife ... after this, Bradley and his wife had broken up and Teresa started dating Bradley. Teresa and Bradley would only have sex, and Teresa did not have any feelings for him and it was only physical. Bradley and his wife were having problems at one time and he would confide in Teresa about his problems."(3)

On the day before she died, Teresa exchanged emails with a supportive friend who encouraged her efforts to grow her adult-oriented photography business.

"Hey Teresa, It was great to hear about your busy life! Sounds like so many things have changed for you in the last year. I'm so happy to hear that business is good. It sounds like you have many hobbies and things going on. It's great! I'm envious and wish I could make the time for that. ... I wouldn't have imagined Adrianne asking you to take nude photos of her. That's cool though that she is comfortable enough. Maybe we could pass your name around for porn shots."(4)

Five weeks earlier, a guy named Ken sent an email to Teresa's photography business thanking her for the letter and package she sent him. "AND the package, well, I think you take better care of me than my mother does, well, I think that's a good thing ... I wouldn't want my mom sending me a porn. I really appreciate everything and damn it I really want to talk with you ... I really miss you and REALLY thank you for sending me messages to my beeper ... I should

---

3. Investigator Mark Wiegert interview of Jolene Bain, Nov. 4, 2005

4. Exhibit 56 Correspondence regarding nude photography

be back online on Monday, hopefully we can talk. I miss you and thank you very much for the goodies. I'll let you know the results! Bye, Ken."

By November 4, 2005, four days after Teresa visited Avery Road in Manitowoc County for a scheduled photo assignment, the Calumet County Sheriff's Office opened a trunk inside her bedroom. She had recently moved into the two-story house on her family's dairy farm, near the town of Hilbert, population 1,100.

"I did locate in a trunk directly next to Teresa's bed several nude photos of a male and a female. Included with these photos were several negatives. There was a portrait order from Pearce Photography which had the name Bradley and Kaycee Czech." (5)

At that point, nobody knew whether these nude photos of the divorced couple were at the heart of her disappearance. The woman had taken out an emergency protection order to keep her ex-husband away from her and out of her life. The photographs recovered from Teresa's bedroom were a focal part of the bitter divorce case. Given Teresa's disappearance, the police would attempt to learn more about Teresa's sexual intimacy with the Green Bay disc jockey.

"By the end Teresa was pretty much leading a double life," Czech said. (6)

5.   Wiegert's activity report for Nov. 4, 2005
6.   Bradley Czech interview with private investigator Jim Kirby

CHAPTER ONE

TURNABOUT

Green Bay's television stations led off their newscasts with a chilling mystery on Thursday night, November 3, 2005. A fiercely independent, happy-go-lucky young woman from the heart of dairy country was gone. No one had seen or heard from her during the past four days. Television anchors painted a grim outlook as photos of Teresa Halbach flashed across the screen. Viewers were left uneasy and fearful of a worst-case scenario. Surely someone watching the distressing news would remember encountering Teresa over the past few days. At least, that's what the small-town Calumet County Sheriff's Office in Chilton, Wisconsin hoped.

But it was not Teresa's face displayed on the television screen that drew a red flag with one of the Manitowoc County residents. It was the image of her missing sports utility vehicle, a Toyota RAV 4.

During that time frame, Kevin Rahmlow lived around Mishicot, a small but proud Wisconsin town of 1,400 people of German, Swiss, and Bohemian heritage. Back in the day, Mishicot had six hotels, three general stores, a movie theater, a grist mill, and a brewery. By 2005, the community's three original churches still stood the test of time but Mishicot looked different. The town's gas station, owned by Cenex, was one of the local hangouts. People came there for fuel, a cup of coffee, and to buy their cigarettes. The popular business was at the corner of State Highway 147 and State Street.

Kevin Rahmlow vividly remembers when he pulled into the Cenex. It was Friday, November 4. Inside the convenience store, the missing person's poster caught his eye. Teresa Marie Halbach, the flier noted, was 5-foot-6, 135 pounds. Brown eyes and light brown hair. (7)

"I remember that the poster had a picture of Teresa Halbach and written descriptions of Teresa Halbach and the car she was driving," Rahmlow said.

As it turned out, Cenex was one of many small-town businesses, bars, and cafes where Teresa's concerned friends and family slapped up posters. They were desperate for answers, hoping somebody, anybody, remembered a sighting. And if the locals didn't see Teresa, perhaps they saw her Toyota RAV4. It had a large Lemieux Toyota sign on the back of her vehicle where the spare tire hung.

When Rahmlow saw the poster, he remembered something.

"On November 3 and 4, 2005, I was in Mishicot. I saw Teresa Halbach's vehicle by the East Twin River dam in Mishicot at the turnabout by the bridge as I drove west of Highway 147. I recognized that the written description of the vehicle on the poster matched the car I saw at the turnaround by the dam."

That Friday afternoon, Rahmlow happened to spot a man in a brown uniform. The man was sporting a badge. "While I was in the Cenex station, a Manitowoc County Sheriff's Department officer came into the station. I immediately told the officer that I had seen a car that matched the description of the car on Teresa Halbach's missing person poster at the turnaround by the dam."

After speaking with the uniformed deputy, Rahmlow went on with his life.

He had no idea whatever became of the matter. He later moved to another Midwest state. He even missed the initial

---

7. July 15, 2017 affidavit of Kevin Rahmlow

Making a Murderer craze on Netflix that captured world-wide attention.

When Kevin Rahmlow saw this flyer at the Cenex gas station in Mishicot, it triggered his memory surrounding Teresa Halbach's disappearance.

***

In December 2015, a true crime documentary about the Steven Avery murder case was released on Netflix, but Rahmlow didn't get swept up in the media frenzy. An entire year passed before he finally turned on Netflix to watch it. And as he watched *Making a Murderer*, the Minnesota man had a flashback. He remembered his encounter at the gas station in Mishicot from more than a decade ago. And besides being familiar with Manitowoc County, Rahmlow knew some of the key people who worked hand in hand with special prosecutor Ken Kratz to cement the guilt of Steven Avery. Avery, as the world now knows, was a previously wrongfully convicted man who lost eighteen years due to a barbaric daytime rape along the Lake Michigan shoreline during the summer of 1985. This was the crime that allowed dangerous sexual predator Gregory Allen to get away by the forces who ran the Manitowoc County Sheriff's Office, notably Sheriff Tom Kocourek, who was about forty years old at the time.

Fast-forward to 2007. Avery stood trial in Chilton for Teresa's murder even though the prosecution's evidence was like a piece of Swiss cheese. And yet despite his side's many holes, Ken Kratz overcame his murder case's numerous physical evidence shortcomings thanks to the unbelievable eyewitness testimonies from a number of unscrupulous people who very much had a stake, a big stake, in the desired outcome of an Avery guilty verdict.

December 12, 2016

Two weeks before Christmas, Rahmlow sent a text message to someone he recognized from *Making a Murderer*. By then, Scott Tadych was happily married to Steven Avery's younger sister, Barb. At the time of Teresa's disappearance, Barb Janda lived in one of the trailers at the Avery Salvage Yard compound, a forty-acre tract out in the middle of nowhere surrounded by large gravel pits. At the time of Teresa's disappearance, Barb and Scott Tadych were steady lovers and she was in the process of getting another divorce, this time from Tom Janda.

After watching *Making a Murderer*, Rahmlow informed his old acquaintance how "I need to get in touch with one of their lawyers."

Rahmlow explained in his text message to Scott Tadych how he recognized Teresa's vehicle as the one he saw by the old dam, either November 3 or 4. He also remembered having a conversation with a man whose face regularly appeared during the *Making a Murderer* episodes.

Scott Tadych did not respond.

Rahmlow reached out again, ninety minutes later. The second time, he texted his phone number to Tadych. He wanted to discuss the matter over the phone.

"OK, I will I am really sick now can hardly talk so I will call tomorrow," Tadych texted back.

But Tadych never did call back.

"I did not hear from Mr. Tadych the next day or any other day responsive to my request for attorney contact information for Steven Avery or Brendan Dassey," Rahmlow said. "I received another message from Mr. Tadych on December 19 (2016) at 6:10 p.m., which was not responsive to my request."

There is no doubt in his mind that Rahmlow saw Teresa's RAV4 along the rural stretch of two-lane State Highway 147 near the East Twin River Dam. The turnaround on the highway was barely a mile from Avery Salvage.

A licensed private investigator in Illinois and Wisconsin, James R. Kirby was hired by Kathleen T. Zellner & Associates to investigate Teresa's murder case.

"I requested abandoned and towed vehicle reports for the time period of October 31, 2005 through November 5, 2005, from the following agencies: Mishicot Police Department, Two Rivers Police Department, and the Manitowoc County Sheriff's Department," Kirby said. (8)

This, of course, was the period when Teresa was last seen in Manitowoc County, near Mishicot. On a Saturday morning six days later, under highly suspicious circumstances, her Toyota RAV4 turned up, double parked, on the far back ridge of Avery Salvage, near a row of junked vehicles. The spot of the find bordered the massive sand and gravel pit operated by Joshua Radandt.

The question lingered. Who moved Teresa's SUV to the far outer edge of Avery Salvage? Was it the killer working alone? Was it the killer working in tandem with an accomplice? Or was it somebody affiliated with the volunteer search party? Or was it one of the Manitowoc County Sheriff's deputies?

Incidentally, at the time of her disappearance, Teresa's RAV4 had no front-end damage. This small but critical detail is substantiated by the fact that the missing person fliers made no mention of any broken auto parts or wreckage. But when her sports utility vehicle surfaced on the Avery property, it showed heavy front-end damage. Weirdly, the broken blinker light from the driver's side was neatly tucked away into the rear cargo area of the murdered woman's auto. Why would the killer do something so strange? Of course, the logical scenario was that the killer had nothing to do with moving the vehicle to Avery's property, and that the mishap occurred, late at night, during the clandestine efforts to sneak the vehicle onto the Avery property without Avery or his family members catching on.

In any event, private eye Kirby's inquiry into the RAV4 spotted by Rahmlow on Friday afternoon, November 4, 2005, revealed the "Mishicot Police Department had no responsive records. Based upon the response of Two Rivers

---

8. Supplemental affidavit of James Kirby, Oct. 20, 2017

Police Department and Manitowoc County Sheriff's Office pursuant to my request, none of these agencies logged an abandoned vehicle on Highway 147 near the East Twin River Bridge."

Obviously, one of the most plausible scenarios for why the police did not log the abandoned vehicle spotted near the Old Dam on Highway 147 in rural Manitowoc County, which was Manitowoc County Sheriff's territory, was because the auto belonged to Teresa, and it got moved as a direct result of Manitowoc County's intercession.

CHAPTER TWO

BOBBY DEPARTS

The four Dassey brothers were: Bryan, twenty, Bobby, nineteen, Blaine, almost seventeen, and Brendan, sixteen. As mentioned earlier, the Dasseys occupied one of the mobile home trailers along Avery Road at their family's Avery Salvage Yard compound. Bryan, the oldest brother, worked in nearby Two Rivers at Woodland Face Veneer, a factory overlooking the scenic Lake Michigan.

Regarding the day in question, Oct. 31, 2005, Bryan Dassey told Wisconsin's Division of Criminal Investigation special agents Kim Skorlinski and Debra K. Strauss that he left for his job at 6 a.m. and visited his girlfriend afterward. He was not on Avery Road "except for waking up and going to work. Bryan said he got home sometime after supper but could not recall when that was." (9)

Eventually, the questions steered toward the missing photographer. She had been a regular visitor to the Avery Salvage Yard during the past year without any problems or hassles, unlike at some of her other unnerving Auto Trader assignments where men tried to proposition her or invite her inside their homes for an alcoholic beverage. Whenever Teresa visited Avery Road, she was given courtesy and respect.

"Bryan said he heard from his mom and Steven that Halbach was only at their residence about five minutes. He heard she just took the photo of the van and left. Bryan

---

9. DOJ report of Bryan Dassey interview.

said the investigators should also talk to his brother Bobby because he saw her leave their property."

At Avery's five-week murder trial in 2007, prosecutor Ken Kratz chose to keep Bryan Dassey off his side's witness stand. Therefore, the jury deciding Steven Avery's fate never heard the following account:

"In October and November 2005, I lived with my girlfriend but I kept my clothing at my mother's trailer, which was on the Avery's Auto Salvage property. On or about (Thursday) November 4, 2005, I returned to my mother's trailer to retrieve some clothes, and I had a conversation with my brother, Bobby, about Teresa Halbach. I distinctly remember Bobby telling me, 'Steven could not have killed her because I saw her leave the property on October 31, 2005." (10)

Bryan Dassey's October 2017 sworn affidavit recalled how he was pulled over by police on November 6, 2005. He was behind the wheel of his uncle Steven Avery's Pontiac.

"My brother Brendan was in the car with me, and he was interviewed by other officers at the same time as me. I told the investigators that they should talk to my brother Bobby because he saw Teresa Halbach leave the Avery property on October 31, 2005.

"I was not called as a witness to testify at my Uncle Steven's criminal trial."

***

Most of the world who watched *Making a Murderer* fell in love with Steven Avery's private counsel, Dean Strang and Jerome Buting. The two criminal defense lawyers worked closely together, putting forth a heroic defense for

---

10. Exhibit G, Bryan J. Dassey affidavit, dated Oct. 16, 2017

their client at his murder trial, but even they now admit that, in retrospect, they overlooked some things along the way.

They had hired Conrad "Pete" Baetz, a retired police detective, as their investigator in preparation for trial. Baetz had moved back to his native Manitowoc County after his retirement in downstate Illinois. He had spent many years at the Madison County Sheriff's Office near St. Louis. (11)

"I have reviewed the police report of the November 6, 2005, interview of Bryan Dassey where he said that Bobby Dassey saw Teresa Halbach leave the Avery property on October 31, 2005. I was unaware of this report. I never tried to interview Bryan Dassey about Bobby Dassey's alleged statement. I was never instructed by trial defense counsel Buting and Strang to interview Bryan Dassey," Baetz said.

"Bobby Dassey was the key prosecution witness at Steven Avery's trial who testified that he saw Ms. Halbach walk towards Mr. Avery's trailer after taking photographs of his mother Barb Janda's van. Bobby also testified that when he left the Avery Salvage Yard, Ms. Halbach's vehicle was still on the property."

In hindsight, Baetz realized that the statement had major significance.

"If the trial defense counsel could have impeached Bobby Dassey with Bryan Dassey's testimony that Bobby admitted he saw Ms. Halbach leave the Avery Salvage Yard, it would have undermined the State's entire case against Mr. Avery, and there would have been a reasonable probability of him being found not guilty."

***

One week after the horrifying news of Teresa's disappearance, two key developments occurred. First,

11. Exhibit H, Affidavit of Conrad "Pete" Baetz, dated Oct. 18, 2017

c.
Da
evide
search
cratches,

ned the
de note,
sentence
in penal
become

tigators
ency to
vember
murder.

among
quietly
igation
plode.
's civil

out to
ga at
back
nside
ered.
when
veral
two

ss of
rder
the

was perhaps the second to last person to
s taken into custody and jailed for her
one event set the wheels in motion for
s $36 million federal civil rights lawsuit
ounty whose insurance company had
y coverage of the civil rights lawsuit
ation the misconduct on the part of
ounty Sheriff Tom Kocourek and
was intentional, not just negligence
her county officials. The insurance
rage served to greatly increase the
al defendants who were named in
they could have been bankrupted
ard in the high-profile wrongful

ar-old Bobby Dassey, who may be
er saw, was confronted by Wisconsin
November 9, 2005, a Wednesday

arrest. You understand that," said
dle-aged, bald detective for the rural
iff's Office. "This isn't an arrest. But
to you so we get our blood, our swabs
ch. Okay?"
earch warrant for Bobby Dassey, who
ounds, brown hair and blue eyes. At the
the other police officers trying to find
w that Bobby Dassey was an awkward
ual deviant who had recurring sexual-
nvolving bestiality, mutilating naked
d drownings. Bobby's obsessions were
m the police and the special prosecutor
er probe. Obviously, Bobby was not about
deviant information when he sat down for
-face police interview regarding the events

At any rate, the search warrant gave these investigators permission to get Bobby's DNA in saliva and blood sample. Additionally, "Bobby A. ordered to provide a forefinger and thumb print The physical person of Bobby A. Dassey shall be and documented including but not limited to bruises, and bite marks."

Manitowoc County Judge Jerome Fox si order on November 7, 2005, at 7:08 p.m. On a s Fox's legacy in the case would be his decision to Brendan Dassey to remain incarcerated at a Wiscons institution until at least 2048, when he will first eligible for parole.

It's unclear why Dedering and the other inve chose to drag their heels and not move with exped obtain Bobby's DNA samples on the night of No 7, 2005. After all, this was an open and unsolved Nobody was arrested yet.

Of course, there may have been some discussions the Manitowoc County Sheriff's officials who were calling the shots and directing the Avery invest because they wanted Avery's $36 million lawsuit to im Their professional livelihoods were at stake if Avery suit was a success.

Sure enough, the next day, November 8, turned the most fortuitous day of the continuing murder s Avery Salvage. That Tuesday morning, the front and license plates to Teresa's RAV4 suddenly appeared an abandoned station wagon that had its windows shat It was an easy place to plant evidence, especially you consider that the station wagon was one of the se thousand wrecked cars that were searched by the police days earlier, on Sunday, November 6.

But that initial police and volunteer firefighter canva the entire Avery salvage yard harvested no damning mu clues. No legitimate reason was given to explain why authorities, at the recommendation of dubious Calumet County Detective Mark Wiegert, were summoned again, two days later, to search the same junked cars shortly after the crack of dawn.

Nov. 8, 2005, was also the same morning when the Manitowoc County Sheriff's Office's crackerjack evidence collection team of Detective James Lenk and Andy Colborn were back at Avery's. As far as they wanted the public to know, they had reached the conclusion that they just had not done a thorough enough of a job during their previous several days of constantly searching through Steven Avery's tiny bedroom and his book cabinet dresser for physical evidence. This time, this Tuesday morning, they were certain that disturbing clues fingering Avery for Teresa's murder were still being concealed inside their murder suspect's bedroom. Colborn maintained that he shook the wooden magazine cabinet near Avery's bed that contained all of Avery's Playboys. Then, out of nowhere a single key, a spare key, shot out of the cabinet at an angle. The spare key landed softly on the blue carpet where the sharp-eyed Detective Lenk walked back into Avery's bedroom and exclaimed, "There's a key on the floor."

That afternoon, another Manitowoc County Sheriff's deputy, Sgt. Jason Jost, happened to be aimlessly wandering around the Avery property. Jost wrote in his reports that he had a suspicion from walking outside that perhaps some of Teresa's bones were here on the property waiting to be found. And Jost was right. He supposedly found a couple of large charred bones out in the grass in Steven Avery's backyard. Because the charred bones were not symmetrical, this raised questions about their baffling discovery. On top of that, the Manitowoc County Sheriff's Office chose not to capture any photographs or make any videotapes showing the condition and location of these human bones being recovered near Avery's burn pit. Instead, the authorities took photos of other things such as dried leaves and other debris used to ignite a bonfire.

In sum, the recovery of the spare key, the bent up license plates, and the backyard bones helped the Manitowoc County Sheriff's Office finally get even with their bitter enemy. Equally important, Steven Avery's arrest signified to Bobby Dassey that he was essentially off the hook as the prime suspect. He could breathe a sigh of relief, a deep sigh.

At the time of Teresa's disappearance, Bobby was proficient at dismembering the carcasses of wild animals, unlike Steven Avery, who didn't have much of an interest in hunting. And unlike most of Manitowoc County, Bobby was developing an appetite for devouring the flesh of road kill. Bobby claimed he came across a deer carcass on one of the roads near his house in the aftermath of Teresa's disappearance. Bobby claimed he grabbed the deer off the road and hauled it back to his family's garage to slice it up. How many nineteen-year-olds do you know who cruise around their gravel roads and side roads looking for dead deer to scoop up and take home for grub? And why all of a sudden during the first week of November, just days after Teresa vanished?

During a subsequent interview with police, Bryan Dassey, the oldest of the Dassey boys, was asked by the detectives "if he could remember anything strange that had stuck out in his mind during that time after Halloween." He said the incident "when Bobby had hung the deer in his mom's garage."

But back in November 2005, nobody was giving serious thought to the scenario that the deer carcass was a crafty ruse, a cunning way to mask the blood spatter and other evidence that may have pointed to Bobby instead of his always unlucky uncle.

Here were some of the key facts about Teresa's disappearance:

She vanished on a Monday afternoon after being on Avery Road.

In the wake of her disappearance, Bobby is on record as having been busy carving up and dismembering animals.

Teresa's incinerated bones actually turned up inside a burn barrel from Bobby's yard, a steel drum barrel that also included a mixture of animal bones.

One would think that an astute detective investigating a young woman's apparent murder would have a natural curiosity about such a coincidence.

"How long had you been hanging the deer, Bobby?" Dedering asked. (12)

"Since Friday night," Bobby answered, referring to November 4.

"Who hit the deer, you know?"

"No."

Bobby suggested he found the deer "right up the road."

"OK again, who claimed the deer?"

"I did. I trussed and hung it up that Saturday."

"Who skinned it?"

"I did."

After asking what Bobby did with the deer skin, Dedering, the bumbling detective from Calumet County, blurted out, "shows how much I've been in your garage, doesn't it?"

At that moment, Dedering's interview partner, Wisconsin DCI Special Agent Kevin Heimerl, made an observation.

"It sounds to me like you've skinned and butchered your own deer before?"

"Yeah," Bobby agreed.

"What would you normally do with the hide then?"

"We took them into town."

"Oh, OK."

---

12. Bobby Dassey Nov. 9, 2005 interview with John Dedering and Kevin Heimerl.

Then Dedering wondered if the local butcher shop accepted deer heads.

"No. We just burn them," Bobby answered. "Over in the burning barrel."

At that point, Dedering admitted he wasn't familiar with Bobby's yard even though it was just a short walking distance from Steven Avery's trailer.

"In the burning barrels?" Dedering wondered.

"Uh-huh," Bobby agreed.

The conversation shifted back to Avery's skills as a hunter and rugged outdoorsman.

"He doesn't hunt that much," Bobby replied.

When Heimerl asked whether the deer's head still existed, Bobby responded by saying that the head was still right side of his mother's garage.

"So which burn barrel do you guys normally burn the heads up?" Dedering asked.

"Uh, ours. This is the first one that we actually got our family … the other one we took in to the butcher."

"Describe to me again, Bobby, where you hunt?" Dedering inquired. "How far is that from your house?"

His hunting spot was about two-and-a-half miles from home, he responded.

Dedering wondered whether Bobby knew the land owner in northern Manitowoc County.

"I don't know."

"But you know, what's his name, Scott Tadych?"

"Tadych," Bobby answered.

Bobby was asked if he and Tadych, the soon-to-be husband of Bobby's mother, hunted together.

"No. That's the first day actually that I hunted."

Now that Bobby's uncle was in custody, Dedering and Heimerl had a strong desire for Bobby to validate their murder theory. It was important for the reputation of Manitowoc County's tarnished sheriff's office to prove

Avery was a cruel diabolical killer who belonged in prison for the rest of his time on earth.

Ever a shifty detective, Dedering decided the best way to solicit Bobby's help in implicating Avery was to drive a wedge between Bobby and his uncle.

"Steve seems to think that he wasn't the last person to see (Teresa) but that you had. He says that you were the last person."

"No," Bobby answered.

"That you followed her out of the driveway."

"No. Her vehicle was there."

"Is that an absolute truth?"

"Absolute truth."

Bear in mind Dedering never seriously considered the young man sitting across from him in the interview as the more likely killer.

At the time of their interview, Dedering did not have a clue about Bobby's deviant sexual side. He knew nothing about Bobby's sadistic appetite for naked, drowned women and mutilated bodies. As a result, Dedering remained singularly focused that November afternoon. He needed to make Bobby mad, raging mad, at his uncle.

"I remember that we talked about why Steve would try to jam you up like that. Why?"

"That's a good point," Bobby agreed. "That's the kind of person he is."

"How does that sit with you?"

"It makes me angry."

"We're getting to the point where we're going to know everything. OK? You understand that we are going to know everything pretty shortly. Now, my concern is this, Bobby, that if you haven't been one hundred percent honest and truthful with me to this point, it's because of two reasons. One is that you're afraid something bad is going to happen to you and your family if you aren't, if you cooperate with the cops … What would be the other reason for you not telling me the truth? Well, I'll tell you, it would be because maybe you had some involvement with it. And like I said, you're shaking your head no, OK?"

Dedering asked if anybody told Bobby how to answer his interview questions with police.

"No.'"

"Nobody?"

"No."

"Your mom hasn't had any contact with you about this? You haven't sat down and had a family discussion about how all this should play out when that bald-headed, old buzzard starts hanging around and asking questions?"

"Nope."

"Nothing?"

"Nope."

Dedering wanted to believe Bobby had no role in Teresa's brutal killing.

"I'm kind of buying into the fact, and like I told you when I talked with you on Saturday, did I tell you that I thought I pretty much believed you then? I still think that pretty much too. OK?"

Still, Dedering wanted to know why Avery "would want to put you in a box? Why would he want to jam you up for?"

"Well, he don't want to go back," Bobby responded.

"You just said something. Something you might be on to," Dedering pondered. "You know maybe, you think maybe, he did this because he doesn't want to go back?"

"Yeah. I know as much as you do," Bobby replied. "You know more than I do. You guys know a lot more than I do."

"Yeah, but you know what you have that we don't have? You got family intuition, man."

"Yeah."

"So what's your gut telling you?"

"Steven's playing his hand."

"Who do you think did it?"

"I dunno."

"You don't know?"

"What I told you guys is all I know about it."

"So if you were a betting man, I'd bet that you didn't do it. Would you bet like that?"

"Yeah," Bobby wisely agreed.

CHAPTER THREE

ALIBI

After investing close to three years of her life reinvestigating Teresa's death, sinking hundreds of thousands of dollars of her law firm's own money into Steven Avery's post-conviction defense, world-famous exoneration lawyer Kathleen Zellner now believes the murder time sequence outlined by special prosecutor Ken Kratz was demonstrably false. According to Zellner, the cellular tower pings off Teresa's cell phone reveal the Auto Trader photographer left Avery's around 2:35 p.m. on Halloween 2005.

From there, Teresa retraced her route of travel from Avery Road. Teresa would have turned left on State Highway 147, traveling for a mile. When she got to the intersection of County Road Q, Teresa headed south. Then she met her disaster shortly afterward, probably along the seldom-traveled Kuss Road, a spooky dead-end road covered by a dense swath of woodlands along both sides of the road. The area's general terrain includes a patch of large sand and gravel quarries along County Road Q, including one enormous quarry that has been around for years, a parcel owned by Manitowoc County Government.

On the day of Avery's arrest, investigators Dedering and Heimerl peppered Bobby with questions about his own movements on the day Teresa met foul play.

"Now, I want to know again about when you left that day," Dedering inquired. "You remember about what time that was?"

"Right around 3 o'clock."

"Did you see anyone when you were leaving the driveway?"

"When I left?"

"Yes."

"No. I didn't see no one coming up the driveway."

"Were there any cars in the driveway?"

"Yeah. It's a little SUV."

"Now, you told me that you were nowhere near that teal colored SUV."

"Nope."

"Never?"

"Nope."

"Never there?"

"Never there."

"Never touched it?"

"Nope."

"Did you go anywhere that night after you got home from your hunting?"

"No."

"You stayed home?"

"Went to work."

Bobby worked at Fisher Hamilton in Manitowoc, a metal processing plant in town.

He told the police he left for work at 9:30 p.m., which is seven hours after Bobby was discretely eyeing Teresa from inside his trailer window.

"So what did you do when you were at home?"

"Napped ... I came right home after hunting."

Suddenly, the interview took a change of direction.

Dedering wanted to boast about his credentials.

"I've been in law enforcement for almost thirty years, and I've done more than an interview or two. OK? ... And what works for me is that, I'll be honest and then I find that usually people are honest in return, OK? I'm going to tell you something. OK? I can tell you that nobody from any sheriff's department planted any evidence anywhere. And that vehicle was found because we thought this through and we figured that something like this could happen ... we made sure that no Manitowoc city or county cop was on the property without another agency right alongside them so that anything that might be falling could be falling honestly."

Dedering wanted Bobby to understand his role investigating the homicide.

"Find the somebody that did something. I know you didn't. I'm pretty confident that you have no play in this. Am I right about that?"

Bobby mumbled something that couldn't be heard.

At that juncture, Kevin Heimerl bragged how he worked at the Wisconsin DCI, the same agency assigned in 2003, two years earlier, to review the Manitowoc County Sheriff's Office 1985 rape investigation spearheaded by Sheriff Kocourek, the one that put Steven Avery unjustly in prison for eighteen years for a violent rape committed by Gregory Allen.

"The Department of Justice, DCI. That's who I work for. We are here. We are in the middle of this thing, the same agency that would ask to review that first case. Those same cops, me and the guys I work with, the guys that are here, OK? Another thing I want to chew on ... people suggested that maybe, me and the people I'm working with, or any other cop like to make stuff up, twist stuff.

"I got it better. They rely on me. I got two kids that rely on me. You know what? There is no case more important to me. And I'm not going to jeopardize my family and my life for anybody and any investigation. OK?"

"That's where I am as well," Dedering added.

"Who is going put their career, because you know, you could be in insurance sales and do a rotten job at it and get fired," Heimerl reasoned. "You can get another job (in) insurance sales somewhere else. But you know, when a cop gets busted for lying, doing something illegal, they lose their job. They don't get another job. They don't get another cop job. OK?"

"OK," Bobby repeated.

"Because if we're not credible, we can't go into court," Heimerl maintained. "That's why. You can't be a cop, if we're not believed."

Dedering echoed those comments.

"Yeah, you know basically a cop whose word is worth nothing, isn't worth anything as a cop. You know. Because why go up on a stand, I swear to tell the truth and for the same reasons Kevin just insisted, I've got a family. I love my family. I need to have a few things to myself.

"You wouldn't lie or do anything illegal but your family comes first, doesn't it?"

"Yeah," Bobby agreed.

Transcripts of Bobby's police interviews show that almost all of his police interview answers were just one word answers.

Yet a bond was forming, between Bobby and the police. They wanted to use him to prosecute Avery. He could strengthen their case. For Bobby, the opportunity to help the police nail his uncle would solidify his purported alibi.

"Everybody else kind of takes a back seat," Dedering reminded Bobby. "You're not different than me. You're not different than Kevin. You're not different than any other cop. That's something that we all have in common. We all love our families. And we want to do the right thing for our families."

The temptation of planting evidence continued to come up.

But Bobby was not bringing up the topic. It was Dedering and Heimerl who kept dredging up the topic.

"It brings shame, humiliation, poverty, we wouldn't want anything like that," Dedering offered. "I'm not taking a chance … I'm fifty some years old. How old are you?"

"Nineteen."

"You can walk down the street. And if there's a job to be, young, healthy, you could work here. You know what? I'm starting to be a liability, health insurance reasons. ... I can't do things wrong because there's too much writing on it for me. You believe that?"

"Yeah."

"I'm sure that the family would love to and probably does believe that there is some sort of conspiracy. But I'm here to tell you something ... You know what? Imagine how many people, how many police officers it would take to orchestrate a conspiracy of this size?"

"Yeah."

"One person could not do it, all right?

"Yeah."

"Do you think two people could orchestrate a conspiracy of this size?

"No."

"OK. Now you're talking more than two dirty cops within one police agency. All the supervisor's eyes and everybody else; the neighboring sheriff's department and state's special agents, and everybody else, and crime lab personnel. You know, you can't fool forensics."

"Yeah."

Dedering brought up the old motorcycle gang saying of how three people can keep a secret if two are dead.

"OK, that means if you don't want somebody else to know anything, you can't involve anybody else because somebody's going to give something up."

Bobby was told he "can believe what you want with your family about the conspiracy ... I can't tell you what to think. OK? But I can tell you that we do have a lot of stuff. I don't understand why Steve would tell somebody something like he wasn't the last one to see her. You know, I don't understand that. What do you think about that?"

Bobby: "I don't understand how?"

"OK. Do you get along with Steve pretty well?"

"Sometimes."

"What was the last thing that caused you to not get along with him?"

Once again, Bobby mumbled something unclear.

Eventually, Dedering asked Bobby whether he dated.

"Do you see anybody?"

"No."

"You are going to break a lot of young ladies' hearts."

"I don't have a girlfriend."

"Ha. You probably will die as a rich man if you keep that attitude. OK?"

Given that a couple of charred human bones apparently did turn up near his uncle's burn pile pit, the next question made sense to ask.

But Dedering had no idea whether his witness was being truthful or deceitful because authorities did not obtain any foot impressions near Avery's burn pit. In effect, it was a wasted question.

"Is there any way or any reason you can think of why your footprints might be near Steve's fire pit or was it Steve's burn barrel?

"No."

"No way that they'd be there?"

"I've been all over the place. Not by the burn barrels and fire pit."

"I just wanted to make sure, OK? Because if something like that'd show up, I worry you'd disappoint me."

Heimerl interjected.

"Well, if something like that would show up. It should potentially disappoint Bobby."

"Yeah," Dedering agreed.

Bobby sat there in utter silence. He knew if he could just sweat out a few more minutes, his interview with these two cops would all be over.

"We got a room available to get your swab, fingerprints and all that, so I think it's time to do that now. It's 3:51 p.m. on my watch. You nervous?" Dedering inquired.

Bobby did not answer.

"That was an eye roll," Heimerl remarked. "Yes or no?"

"No," Bobby responded.

CHAPTER FOUR

ZELLNER FACTOR

Just four days before the twelve-year anniversary of Teresa's mysterious Manitowoc County murder, the condemned prisoner made a prepaid collect call from his permanent residence behind the walls of the Waupun Correctional Center. The simple man had gained the unwavering support of millions of men and women across the globe, people whose lives were forever touched by the Emmy-winning documentary.

But their lives have never intersected with the plight of Steven Avery, a man unjustly imprisoned and snatched from society for eighteen long years, starting in his early twenties. This same man, at age forty-three, was on the verge of collecting a multi-million dollar federal lawsuit settlement at the hands of law enforcement in Avery's native Manitowoc County. Suddenly, just days before he got to sit inside the law offices for the sworn deposition of the man responsible for his disastrous life, retired Manitowoc County Sheriff Tom Kocourek, Avery found himself ripped away from his mother and father, Dolores and Al, his brothers Chuck and Earl, and his sister, Barb. This time, unlike the last time, there was a major news media marketing campaign, long before any trial, to brand Avery a demon, a sicko, a pariah, the pond scum of the earth. The people involved in this effort included the likes of Manitowoc Sheriff Kenny Peterson, Undersheriff Rob Hermann, Manitowoc County Special Prosecutor Ken Kratz, Calumet Sheriff Jerry Pagel, Calumet

County Sheriff's Investigator Mark Wiegert and Special Agent Tom Fassbender, worked at the Wisconsin DCI.

All six liked-minded men, between their forties and sixties, were in complete agreement. Steven Avery was going to go down hard for Teresa's murder and everyone in Wisconsin would be assured that he was a bloodthirsty monster.

The Steven Avery-is-guilty pretrial publicity mantra was bigger than a tidal wave. It was a typhoon, a monsoon. At the end of the day, after a few days of back-and-forth jury deliberations, including questions surrounding the testimony of Kratz's leadoff witness, Bobby Dassey, Avery was tried and convicted of the first-degree murder, though many people still had lingering doubts, even after trial had ended. Indeed, Avery was one of the last persons to see Teresa, but most people now believe what Avery has always professed from the get-go, that he is innocent, that he had nothing to do with her killing. What motive did he have to harm the freelance photographer from Green Bay? Rational people, objective people, people who are deep critical thinkers, struggle to find the motive.

Of course, there is another nagging question weighing on the minds of many. If Avery did not murder Teresa, then who did? And why?

Since January 2016, Avery has had a tireless advocate who dropped into his life from Wisconsin's dreaded rival, Illinois. Lucky for him, the suburban Chicago woman out of Downers Grove happens to be regarded as one the country's foremost lawyers in exposing police corruption and prosecutorial misconduct. She has achieved a miraculous streak of overturning more than twenty wrongful convictions since the 1990s.

"In 23 years, Kathleen Zellner has righted more wrongful prosecutions than any private attorney in America. No private attorney in the United States has successfully won for the release of more innocent defendants," her website proclaims.

As of September 27, 2018, the United States had 2,270 exonerations.

Suburban Chicago lawyer Kathleen Zellner has achieved more exonerations of wrongfully convicted prisoners than any other lawyer in the country.

"My interest in this area of law resulted in being appointed on a death penalty case, representing a serial killer. I represented an individual named Larry Eyler in the early 1990s and so I had to prepare a post-conviction. I had started my own law firm. I was the in-house counsel for a large HMO, and I was doing medical malpractice, but my clerks thought it would be interesting to see if we could tackle the complexity of a post-conviction case in 1992, with someone that everyone believed was guilty." (13)

13. Kathleen Zellner Sept. 27, 2018 at Maryville University, Peace and Justice Award lecture

Zellner said she made incredible discoveries that Eyler had only been convicted of one murder.

"I realized, as we were progressing, that we were really good at what we were doing and yet I'm getting ready to overturn the one conviction for someone that I know has committed twenty-one murders. So the dilemma I was in was to try to figure out how to turn it into something positive, something good.

"What I figured out was, my client was probably infected with the HIV virus, and I decided to have medical testing done, and I confirmed that he had a full blown case of AIDS. So I went to him ... I persuaded him to give to me the twenty-one confessions to all the murders he had committed, in tremendous detail. And I ended up helping to close all of those cases with three jurisdictions and the FBI ... and we closed all of the murder cases. I decided at that point that I would never represent someone again that I believe was guilty. I did not see myself as a criminal defense attorney, but I thought that our skill level on the Eyler case indicated that we, as small a firm as we were, could investigate and uncover evidence that the police had not and the prosecutors had not."

In 1994, Zellner took on her next case, the Joseph Burrows murder case.

The murder victim in that crime southeast of Kankakee, Illinois, was a frail eighty-eight-year-old retired farmer named William Dulin. The Iroquois County killing occurred on November 8, 1988. Dulin's bloody body was found inside his home. Four years later, in 1992, Joseph Burrows' murder conviction was affirmed by the Illinois Supreme Court, and he was scheduled to die by way of lethal injection, prior to Zellner's arrival on the case.

"I was called by the same group that had national funding and had given me the Eyler case so I really didn't want to take the call," Zellner said. "But they said to me, 'He's innocent. We're very sure he's innocent. And it's going to take a tremendous effort because he's facing the death penalty and he had an execution date set, within 120 days of when we took the case.'"

Zellner goes on explain how "we took Mr. Burrows' case and we began an intensive effort to save his life and vacate his conviction and because I had been with someone who was so profoundly guilty and evil, I became an expert in recognizing innocence. And I knew that Mr. Burrows was innocent, and this was not a DNA case. This turned on the testimony of his codefendant who had committed the murder."

As she dug into the case, Zellner realized the slaying was all about the ballistics from where the eighty-eight-year-old farmer was slain.

"After consulting with ballistics experts, I figured out that a woman had committed the murder, the murder of an eighty-eight-year-old farmer in downstate Illinois and there had been a struggle where shots had been fired into the ceiling, and I knew that the gentleman that was killed was so frail there wouldn't have been a struggle with my client, who was 6-foot-2 and weighed about 240 pounds."

The codefendant, Gayle Potter, age thirty-two, got a twelve-year prison sentence under a plea agreement with prosecutors where she fingered the thirty-five-year-old Burrows as the killer and another guy as an accomplice in the small-town robbery murder. Burrows and Ralph Frye, who was also wrongfully convicted of the killing, were actually about sixty miles away in the Champaign-Urbana area at the time of Dulin's death in tiny Iroquois County.

"And she was going to be out in about twelve months," Zellner said. "So I decided to focus all of my efforts on getting her, since I had become so skilled at getting confessions, getting her to confess to me that she had committed this murder."

Zellner said she knew that because of double jeopardy laws, Potter could not prosecuted for murder at that stage.

"So I visited her, fifty times. And we got to know each other and we talked about Mr. Burrows' children and the fact that he was months away from being executed and they were executing people in Illinois at that time. And she gradually came around to the position that she would testify at an evidentiary hearing which was in Kankakee, Illinois."

At that point, there had been hardly any death penalty cases in America that had ever been overturned by someone claiming to be innocent as Burrows.

"So I put her on the stand, not a lot of confidence in what she would do because she was very sociopathic. So the first question I asked her was 'Who shot William Dulin?' And she paused and she said, 'I shot William Dulin.' And it was that example of the narcissistic sociopathic, but the words came out of her mouth and it saved Mr. Burrows' life."

In the end, Potter was charged with perjury, and she served three more years of Illinois prison time. She never did get the death penalty.

"But I walked out the front door with him, and they took his handcuffs off, chains, we walked out the door, it was on the front page of the New York Times. And I thought to myself, this is what I want to do with the rest of my professional career. I have gotten big verdicts. I've won millions of dollars in verdicts, I know that I can convince a jury …but nothing in my mind topped the experience of thinking that you'd saved someone's life or you at least made a major contribution to saving a life."

Avery's crusaders believe it's only a matter of time before he will walk outside the Waupun Correctional Center in south-central Wisconsin as a smiling, teary-eyed free man, vindicated for a sloppy and corrupt murder investigation. But it took Avery eighteen years the first time around to convince the rest of the world of his innocence in the brutal attack that victimized Manitowoc businesswoman Penny Beerntsen in the late summer months of 1985.

Naturally, a second Avery exoneration would cause heads to spin in the Wisconsin criminal justice arena. Powerful politicians from both political parties, Democrats and Republicans, would be tarnished and shamed. For the time being, Wisconsin's judicial system, which does not have a reputation for honesty and integrity, is the last line of defense for the Avery-is-guilty faction. Wisconsin's politically connected people are uncomfortable with the latest worldwide *Making a Murderer* sequel. The first documentary was downright embarrassing enough. It exposed how Wisconsin's criminal justice system, how its small town police forces, still operate. Most of the dairy state consists of judges who are elected on popularity votes, not appointed after a rigorous interview and screening process as a number of states have established.

Although Wisconsin once had a proud reputation for being reform-oriented and one of the most progressive states in the country, it is not that way any longer. There are no meaningful reforms in Wisconsin to improve the state's blemished reputation when it comes to small-town police work, criminal forensics, and avoiding conflicts of interest in law enforcement. These are taboo topics that are not publicly talked about. And yet Wisconsin has an overabundance of unsolved murders and cold cases, because these crimes tend to occur inside the jurisdiction of largely untrained and inexperienced police agencies and sheriff's offices, people who are generally ill-equipped, inept, and simply not up to the task of solving complicated murder cases.

It is one thing for police cars to show up at the scene of the bloody murder and the killer is sitting on the front porch stoop with a cigarette dangling from his mouth, his hands in the air, and the bloody knife resting at the foot of his bloody sneakers. But what about the many unspeakable crimes of violence when the motive is not immediately apparent, when the killer is lurking in the shadows of society?

If these are the cards you are dealt, and you are a condemned but innocent prisoner, then you need a lawyer who can do more than just poke holes in the original testimony and evidence offered at your first murder trial. You need a lawyer who is not just regarded as an all-star in his or her neck of the woods, but a seasoned and skilled lawyer who has the reputation of being world-class, the most valuable player in his or her legal specialization. And you need that MVP lawyer who can get you access to an entire roster of internationally renowned experts, the cream of the crop, in complicated topics like biological and genetic science, criminal behavior, computer forensics, and prosecutorial misconduct.

If you are Steven Avery, you need the best of the best working on your side. You need someone such as attorney Kathleen Zellner from Illinois.

"Steven Avery started writing to me in 2011. I was in the middle of a civil rights case in Washington and so I really didn't have time to work on it and then his current girlfriend did contact me in September (2015). I did watch the documentary on Netflix. And the reason I took the case is because I felt that he had been discriminated against because his family was poor and they were uneducated. I know he's innocent. Now, I just have to prove it." (14)

But starting from scratch, trying to unwind a decade-old solved murder is no easy task. The Avery case is like climbing Mount Everest. It's wicked and nasty and there are numerous unexpected avalanches tumbling down the mountain trying to flatten Zellner and her crusaders in their quest for fairness and justice.

"I do not like people that are bullies," Zellner said. "I felt from a very young age that I was strong enough to protect people that were weaker or were victims.

14. Zellner interview with Newsweek, March 29, 2016

"Half of my exoneration cases have led to the apprehension of the real killer. I've probably solved way more murder cases than most homicide detectives. I think the good thing about the Netflix documentary was that it educated the public. Investigations can be corrupt, the evidence can be planted. Police officers can feel sufficiently pressured."

It goes without saying Zellner has few friends who are rooting for her to overturn Avery's murder conviction among Wisconsin's police law enforcement agencies.

This is hardly a surprise. In Wisconsin, it's quite common for police departments to keep their mouths shut and circle the wagons when someone in their profession gets outed for being a dirty, crooked cop.

Zellner is now in her third full year of providing free, pro bono legal representation to the world-famous Manitowoc County condemned inmate. Without Zellner's efforts, Avery is doomed. He has no chance for parole and will surely die inside of his lonely little prison cell and many of the deep, dark and disturbing secrets regarding the true facts of the crime would remain bottled up forever.

But now, so it seems, Zellner is in her best position to expose the shenanigans, the evidence planting, the dirty tricks played by the likes of special prosecutor Ken Kratz. She is in prime position to pull down the curtains and show to the rest of the world the many instances where the evidence pieces magically appeared at the most opportune times of the murder investigation against Avery and later his sixteen-year-old developmentally disabled nephew, Brendan.

Given the international fervor generated by the Avery murder case, and given the backlash against the brave Emmy-award winning documentarians, Moira Demos and Laura Ricciardi, who have brought Wisconsin's boils to the rest of the world's attention, there is only one logical way for Avery to regain the freedom he lost on November 9, 2005.

Attorney Kathleen Zellner must be overwhelmingly successful in convincing America's judicial system that the person who killed Teresa, incinerated her body and then cut her up into tiny pieces, was someone other than her client.

She must, in convincing fashion, put forth a compelling argument before the appeals court judges that the real evidence, the overlooked evidence, the concealed evidence, sheds light on the one or perhaps two culprits still roaming around and lurking in the shadows of society, bad people, terribly deranged, but people who still come and go freely in their Wisconsin communities to this very day, just as Manitowoc County's dangerous sexual predator Gregory Allen was allowed to do for another decade until he was finally captured and put in prison for life because he could not stop attacking and raping women during the 1980s and 1990s.

What if Zellner at this stage of the post-conviction process is on the right path?

What if she has uncovered the long suspected hidden truth, disturbing evidence that points to somebody other than Avery, but perhaps somebody who is still connected back to the family, somebody who was already familiar with the immediate landscape including Avery Road and Bear the dog?

Regardless of your opinion about Avery's guilt or innocence, you cannot deny that there were two strange people whose courtroom testimony helped sack Avery at his jury trial. One was Bobby, the nephew. The other was Scott Tadych, the abusive woman beater who is the current husband of Avery's dysfunctional sister, Barb, who has become an outcast within her family.

Tadych has a reputation of being a thug and a compulsive liar. Nothing out of his mouth can be trusted. He is regarded as one of the meanest monsters who live in the Mishicot-Two Rivers area, and he's behaved that way for years, court documents and police reports outline.

In November 2017, Zellner presented Wisconsin's circuit court with reams of evidence pointing at Bobby Dassey and Scott Tadych as being the most likely people involved in Teresa's death and dismemberment of her body.

"This new evidence establishes a reasonable probability that a different result would be reached at a new trial based upon the totality of the new evidence. In summary, this evidence consists of brand-new admissions from Barb Tadych and Mr. Tadych that they were aware that Ms. Halbach left the Avery property prior to her murder and an affidavit from Barb's stepson, Brad Dassey, that Barb tried to remove relevant and probative evidence from the Dassey computer before it was seized by police on April 21, 2006." (15)

---

15. November 1, 2017, Zellner's amended supplement to previously filed motion for reconsideration.

CHAPTER FIVE

SKINNY

On the day after Avery's arrest in Manitowoc for Teresa's killing, a strange, cryptic letter made it thirty miles north.

The "Green Bay Post Office pulled a piece of mail off their conveyor and reported it to Green Bay authorities." That piece of mail consisted of a letter without any envelope. It "was folded in thirds ... there was no stamp attached. The note, upon inspection, revealed that the writer indicated a body was burned up in the aluminum smelter at 3 a.m. on Friday morning ... the note was signed SIKIKEY ... the note was written in blue ink and had both printing and cursive writing in the body of the note." (16)

Indeed, the note was bizarre and baffling. One thing was certain. It was not Avery's handwriting. Was it from a crackpot or perhaps somebody with inside knowledge of Teresa's murder? The police were never able to decipher the letter's origin. Actually, they chose to downplay its relevance. After all, if the letter pointed at somebody else instead of Avery, that would have posed a public relations nightmare of epic proportions for Manitowoc and Calumet Counties as well as the Wisconsin Department of Justice. These agencies wanted Avery locked up and gone. They were tired of him being the public crusader for criminal justice reform in Wisconsin. None of the bad and incompetent cops of Wisconsin wanted anything to change. They wanted to maintain status quo and Avery's constant appearance in the

16. John Dedering activity report, Nov. 10, 2005 contact with Green Bay Police Department

press only reminded the public at large about the weaknesses and flaws in Wisconsin's fractured judicial system.

As it turned out, John Dedering, the Calumet investigator who interviewed Bobby, drew the assignment to follow up on the mysterious letter. He learned "the mail that was being sorted in Green Bay comes from Manitowoc, Two Rivers, Green Bay and De Pere. The Green Bay police officer, Fred Laitinen, advised that gloves were used to handle the piece of mail and the SIKIKEY letter would be held at Green Bay's Police Department."

Despite the intense statewide media feeding frenzy surrounding Avery's arrest, there had been no stories published regarding the prospect of Teresa's bones being burned. Then, two days after the mysterious letter, The Herald Times Reporter of Manitowoc ran a front-page newspaper article explaining "burned human remains, key to Halbach's SUV, found on Avery's land."

The mysterious letter writer had prophetically revealed, "Body was burnt up in Alunamon (sic) Smelter. 3 A M Fridy (sic) Morn. SIKIKEY."

The odd letter was not signed with the writer's real name. Rather, it ended with the following key identifiers: "Manitowoc Sherff (sic) Avery."

Finally, a dozen years later, private investigator James Kirby traveled to Manitowoc to interview Lisa Novachek, payroll employee at Wisconsin Aluminum Foundry. She also worked at the foundry in 2005 and has familiarity with her company's employees. The business has been a mainstay in Manitowoc since the early 1900s. It's tucked inside an old industrial neighborhood and remains a vibrant blue-collar operation to this day.

"I showed Ms. Novachek the 'SIKIKEY' note which was reportedly found during sorting at the Green Bay post office … Novachek told me there were twenty people who worked the night shift at the aluminum foundry in early November 2005 and that about half of them were illiterate or partially literate and that the 'SIKIKEY' note could have been written by one of them. Ms. Novachek told me that Scott Tadych's nickname at work in 2005 was 'Skinny' and that 'SIKIKEY' may be a reference to Scott Tadych." (17)

The Wisconsin Aluminum Foundry has been in Manitowoc for decades. It's where a portion of Teresa Halbach's bones and teeth may have been thrown into the industrial fire.

When Scott Tadych was twenty-nine, he was hauled into the Manitowoc County Jail on charges of battery, disorderly conduct and criminal damage to property. And it would not be the only time he would end up in one of the local jails for criminal acts of violent tendencies.

According to the criminal complaint, officers in nearby Two Rivers met with a woman on July 7, 1997, at her residence. "She had an altercation with her live-in boyfriend, Scott Tadych. (She) stated Scott had accused her of seeing another male and she told him to leave the residence ... Scott

17. Third supplemental affidavit of James Kirby, Nov. 16, 2017

began packing up some clothing and personal items ... at one point she walked past Scott and he was swinging at the back of her head with his left hand but he missed her ... she told Scott that was the last straw and she went into the TV room to get his duffle bag and take it to the kitchen." (18)

At that point, "Scott went out of control and picked up the water cooler and slammed it down hitting the kitchen chair and the microwave cart ... she then called her mom and dad to come over because she feared for her life and her son ... Scott kept making comments to her and he pushed her two times."

Tadych decided to take out his anger and rage upon the woman's laundry.

"Scott went downstairs and threw all her laundry, clean and dirty, all over the basement floor and in the drain. Scott also punched her in the chest with his right fist. Scott walked back up the stairs and (the victim) was going to follow when Scott locked the basement door ... when she opened the door, Scott punched her again ... Scott's mother and father had arrived and both she and (his) mother had seen Scott strike her. Scott tried to push her down the basement stairs and shut the door."

When Tadych went into the garage, a fight erupted over the fishing rods.

"She was going to take the rods away from Scott, and he slapped her on the right arm. Scott filled up his car with his items and told his mom to get his brother."

As tensions escalated, Tadych drilled his girlfriend's son, who was only a boy.

"Scott punched (him) in the upper left chest with his right fist. (The boy) fell to the floor and was crying ... her son ... is 11 years old."

More chaos ensued.

---

18. State of Wisconsin vs. Scott A. Tadych 1997CF237

"Scott went outside and ripped the CB out of her truck ... She went into her truck to check for damage, and Scott was screaming at her and he pulled her hair ... after Scott pulled out the radio, her radio, clock, blinkers, and back up lights would not work. At no time did she give anyone permission to damage her property."

The victim's eleven-year-old son gave this account to Two Rivers Police: "he saw Scott pushing his mom ... Scott went downstairs to get some clothes and Scott began to throw clothes all over and Scott tried to rip up (his victim's) sweatshirts. (The boy) stated he was fearful Scott would hurt his mom ... Scott began screaming at him and calling him a lard ass and a fat ass."

Things got nasty when the child tried to stop Tadych from harming his mother.

"Scott went back upstairs and was pushing his mom around inside the kitchen ... he stepped between the two and Scott knocked him to the ground ... he fell to the floor and he was crying because it hurt."

Under a plea bargain, Scott Tadych was found guilty of criminal battery. On October 13, 1998, he was ordered to stay in the local jail for 135 days.

Seven years later, at the time of Teresa's disappearance, Tadych worked the overnight shift at the aluminum foundry near Manitowoc's downtown. All of a sudden, the SIKIKEY letter arrived in Green Bay suggesting Teresa's body was incinerated. Was the Wisconsin Aluminum Foundry plant in Manitowoc central to the missing photographer's dismemberment?

Was "SIKIKEY" an illiterate worker's best attempt at trying to identify Tadych by his nickname of "Skinny" at the foundry?

As of 2006, plant foreman Keith Schaefer had known Tadych for nine years.

"Keith went on to say he had been hearing Scott Tadych telling some of the workers in the plant about information on the Teresa Halbach murder/homicide investigation. Keith had heard that Scott had not shown up for work on October 31, 2005, however, he had heard he went to see his mother in the hospital. Scott had been telling people he had seen the fire on Halloween by Steven Avery and Scott, or the other people, made it sound like he had gotten out of the vehicle and actually talked to Steven by the fire. Keith also heard from other guys that Scott had noticed stains on the pants and shirts of one of Barbara's kids." (19)

As many people may remember, the prosecution maintained the infamous bleached blue jeans belonged to Avery's mentally disabled nephew, Brendan. Attorney Zellner strongly suspects that any cryptic conversations were not in regard to Avery's slow nephew. Rather, any phone calls made to Tadych at the Wisconsin Aluminum Foundry concerned Barb's other son, Bobby. After all, Brendan, sixteen, and Scott Tadych had nothing in common and had no real relationship whatsoever. On the other hand, Bobby and Tadych were tight.

After Teresa went missing, "Keith described Scott as being extra edgy lately, a short-tempered, angry person. Keith said he is a chronic liar and does not really get along with a lot of people at the plant and would never know when he would blow up at somebody. Keith felt Scott also knew more about the murder than he had told people, and Keith felt Scott could be very capable of the murder or knowing something more."

Yet, all the while, Tadych's romantic relationship with Barb remained fine.

"However, because of the case, he did seem disturbed by what was going on," Schaefer said. "After Steven was arrested, Scott had thought it had been a set up and that

---

19. Interviews of Keith Schaefer, Leonard Brouchoud, Thomas Culp, March 30, 2006, Investigator Wendy Baldwin

he was being framed; however, a week later, Scott did not believe this anymore and thought Steven was guilty."

CHAPTER SIX

AVERY'S PHONE CALL

Although he remained condemned to live out the rest of his days here on earth inside a Wisconsin Department of Corrections prison cellblock, Avery's spirits were high and his mood upbeat toward the end of 2017.

After all, his prospects of regaining his freedom or gaining a new trial were stronger than ever, thanks to Zellner's energy and fighting spirit. But back in Manitowoc County, the skies were dark and growing more ominous. People were becoming unhinged as the master at overturning wrongful convictions was starting to reveal her cards. As he remained at Waupun, Avery made a phone call to his sister, Barb, on October 24, 2017. Here's a synopsis of the call, which was recorded and included in the court record of Avery's post-conviction appeal.

The call concerned the personal computer inside the trailer of Avery's sister, Barb. This was the computer that her son Bobby used to fuel his wicked sexual fantasies involving gore, violence, and death.

"Why is all that shit on the computer?" Avery asked.(20)

"There was nothing on my fucking computer. All this, I didn't even have fucking Internet back then," his sister lied.

"Yes, you did."

"No, I didn't."

"What do you mean you didn't?"

---

20.   Steven Avery call with Barbara Tadych on Oct. 24, 2017 and Scott Tadych transcript, amended supplement to previously filed motion for reconsideration.

"No, I didn't have Internet."

"You did."

"No, I didn't."

"At that time you did. Before that you did."

"No I didn't."

"You didn't? Well, it's on the computer."

"I did not have Internet."

"Well."

"Well nothing. I didn't."

Zellner has pointed out to the court handling Avery's post-conviction appeal that "Barb's vehement denial that her computer had access to the Internet at the time of Ms. Halbach's murder is probative because it is unequivocally false."

But why lie?

Was Barb lying to protect her older son Bobby? Was she content to see her youngest son, her feeble-minded son, Brendan, carted off to prison if it meant protecting someone else in the family for the murder?

Prior to the confrontational prison call, one of Zellner's expert witnesses, forensic computer expert Gary Hunt, conducted a forensic examination of Barb's desktop computer.

"The computer was used to access violent images of young deceased females, rape, torture, incest, and pedophilia on the Internet at times when only Bobby was home." (21)

Hunt's analysis also turned up evidence that someone inside the home had gone to great lengths to destroy information off the computer's hard drive. The computer record deletions were specific to the time frame of Teresa's disappearance and murder.

"Barb's denial is especially telling given that she took steps to delete the disturbing images before police seized her

---

21. 2017 affidavit of Gary Hunt, senior forensic examiner with QDiscovery LLC

computer on April 21, 2006. This is additional new evidence that supports Mr. Avery's claim that the recovered images on the Dassey computer meet the legitimacy tendency test established by Denny by implicating Bobby in Ms. Halbach's murder." (22)

Not only did Barb remove incriminating evidence against her son, Bobby, she also apparently knew that Teresa left the Avery property, alive, during the afternoon of October 31, 2005.

"Barb and Mr. Tadych have recently made admissions that Ms. Halbach left the Avery property before the murder," Zellner revealed.

These bombshell admissions came during the same recorded phone call of Avery and his sister Barb, October 24, 2017.

"Bobby's home," Steven Avery reminded his sister.

"He wasn't always home," she answered.

"Well, most of the time he was home."

"No."

Then out of nowhere, a male voice interjected.

"He doesn't know fucking shit."

It was the violent man from Manitowoc County who was eavesdropping. But why was Scott Tadych eavesdropping? Why was he so paranoid about his wife's conversation about Teresa's murder a dozen years afterward?

As Tadych listened intently, Avery informed his sister that Bobby saw Teresa leave the property.

"She left," Avery repeated.

"That's right," Scott Tadych interjected.

"Yeah. She left," Barb Tadych repeated.

"Yeah," Avery said.

"Yeah," his sister repeated.

"Well," Avery explained, "he didn't testify for that."

---

22. Steven Avery's amended supplement to previously filed motion for consideration, dated Nov. 1, 2017

Zellner now had tape-recorded statements from Barb and Scott Tadych agreeing that Teresa left the Avery compound on her final day of life, information that doesn't mesh with their original trial testimony.

"Mr. Tadych's response indicates either that Bobby had told him that Bobby observed Ms. Halbach leave the property or Mr. Tadych's response indicates that Mr. Tadych observed and or had contact with Ms. Halbach after she left the property."

But if Tadych and Barb were now admitting Teresa left Avery Road, not realizing their conversation was being recorded by the prison, what does that say for the crucial trial testimony served up by disgraced special prosecutor Ken Kratz's main trial witness?

Kratz highlighted Bobby's testimony, knowing full well it was sure to be the biggest televised criminal trial ever in Wisconsin.

"Barb and Mr. Tadych's admissions are crucial to Mr. Avery's defense because the most important eyewitness for the State was Bobby, who testified that Ms. Halbach was still on the Avery property and that he saw Ms. Halbach approaching Mr. Avery's trailer before he left."

On the other hand, if Bobby committed the murder, is it realistic to expect he would testify with truthfulness? Or, would he lie on the witness stand, realizing a guilty verdict against his uncle served his own needs?

Anyhow, here's how Tadych behaved during the October 2017 call between Avery and Barb where Tadych was eavesdropping the entire time.

"Let me talk to the cock-sucking loser. Fuck him. All you do is, the only evidence they got is against him, and he's trying to gasp for air to blame it on somebody else. He's a fucking loser. I wasn't even on that property that day, you goddamn idiot. That's how fucking intelligent you are. You want to get out yourself so you can get out and do something stupid again, you dumb fuck. I can't wait to kick your fucking ass. Fucking little fucker!"

Avery: "I ain't scared of him. I ain't scared of him."

Tadych: "You ruined my fucking life. You ruined my fucking name, dumb cock sucker. You fucking jailbird motherfucker!"

"Yep."

"I hate the cocksucker. You ruined my fucking life!"

"Yeah."

Avery reminded his sister how her husband was solely responsible for making outrageous false claims to the police suggesting Avery was molesting her sons including Brendan.

"It came from him. So he wanted the cops to put all the blame on me. So who would say something like, that I did something to the boys?"

"I don't know. I didn't read none of this shit, OK?"

"Yeah. That's why nobody wanted to read nothing and see about nothing. Any guilty person, uh, would say and try to blame it onto somebody else. Oh, I was fucking with the boys."

Now, the conversation fueled Tadych's rage.

"Yeah, fuck him, the cocksucker. He's a stupid fuck. Going down to fuck your family when he got out of prison the first time!" Tadych roared.

"Yeah? See. That fucker needs to be locked up. How about his mother?" Avery asked his sister.

Avery alluded to the fact that Tadych tried to attack his own mother during one of Tadych's domestics that resulted in an arrest.

"What about his mother?" his sister inquired.

This time, Tadych blew a gasket. He began screaming at Avery, loud as ever.

"Yeah, you talking about my mother, you cock-sucker? I'll put you in the fucking ground!"

"Yeah?" Avery asked.

"Fucking bastard," Tadych screamed. "I don't give a fuck. The cock-sucker's a loser. He's grasping for air. The only evidence they got is against him."

"Uh, his mother had to call the cops on him," Avery reminded his sister.

"He never touched his mother," Barb professed.

"You stupid fucker," Tadych yelled.

"I already asked her all of that," Avery told them both.

"Smart man you are. Thirty-six years in prison and you know the world. I hate him," Tadych shouted.

Avery's sister had enough.

"This needs to stop."

"It's gonna stop when it's over."

"It needs to stop now."

"I can't," Avery said.

"Well, like I said, you will end up with a dead sister because I can't take this shit no more."

"Well then shut the computer off then. Shut everything off. You don't need a phone. Just go to work."

"Yeah, OK, whatever."

From Zellner's perspective, the heated phone call was revelatory.

"Bobby and Mr. Tadych placed themselves in the same location as Ms. Halbach when she received her last phone call. Mr. Tadych's multiple inconsistent statements severely undermine his credibility at trial. His recent telephone call with Mr. Avery demonstrates his knowledge that Ms. Halbach had left the Avery property on October 31, 2005. The October 24, 2017 telephone call also demonstrates that Mr. Tadych has violent, homicidal propensities manifested by his uncontrollable temper. Mr. Tadych threatens to physically assault Mr. Avery and even more disturbingly, to put Mr. Avery 'in the fucking ground.'"

Back in 2007, special prosecutor Kratz glossed over the uncomfortable fact that the majority of Teresa's charred bones, supposedly burned at Avery's outdoor backyard pit on a cool autumn night, were never found. Practically all of her teeth were absent from Avery's burn pile pit. Meanwhile, some of the charred bones pointed to the neighboring property along Avery Road.

"It is an undisputed fact that some of Ms. Halbach's bones were found in the Dassey burn barrel," Zellner argued. "No credible explanation has ever been provided by the State as to why Ms. Halbach's bones would be in the Dassey burn barrel if Mr. Avery had burned her whole body in his burn pit."

CHAPTER SEVEN

COMPUTER BLUES

At the sixth month mark of the murder probe, Avery and his mentally challenged sixteen-year-old nephew, Brendan, were both incarcerated, but something wasn't right back on Avery Road.

Wisconsin police were becoming intensely focused on Barb's desktop computer. This was the home computer primarily used by her nineteen-year-old loner of a son, Bobby. The computer was kept inside his bedroom.

But before Wisconsin's police got a search warrant to seize the computer, Barb Janda was one step ahead of them.

"Mr. Avery has discovered new evidence that Barb hired a person to make deletions of incriminating evidence prior to the computer being seized by the police on April 21, 2006." (23)

Bolstering Avery's case, Brad Dassey shed light on a conversation he vividly remembers taking place during a drive to the Sheboygan County Jail to visit his half-brother, Brendan back in 2006.

"My father Peter Dassey was with us. Barb stated that she had hired someone to reformat her home computer. She wanted to know if 'reformatting' would remove what was on the computer. Barb admitted her computer had some pornography stored on it, and she claimed the computer had 'viruses' on it. She had the reformatting done shortly before the authorities seized her computer. Barb commented that she did not think the person she hired knew what he was

23. Motion for Reconsideration, November 1, 2017

doing. She said she did not want anyone to get what was on her computer." (24)

Brad Dassey said he "thought that Barb was trying to remove evidence relevant to Ms. Halbach's murder. The authorities interviewed Brad after he reported this information, but he was not called as a witness, by either side, to testify at Mr. Avery or Brendan's trials."

In July 2017, Zellner's computer forensic expert, Gary Hunt, unearthed some, but not all, of the dirty little secrets from Bobby Dassey's home computer. The missing files only deepened the mystery surrounding Bobby and the time frame in question.

The home computer deletions were as follows:

August 23-26, 2005

August 28 - September 11, 2005

September 14-15, 2005

September 24 - October 22, 2005

October 23-24, 2005

October 26 - November 2, 2005

November 4-13, 2005

November 15 - December. 3, 2005

Of the computer files that were recovered, they paint a dark picture. Foremost, they undermine Bobby's incriminating trial testimony as Kratz's first witness.

"Bobby testified at Mr. Avery's trial that after he arrived home on October 31, 2005, from working the 10 p.m. to 6 a.m. shift, he went to sleep until 2:30 p.m. Bobby's testimony is demonstrably false. Mr. Hunt has determined that the Dassey computer was used to access the Internet at 6:05 a.m., 6:28 a.m., 6:31 a.m., 7 a.m., 9:33 a.m., 10:09 a.m., 1:09 p.m., and 1:51 p.m.

"Bobby was the only person home during those hours because his mother, Barb, was at work, Blaine and Brendan were in school, and Bryan lived with his girlfriend.

---

24. Brad Dassey affidavit October 30, 2017

"(This) is powerful evidence that Barb was aware that her computer had incriminating files on it that were relevant to Ms. Halbach's murder. Barb's efforts to delete the files before the computer was examined by authorities – in addition to her recent denials that she even had the ability to access the Internet during the time in question – reinforces this conclusion." (25)

In my 2015 WildBlue Press true-crime book, *Body of Proof*, nineteen-year-old Christopher Edwards of Omaha, Nebraska, emerged as the prime suspect in the disappearance of his missing girlfriend, Jessica O'Grady. The two worked at the Omaha Lone Star Steakhouse. Her body was never found, but the Omaha Police and Douglas County Sheriff's Office moved forward with an arrest in the hopes of achieving Omaha's first-ever no-body murder conviction before a jury.

One of the key pieces of evidence came from Edwards' laptop computer. The forensic examination of his computer determined that he was trolling the Internet in the days prior to killing his girlfriend, searching on medical websites for morbid details about the human body, including a Google keyword search for information relating to "arteries." The day after Jessica O'Grady disappeared, Edwards was caught on videotape at his local Walgreens store, where he purchased several bottles of white-out and cleaning supplies. When the police asked to look underneath his bed and his bedroom mattress, he initially balked at the idea, but then consented.

When his bedroom mattress was flipped over, it was saturated with blood. Later, the jury heard all of the evidence and found Christopher Edwards guilty of murder. He remains in the Nebraska Department of Correction. To this day, he refuses to reveal where he disposed of O'Grady's body.

---

25. Steven Avery's amended supplement, November 1, 2017

Meanwhile, Zellner also believes the computer forensics found on Bobby's computer can connect the dots for Teresa's demise and dismemberment.

"The forensic examination of Barb's computer performed by law enforcement did not permit law enforcement to detect Barb's efforts to delete computer records of eight periods in 2005. The missing records, which were presumed deleted, were only discovered using 2017 forensic technology."

Had that information been known at Avery's trial, it could have been a game changer for the defense. Unfortunately, Avery's lawyers Jerry Buting and Dean Strang were operating in the dark.

"Mr. Avery cannot be faulted for failing to detect Barb's efforts at concealment prior to his trial; in fact, as recently as October 24, 2017, Barb denied that she even had Internet during this period of time. The evidence is material because it supports Mr. Avery's theory of an alternative perpetrator … there was no evidence elicited at trial concerning Barb's efforts to remove evidence of the Halbach murder on her home computer," Zellner said.

But questions linger to this day. What had Barb come upon on her family's computer? Was she out to protect someone sinister in her family, someone the authorities had chosen to overlook? Was she willing to sacrifice her relationship with Brendan in order to keep her other more desirable family members out of law enforcement custody?

Had someone in law enforcement or the prosecution team tipped her off about the upcoming planned search of her family's computer?

"Shortly after my conversation with Barb I contacted the authorities because I thought Barb was trying to remove evidence relevant to the Teresa Halbach murder from her computer," Brad Dassey said. "I do not know who reformatted Barb's computer. I was interviewed by the authorities after I reported this information to them."

CHAPTER EIGHT

BOBBY'S OBSESSIONS

The mystery person Barb paid to obliterate data on the desktop computer stored inside Bobby's bedroom on Avery Road did a good job, but the computer tech was not perfect, as outlined by Gary Hunt, the senior forensic examiner with QDiscovery. He has been certified as an AccessData Certified Examiner since 2012 and a Certified Computer Examiner since 2013.

Gary Hunt is senior forensic examiner with QDiscovery. His work on the post-conviction process uncovered dark, violent pornography on Bobby Dassey's home computer.

"At the time of the 2006 investigation, there were three leading forensic examination utilities: Encase, Forensic Toolkit, and X-Ways. It is important to note that the platforms have significantly evolved since the 2006 investigation," Hunt explained. "FTK specifically added new features and parsing capabilities allowing for more efficient investigations and greater insight into the data at stake. Additionally, Internet Evidence Finder was not first released until March 22, 2009. The bulk of my analysis revolved around web activity which was streamlined by the use of IEF."

Approximately twelve years after Teresa's terrorizing death, Hunt uncovered startling new information on Bobby Dassey's home computer. This information was not(26) known to Avery's trial lawyers, Dean Strang and Jerry Buting. It also wasn't known to the producers and documentarians of the original *Making a Murderer*.

This information was uncovered by Kathleen T. Zellner & Associates, but not until 2017.

"There was a single user account on the computer named 'HP Owner,'" Hunt found out. "The HP Owner user conducted the following Internet searches on various dates: teen pussy, 11 year old sex, 12 year old sex, 15 year old girl, 15 year old girl naked, aaa teens, cute kid naked, fuck preteen girl, hot teen pussy, kid slut, kid sluts, naked teens, naked young girl, naked young pussy, nude teenage girl, nude teenage girls, pre teen sluts, pree (sic) teens naked, preteen boobs, preteen busty, preteen girl model naked, preteen girl nude, pre-teen girls naked, preteen naked, preteen pussy, preteen sex, preteen sluts, pre-teen girls naked, preteens naked, pre-teens naked, teen black pussy, teen girls naked, teen porn, teen pussy, teen redhead pussy, teen sex, teen twits, teen twat, teenage pussy, teens naked, teens spread wide open, wet teen pussy, young 13 girl nude, young 13 year old girl nude, young 13 year old naked, young 13 yr old naked, horsecum, car accident, car accidents, deseised (sic) girls, dessesed (sic) girls, diseased girls, drawned (sic) girls, drawned pussy, drowned girl, drowned girl nude, drowned pussy, fast car accident, gun to haed (sic), gun to head, knife

---

26. Affidavit of Gary Hunt, October 26, 2017

goes through skin, rotten girl, seeing bones, hot girls, and tempo car accident."

At the time of these repetitious searches, Bobby was nineteen and worked the 10 p.m. to 6 a.m. shift at the metal processing facility in Manitowoc, not too far from his home.

From Bobby's bedroom computer, Hunt recovered two pictures "in the unallocated space, the first showing Teresa Halbach and Steven Avery, the second showing only Teresa Halbach."

Both images were carved from the unallocated space of the computer hard drive. Since the files were recovered via data carving, there is no file system metadata available. In other words, the files' original paths, names, and creation dates, accessed or modified timestamps are not available.

"In conclusion, the computer was used to run Internet searches including but not limited to those identified in (the previous paragraph) and Exhibit B. Some images displayed as a result of the searches were clicked on by the user. Additionally, two pictures of Teresa Halbach were recovered from the unallocated space. These images do not have any date attributes or information suggesting how they arrived on the computer."

Meanwhile, a law enforcement heavyweight who dedicated his career to putting ruthless killers in prison also came to Zellner's aid in her quest to regain Steven Avery's freedom.

Gregg McCrary is a distinguished retired FBI agent who teaches policing at Marymount University in Arlington, Virginia. He is a nationally regarded violent crime behavioral expert. He signed a sworn affidavit on October 23, 2017.

"I have reviewed the Wisconsin DOJ report summarizing the forensic computer examination of the Dassey computer. It is my opinion, based on this report, in addition to the report of Kathleen T. Zellner & Associates' forensic computer examiner, that Bobby Dassey's Internet searches reflects a co-morbidity of sexual paraphilias. The sexual and violent content he was searching for and viewing should have alerted investigators to Bobby Dassey as a possible perpetrator of Teresa Halbach's murder. (27)

"The content of these images, combined with the obsessive use of the computer to view these images and Bobby Dassey's entanglement in the investigation into the murder of Teresa Halbach, should have alerted the investigators to Bobby Dassey as someone having an elevated risk to perpetrate a sexually motivated violent crime such as the violent crime perpetrated on Teresa Halbach."

In hindsight, McCrary found it troublesome that Bobby turned into a star witness against his uncle.

"The fact that Bobby Dassey became the key witness for the prosecution and that his testimony placed Teresa Halbach on the property 'walking over to Steven's trailer' after she completed her assignment, interjected himself into the prosecution in a way that should have raised the suspicions of reasonably trained detectives, if that testimony is untrue. Based upon the affidavit of Bryan Dassey, it appears that Bobby Dassey's testimony was untrue."

McCrary is regarded as a foremost expert witness in violent crimes. He worked at the FBI for twenty-five years. On the other hand, John Dedering, the Calumet County Sheriff's Investigator, who interviewed Bobby, had practically no real world experience handling murder cases because it was largely cow country.

In fact, Dedering even admitted during his questioning of Bobby how he had basically shied away from entering the Dassey's property off Avery Road. The investigator chose to keep himself away from the inside of Bobby's garage where Bobby was dismembering a deer carcass that he chose to grab off the road shortly after Teresa vanished. The deer carcass was taken home by Bobby after the Manitowoc

---

27. Second Supplemental Affidavit, Gregg McCrary, October 20, 2017

County Sheriff's Department had already made visits to Avery Road on successive days to interview his uncle, who denied any involvement in Teresa's disappearance and freely gave detectives permission to walk through his trailer to look for signs of foul play.

"In my opinion, a prudent investigator would have considered Bobby Dassey a suspect and would have investigated him as such," McCrary said. "There is no evidence that authorities ever investigated, much less eliminated, him as a suspect or investigated the discrepancies in his trial testimony."

***

After Dedering and Wisconsin DCI agent Kevin Heimerl finished their non-accusatory interview with Bobby on November 9, 2005, they led him down a hallway to undergo a physical examination with Faye Fritsch. She was a nurse at the Aurora Medical Center near Manitowoc.

Dedering noted he questioned Bobby Dassey regarding scratches on Bobby's upper back. Bobby Dassey stated these were due to his Labrador puppy jumping on his upper back.

"He stated he was bent down to put on his shoes (this morning) when the dog jumped up and scratched him," Dedering wrote. "I did examine Dassey's shirt and could find no obvious holes or tears."(28)

The investigator spoke with Dr. Laura Vogel-Schwartz to get her assessment.

"She stated it was not likely they were over a week old. She stated it is her opinion that the scratches were fairly recent. The scratches to Bobby Dassey's back were photographed. We did escort Bobby Dassey from the

28. Interview of Bobby Dassey by Investigator John Dedering, November 9, 2005

hospital. He was released, and I observed him speaking with his mother in the parking lot."

A baby Labrador puppy supposedly dug its claws deep into Bobby's back, so he claimed. Nobody in Wisconsin law enforcement ever bothered to follow up and investigate the veracity of Bobby's claim. After all, the case's lead investigators, who had no business lurking around the Aurora hospital, were intently focused on something far more important to them. They wanted to personally monitor the DNA collection from their new prisoner, Avery, who was being asked to submit fresh new DNA samples to the lead Wisconsin detectives even though he was only being arrested on a charge of being felon in possession of a gun, not murder. Prosecutor Kratz would not charge Avery with first-degree murder and mutilation of a corpse until a week later, November 15, 2005.

But why did Mark Wiegert and his sidekick, Tom Fassbender of the Wisconsin DOJ, need to collect more DNA samples from Steven Avery? After all, Avery had given up his DNA samples to the state of Wisconsin when he was serving state prison time for Gregory Allen's crimes.

Nonetheless, Fassbender and Wiegert teamed up on the afternoon of November 9, 2005, to pick up Avery at his residence and bring him straight to the hospital where they could be inside the room as they observed the events unfold.

"Steven asked what the DNA samples were for," Fassbender's report showed. "He was essentially advised that samples were being obtained from everyone that has been around the area and that they are used for standards for comparison. He advised that they already have his."

Theoretically, if Wisconsin already had Avery's DNA samples on file in 2003, this raises a legitimate question. Why did Wiegert and Fassbender decide they needed to make a special trip to the hospital to take yet another DNA specimen from Avery? Also, why were Wiegert and Fassbender absent from the physical examination of Bobby and the collection of Bobby's DNA sample yet the two were inside the doctor's office as so-called passive observers when the nurse took an abundance of additional DNA from Avery?

"After the physical examination, Faye Fritsch did the buccal swabs on Steven Avery. The buccal swabs were taken from Steven Avery's mouth at 1:51 p.m. and I saw Faye Fritsch place the swabs into an envelope and seal the envelope. The envelope containing the buccal swabs was turned over to me by Faye Fritsch at 1:53 p.m.," Calumet Sgt. Bill Tyson's reports show.

From there, Avery was taken into another examination room for palm prints and fingerprints. A correctional officer handed off those prints to Tyson at 2:10 p.m.

Regardless of Avery's guilt or innocence, however, it appears that monkey business was going on at the hospital and that the registered nurse, Faye Fritsch, then thirty-five, of Two Rivers, was complicit.

"During the physical examination of my body on November 9, 2005, the nurse took two swabs near my groin at the request of Calumet County Investigator Wiegert," Steve Avery said. "I saw the nurse who took the groin swabs hand them to Investigator Wiegert as I was being taken out of the exam room by Agent Fassbender and the nurse. I saw Investigator Wiegert pretend to put the swabs in the hospital-type waste basket but I did not actually see the swabs leave his hands and fall into the basket." (29)

Fassbender's report noted there were numerous small scratches, scars, and sores documented on Avery's body. This was all understandable since Avery did metal scraping at the salvage business. "There was one particular wound that entailed a cut to Steven's middle finger on his right hand. The cut had scabbed over."

During the exam, Fassbender left briefly to fetch Avery a can of soda. "Fassbender asked Steven if he wanted

29. Affidavit of Steven Avery, November 23, 2016

something to drink, and he said he would take a soda. Fassbender left the room and got him a soda."

Unknown to Avery at the time, this was another way for Fassbender to obtain another DNA sample of Avery, without Avery's knowledge.

But Fassbender made sure he was back in the doctor's room, with Wiegert, when the DNA harvests were taking place. Both men kept their mouths quiet when the nurse carried on and began to take additional DNA samples from Avery that were totally unnecessary and outside the scope of their court-obtained search warrant. Incidentally, these were DNA samples that the same nurse would not attempt to take from Bobby that same afternoon.

"Towards the end of the examination," Fassbender's report reflected, "(Nurse Faye) Fritsch had the lights turned out in the examination room and utilized a Woods light to illuminate any secretions on Steven's body. Fritsch subsequently took two swabs in Steven's groin area. After that, she continued and was going to take more swabs when (myself) and Investigator Wiegert conferred and determined that the search warrant did not call for that type of exam.

"Investigator Wiegert immediately stopped Fritsch and the exam was concluded. Investigator Wiegert had Fritsch dispose of the two swabs into the Biohaz/sharps bin. Fritsch also took buccal swabs from Steven's saliva."

It's quite curious to look back years later and realize that both Wiegert and Fassbender thought it was crucial they needed to be sitting in the very same room as the Manitowoc nurse who collected Avery's DNA, only to mess up and obtain more DNA samples than necessary. But if being present to watch Avery's DNA collection was so essential, why did both Wiegert and Fassbender choose not to accompany Avery down the hall to obtain his fingerprints and palm prints as well?

"Agent Fassbender's report is not credible because Nurse Fritsch never mentions in her charting disposing of the groin swabs," Zellner said. "Agent Fassbender's report directly contradicts Mr. Avery's account of this examination as described in his affidavit.

"Contrary to Agent Fassbender's report, Investigator Wiegert told Nurse Fritsch that he would discard the swabs while Agent Fassbender escorted Mr. Avery into a separate room to get his fingerprints. As Mr. Avery followed Agent Fassbender and Nurse Fritsch out of the examination room, Mr. Avery heard investigator Wiegert tell Nurse Fritsch to give him the groin swabs and Mr. Avery observed Investigator Wiegert walk to the examination room receptacle as if to discard the groin swabs. Mr. Avery observed that Investigator Wiegert did not drop the groin swabs into the receptacle." (30)

The illegal collection of the groin swabs is yet another reason why Avery's murder conviction warrants being overturned, according to Zellner.

"Investigator Wiegert, as an experienced investigator, would have known that taking groin swabs was not authorized by the search warrant, which permitted only the collection of saliva and blood samples. It is therefore reasonable to conclude from this clear violation of Mr. Avery's Fourth Amendment rights that Investigator Wiegert planned to use the illegally seized groin swabs from Mr. Avery to plant Mr. Avery's DNA on other crime scene evidence," Zellner stated.

---

30. Zellner Motion for Post-Conviction Relief June 7, 2017

CHAPTER NINE

SHADY DEPARTMENT

Where there are shuttered factories and boarded up businesses, one of the most desirable jobs in an economically depressed blue-collar area is one that provides a shiny badge, holster, and loaded gun.

A fear factor and an intimidating law enforcement presence often keep the locals in check, and cast an eye of suspicion on the community's outsiders, notably minorities. In communities like this, a job as a county sheriff deputy means power and prestige. These jobs are hard to come by.

Positions in full-time law enforcement carry generous fringe benefits, enormous job security and generous taxpayer-funded retirement pensions that most of the taxpaying public won't have in their line of work. Work in the public sector, particularly in law enforcement, and you tend to make above-average wages. Usually, there's a steady flow of overtime pay and built-in annual pay raises that most people in the private sector would envy.

Being a sheriff's deputy in a small town means something. It means clout. It makes you somebody. You are given enormous power to mess with somebody's civil rights and freedoms. Want to harass somebody? Want to make somebody's life miserable? Want to intimidate someone? Want to rough someone up? Most cops who operate on the dark side of the law know what they can get away with. Fortunately, most people in law enforcement are honorable, righteous, and truly want to do the public's good. They are our true public servants, and they try hard to keep our communities safe. For them we owe a debt of gratitude.

But not all cops are cut from the same cloth and that's just as true in Wisconsin. Around northeastern Wisconsin, the Manitowoc County Sheriff's Department gained notoriety on a number of cases involving strong suspicions of a police cover up.

Upon taking office in January 2007, Sheriff Rob Hermann promoted his younger brother Todd to the position of deputy inspector of operations – third in command of the entire sixty officer department. In effect, the sheriff put his little brother into one of the best paid positions and most powerful roles in all of county government.

During Rob Hermann's tenure as sheriff, his undersheriff remained Gregg Schetter. Schetter and the Hermann brothers all grew up together in southern Manitowoc County. In fact, Schetter happened to be one of the groomsmen in Todd Hermann's 1993 wedding, along the sheriff himself. Wouldn't it be nice to have your wedding party doing your performance reviews, setting your salaries and pay raises, especially in a county government job?

As for Schetter, he was sandwiched in the middle of both Hermann brothers in the upper administration. He was the boss of one and answered to the other. This was small-town cronyism at its finest, and this was the way the political movers and shakers of Manitowoc County preferred to run their downtown sheriff's office. The Manitowoc Sheriff's Office did not have an internal affairs unit for citizens to bring their complaints about corruption or abuse of power involving the sheriff's deputies. Instead, complaints from the citizenry were funneled to Schetter, and he decided what complaints were legitimate and which ones to dismiss.

The opportunity to wear the brown uniform and the shiny star as a Manitowoc County Sheriff's deputy was historically based on who you knew – not what you knew. Deputy candidates who may have been highly qualified but failed to have an inside connection were often part of the reject pile. Their job application materials often collected dust, and they would need to look elsewhere to pursue a career in law enforcement.

As far as the top of the administration was concerned, Sheriff Rob Hermann and Undersheriff Gregg Schetter were afforded a long-standing generous perk that was off-limits to virtually all other county government employees. They got a yearly fuel stipend to the tune of nearly $10,000 each just to drive to and from their office desk jobs in downtown Manitowoc. The generous stipend, approved by the Manitowoc County Board of Supervisors, came in addition to their annual salaries in the neighborhood of $100,000, all for managing a mostly rural sheriff's office, rarely ever handling serious crimes such rapes, kidnappings, bank robberies, and murders. Most of the serious offenses tended to occur within the jurisdiction of the Manitowoc Police Department, a city police agency that strived to hire more qualified police officers. The city department was regarded as being far more professional, ethical, and accountable to the residents, but it was often dragged down and sullied because it shared the same name as the county sheriff's office.

For those who desired to climb the ladder within the Manitowoc County Sheriff's Office, there were two easy ways to get there. One was to brown nose your way to the top. The other was to have dirt on your superiors. A number of employees who climbed to the top of the troubled department were skilled at both.

***

Back in the 1970s, Bob Hermann, president of Cleveland Auto Sales & Salvage Inc., helped elect a mediocre city cop in his thirties named Tom Kocourek as the new sheriff of

Manitowoc County. In 1978, Kocourek garnered the most votes in a crowded five-man political primary that ousted the incumbent sheriff. By all accounts, Bob Hermann was an all-around likeable fellow. He had recently retired from his position as a Manitowoc County traffic patrolman. On the other hand, Kocourek brought few redeeming qualities to the sheriff's office. Yet he would hold down the fort for the next twenty-two years, retiring in 2001, so he could start collecting his government pension as he went to work in Manitowoc's non-profit sector as a well-paid executive director of the Big Brothers Big Sisters organization.

As sheriff, Kocourek's legacy is that his name is synonymous with crookedness and corruption. Along the way, Kocourek made sure to mold a number of disciples within his sheriff's office. After all, he wanted some of the minions to follow in his footsteps and uphold his legacy.

Incidentally, just five days before Teresa vanished after visiting Avery Road, recently retired chief investigator of Manitowoc County, Gene "the sketch pencil" Kusche, was compelled to give a sworn deposition at a Manitowoc law office. During that late October afternoon, Kusche was asked to recall the circumstances of his demotion by Sheriff Kocourek during the 1980s. Kusche had been the undersheriff at one time, second in command of the entire agency, but then, out of nowhere, Kocourek removed him from the post.

"I asked him, 'Why did you do this?'" Kusche testified. "And he said, 'Because I lacked tact.'"

Kusche remembered his two-decade-old conversation with Kocourek like it happened yesterday. (31)

"I said, 'Tom, tact on your department was the ability to smile at someone's face while you stabbed them in the back.' I don't think he responded," Kusche smirked.

---

31. Gene Kusche, deposition in Avery civil rights wrongful conviction lawsuit, October 26, 2005

Actually, Kusche was no honorable cop himself. And that's why, despite his baggage, he was worth keeping around inside the Kocourek regime. Plus, Kusche acquired a special skill that no one else in the sheriff's office had. Kusche was a pretty good sketch artist. As people who watched *Making a Murderer* will remember, Kocourek used Kusche as one of his henchmen to accomplish the false imprisonment of Steven Avery, the bushy bearded young punk, age twenty-three.

On the hot summer afternoon of July 29, 1985, a prominent young businesswoman was badly beaten and viciously raped as she jogged in her bikini along the sandy shores of Lake Michigan. Sheriff Kocourek put himself in charge of solving the brutal rape, although virtually no investigation would be done. Within hours of the attack, Kocourek selected Steven Avery, a local rascal, as the horrific crime's scapegoat. That night at a local hospital, Kusche was furnished a recent jail mugshot of Avery. Kusche traced the mugshot on his sketch pad. His drawing was presented to the semi-conscious rape victim as she lay in her hospital bed, recovering from her near-fatal beating.

Before the clock struck midnight, the sheriff got on the phone with another of his henchmen – Kenneth Petersen, a sergeant in road patrol. Petersen, in turn, got a hold of traffic patrol deputy Mike Bushman.

In due time, Petersen and Bushman would both ascend into top level leadership positions – tokens of gratitude for their unwavering loyalty and ability to follow orders from their sheriff. As for Bushman, he grew up in St. Nazianz, a tiny German village in southern Manitowoc County surrounded by farms, hillsides, and wilderness. There, his family ran the Bushman Hardware Store. After high school, Bushman tried college, but he lacked ambition and dropped out. During the 1970s, he found a job as a local school bus driver, but driving a yellow bus wasn't glamourous. A job as a Manitowoc County Sheriff's deputy was way more appealing. Although Bushman had no prior law enforcement experience or special qualifications that suited him to become a cop, that would not be a problem.

When Bushman filled out the job application, the form asked for references. The first reference Bushman put on his application was Bob Hermann, the popular Manitowoc County traffic patrol deputy who ran the Cleveland Auto Salvage yard about fifteen miles from St. Nazianz. The name of Bob Hermann meant something in a county where law enforcement jobs were based on who you knew.

Sure enough, Bushman got the job. Now, he too was a full-time county road patrol deputy like Bob Hermann. Of course, Bushman owed a tremendous debt of gratitude to the Hermann family and that would not be forgotten.

As for Ken Petersen, he wasn't the type of guy you'd expect any reputable law enforcement agency would to be begging to take a job, either.

Growing up in Manitowoc, Petersen had no ambitions to pursue a career in law enforcement. He graduated from Lincoln High School in 1968. From there, he attended Lake Shore Technical College in nearby Cleveland, Wisconsin, earning an associate's degree in marketing. But over the next six years, Petersen bounced from job to job. He struggled to find stable employment. Among his many low-paying jobs during the 1970s that did not pan out, Petersen worked at the Montgomery Ward retail store in Manitowoc. But in 1975, Petersen had a stroke of good fortune. He got hired by the Manitowoc County Sheriff's Office. For Petersen, 1978 was a transformative year that paved the way for his future success. That was the year Tom Kocourek was elected sheriff.

Three years later, in 1981, Petersen was involved in a big slip-up that made the daily newspaper. His actions involved a questionable death, possibly a preventable death.

Petersen was involved in a traffic crash that left dead a twenty-two-year-old woman from Manitowoc County's small community of Newton. The case may have ruined his law enforcement career had he worked for someone other than Kocourek. A number of sheriff's deputies who worked at the agency have said that Petersen was driving his squad car excessively over the speed limit in a reckless manner at the time he ran over the young lady during a thick, late night fog.

The fatality was chronicled in Manitowoc's newspaper on July 21, 1981:

"County Coroner Marion Cumming today identified the woman killed in a crash of two motorcycles early Monday as Gina M. Herzog, 22, Route 1, Newton. Cumming said the cause of death was a head injury sustained in the crash of the motorcycles. A squad car later collided with the wreckage and the victim."

Shortly after midnight, two young men on motorcycles left a bar out in the country as Petersen was gunning the gas on his squad car racing to the bar to investigate allegations of underage drinking. The motorcycles got tangled in the thick dense fog, causing the riders to tumble to the ground. Minutes later, Petersen's squad car came barreling down the two-lane highway. Fellow members of the Manitowoc County Sheriff's Department have said that Petersen was racing toward the bar like a madman when he struck and ran over Herzog, who may have been sitting on the side of the roadway, shaken up from the initial motorcycle tumble, according to other sheriff's deputies who worked for the county at the time of the tragedy.

Nobody else was seriously hurt during the motorcycle spill.

Two days later, a number of top public officials for Manitowoc County orchestrated a press conference. Deputy Petersen was absolved of any wrongdoing and negligence regarding the tragic loss of life.

According to the newspaper account, a coroner's inquest into Herzog's death was not even necessary. The Manitowoc press was assured the matter was cleared up even though it was unclear whether interview statements were even taken from the other motorcycle riders involved in the bike spill.

There was also no mention in the newspaper article regarding how fast Petersen was traveling. It was unclear whether any crash reconstruction occurred. The story in the paper was headlined, *"Coroner says police car no factor in traffic death."*

"The pathologist, Dr. John H. Fodden, said severe skull bone and brain damage caused the almost immediate death of Herzog and this was due to the motorcycle crash. Herzog also was injured internally after death and that could have been caused by a wheel of one of the motorcycles or an automobile. But, it was very, very, clear this was after she was dead," Dr. Fodden told the newspaper.

But was Herzog alive when Petersen's squad car ran her over? Since Petersen was barreling down the two-lane highway under the thick fog and darkness, he did not know. Was the young woman's death avoidable? There's not even a paper trail surrounding the crash in Petersen's personnel file.

My review in 2016 of Petersen's Manitowoc County employment file showed there was no mention at all of the fatality. There was no mention whether twenty-two-year-old Gina Herzog's fatality went before the sheriff's office accident review board even though it was standard practice to do so whenever one of the Manitowoc County squad cars sustained damage.

At any rate, both Petersen and the Manitowoc County Sheriff's Office escaped liability. Perhaps most telling, there were no more follow-up newspaper articles regarding Herzog's death after July 23, 1981. The local newspaper agreed to bury the story and nothing more was ever written about the infamous "Kenny Petersen incident." One sheriff's official told the author that Herzog's father was heartbroken and devastated by his daughter's untimely tragedy, but decided not to pursue a lawsuit against the Manitowoc County Sheriff's Department because nothing could change the outcome. A civil lawsuit against the county and Kenny Peterson would not bring the grieving man's daughter back.

As a result, the "Kenny Petersen incident" became a successful whitewash for Sheriff Kocourek. He was skilled at manipulating the local press to do what he wanted, and part of that skill also involved making sure that some stories that may have reflected poorly upon him and the Manitowoc County Sheriff's Office never saw the light of day.

As for the victim, Gina Herzog's newspaper obituary noted she was born in Manitowoc, a Class of 1977 graduate of Kiel High School, and she worked in Sheboygan for the state of Wisconsin's Division of Vocational Rehabilitation Office. She was survived by her parents of rural Newton, a sister, two brothers, and one grandmother.

The Herzogs had to persevere after the pain and heartache of their profound loss that many people blamed on Kenny Petersen's reckless driving.

As for Petersen, his law enforcement career hardly hit the skids because of the episode. In fact, his county sheriff's career would undergo a dramatic rise – three major promotions within the next eight years.

In 1982, Kocourek promoted Petersen to road patrol sergeant. In turn, Petersen became an obedient foot soldier. That was never more so than on July 29, 1985, hours after Penny Beerntsen's brutal attack on the Lake Michigan beach.

"That evening I would have received a phone call from Sheriff Kocourek informing me to arrest Steven Avery to see if he was at home and arrest him for attempted first-degree homicide," Petersen testified. "That night the only person I had any contact with was the sheriff. There was no one else that I was aware of." (32)

---

32. Deposition of Sheriff Kenny Petersen in Steven Avery's civil rights lawsuit, October 13, 2005

The previous winter, Avery had forced Sandra Morris, the wife of sheriff's deputy Bill Morris, off the road in front of Avery's trailer. Avery pointed an unloaded shotgun at her, accusing her of spreading false rumors that Avery had been outside naked on one of his cars laying down and masturbating on the hood of the car. The Sandy Morris incident was fresh on the minds of the Manitowoc County Sheriff's Office in the summer of 1985, and that made Avery a prime scapegoat for Sheriff Kocourek. He would look good to the community if he could take a heap of credit for single-handedly solving the rape of a prominent businesswoman in lightning quick fashion.

So that night, July 29, 1985, one of the deputies Petersen asked to tag along, to carry out the sheriff's wishes of arresting Steven Avery, was road deputy Mike Bushman. Thanks to Kocourek, Bushman was now serving as Manitowoc County Sheriff's Office's first-ever dog handler. Under Petersen's watch, Avery's arrest – for a brutal crime he was being framed of – went down without a hitch.

At his December 1985 jury trial, Avery provided more than a dozen witnesses who insisted he was doing concrete work at his family's salvage yard on the afternoon in question. Avery's public defenders produced store receipts from the ShopKo retail store in Green Bay indicating Avery and his wife were inside the store at 5:13 p.m., a mere seventy-five minutes after the time of the vicious rape north of Two Rivers. The jury of Manitowoc County residents rejected Avery's pleas of innocence.

The jury was in line with District Attorney Denis Vogel and Sheriff Kocourek. Avery was convicted of attempted first-degree murder, first-degree sexual assault, and false imprisonment. On March 10, 1986, Judge Fred Hazlewood sentenced Avery to spend thirty-two years inside a Wisconsin state prison facility. In August 1987, a Wisconsin appeals court rejected Avery's attempt to overturn his conviction, even though it appeared Avery was truly innocent of the awful crime.

In the back of his twisted mind, Sheriff Kocourek knew he had pulled a fast one. He had hoodwinked the entire Manitowoc community, a jury, and even the rape victim. He had tricked them all into believing Avery was the villainous monster who raped the woman who ran the popular candy store in Manitowoc. Now that Kocourek's career was going places, he needed other foot soldiers he could trust as part of his army.

On December 21, 1987, he typed a two-paragraph memo for Petersen's personnel file.

The subject was titled "PROMOTION."

"During the past twelve months at the Manitowoc County Sheriff's Department you have been in training for one of the most important positions at the department … Because of the excellent job which you have been doing … effective January 15, 1988, you will officially assume the duties of Deputy Inspector of the Operations Division. Congratulations on your new appointment and I look forward to working with you in your command position for many years to come."

On December 18, 1989, Petersen drew another huge promotion from the boss.

"As Inspector at the Sheriff's Department you will represent the Sheriff in his absence and supervise the day-to-day operations of the entire Sheriff's Department … Your past work product in the various positions held by yourself at the Manitowoc County Sheriff's Department has always been excellent and I feel confident that this pattern of productivity will continue in your new position as Inspector … I look forward to working with you and having you as my right-hand man here at the Manitowoc County Sheriff's Dept." – Sheriff Kocourek

Petersen's promotion to sheriff's inspector came with a nine percent salary increase and another exclusive perk given only to the top two sheriff's officials.

"As Inspector, he is now eligible for $100 per month car allowance plus 1,000 gallons of gas per year," Kocourek notified county personnel.

As for Bushman, documents contained within his employment personnel file from Manitowoc County government show he had wrecked one of Manitowoc County's new Chevrolet Caprice squad cars on September 4, 1989. Bids to repair the damage ranged between $2,004 and $3,792 – a lot of money by 1989 standards.

"Sgt. Bushman, while on patrol, observed what appeared to be a drunk driver. While watching this vehicle in his rear view mirror, Sgt. Bushman lost his bearings in relationship to the intersection. Sgt. Bushman was unable to stop the squad car before it ran off the road through the T intersection … The squad car, at just less than highway speed, struck the embankment and came to a rest … Investigation into the accident showed the case to be a result of inattentive driving. Accident investigated and written by the Wisconsin State Patrol."

Bushman's incident was presented to the sheriff's office's accident review board. One of the reviewers happened to be Petersen, who ran over Gina Herzog eight years earlier.

"We recommend Sgt. Bushman be issued a written reprimand relating to this accident," Petersen advised Sheriff Kocourek.

As Petersen knew from prior experience, a royal screw up as a Manitowoc sheriff's deputy was not necessarily a professional setback under Kocourek's leadership. Just a few months later, on February 9, 1990, Bushman received a memo in his personnel file from the sheriff.

"I wish to congratulate you and advise that you have been selected to fill the position of Lieutenant/Shift Commander … Your excellent service to Manitowoc and the Sheriff's

Department in your past positions of patrol officer and patrol sergeant have prepared you to assume the responsibilities of lieutenant, and I am sure you will do an excellent job as you have in the past."

In Bushman, Kocourek knew he had added another sheep to his flock.

***

Because the 1985 Avery prosecution was a sham from the get-go, the Manitowoc sheriff was growing increasingly paranoid. He was willing to target anybody who posed a threat at blowing his cover.

In 1990, as Avery was serving his unjust attempted murder prison sentence, Kocourek got wind of someone in town who was not convinced of Avery's guilt. Freedom of speech may be afforded by the U.S. Constitution, but the following information, obtained from a Manitowoc County Sheriff's police report, reveals the dangers of speaking out in a small town where law enforcement runs roughshod over the citizenry. One man in Manitowoc was threatened with arrest and felony charges if he made his beliefs known again about Avery's innocence.

In March 1990, Kocourek, the sheriff himself, wrote up a formal report, classifying the incident as "Harassment."

According to the sheriff, a customer of the Beerntsen's Confectionary candy store stopped inside and asked if co-owner Penny Beerntsen was there. She and her husband were out of town at the time. The customer, Erik Moen, thirty-three, told the store clerk he was a friend of Avery and that Avery was innocent of assaulting the candy store lady.

A week later, the sheriff of Manitowoc County made a personal visit to Moen's residence on South 38th Street in Manitowoc. "Erik stated that he was in fact at Beerntsen's Confectionary several days ago and had stopped in to purchase some chocolates. He stated that he meant no harm and only wanted to tell Penny Beerntsen that, in his opinion, Steve Avery was innocent," Kocourek's report reflected.

The sheriff who had framed Avery also knew about Gregory Allen, the dangerous sexual predator who was allowed to get away with the near fatal assault and remain a danger to the community at large. Yet this is how Kocourek summarized his exchange with Moen.

"Erik admitted that he had no new factual data that was not already brought out during the trial and that the belief of Steve Avery being innocent was only a personal belief on his part. I advised Erik that his presence at the store in attempting to contact Penny Beerntsen reference this case could be interpreted as a felony charge reference harassing a witness.

"Erik was warned that any future attempts to contact the Beerntsen family and discuss the matter would result in felony charges being brought against him. He was also informed that if he had any new information that was not already brought out at the trial, that he should contact the sheriff's department, which was the investigating agency, and we would be glad to look into that information. Erik stated that he understood," Kocourek wrote.

Obviously, Kocourek's report was a web of lies. He was not about to reopen the rape investigation, and he most certainly was not about to investigate somebody else as the rapist. Rather, the sheriff's face-to-face interview with the local man served a higher purpose. Kocourek had iced the concept of Avery's innocence from gaining traction around Manitowoc. For him, this was an important event, much more so than punishing real criminals.

In the days following the brutal attack along Lake Michigan's beach, the traumatized rape victim began receiving anonymous threatening phone calls at her house from the rapist, Gregory Allen, who was notorious for calling his victims afterward.

But Sheriff Kocourek convinced the candy store owner not to worry, she was just confused. Avery was already in jail, he informed her. Rather than trust her own instincts, she believed the sheriff.

Because the residents of Manitowoc County were in no position to rise up and oust Kocourek from office, he remained the most powerful politician of Manitowoc County for many more years to come. Finally, when the numbers lined up for him to collect his police pension, he decided to leave the office on his own terms. In 2000, he decided to pass the torch of corruption to someone else. But his heir apparent, Ken Petersen, still didn't know where all the bodies were buried and all the skeletons were being hidden. The Manitowoc County master needed to let his understudy in on one more devious secret. Once again, all things centered on the high-profile rape conviction of Avery, from the 1980s. At the time, Avery was pushing forty and in the middle of his prison term behind the walls at the Wisconsin Department of Corrections. As for the retiring sheriff, Kocourek was cutting cakes, receiving going away gifts, and bidding his farewells to fellow county government employees and local dignitaries as part of his grand farewell retirement send-off.

And now that Petersen had earned the outgoing sheriff's sacred trust, the time arrived to make Petersen aware of a secret document being kept inside a special safe, a safe to which only the sheriff of Manitowoc County had access. Although the sheriff's office had a large vault where it housed thousands of old records from major criminal cases over the years, this particular report was apparently off-limits to the rest of the sheriff's employees. The secret document turned out to be a letter, purportedly written by a prison inmate, outlining an alleged confession that convicted prisoner Avery gave to the inmate regarding the 1985 rape of Penny Beerntsen.

The letter was mentioned as part of Avery's $36 million civil rights lawsuit. It was more unflattering testimony about Kocourek and the topic of the letter's existence came up just a couple of weeks before Teresa vanished and was killed.

"He said somebody from, some inmate from Brown County sent it to him," Petersen testified. "That's all I know … I don't know if it came direct or where it came from. All I know is it was there."

Regardless of how it was contrived, the letter in the sheriff's safe was phony.

In reality, Avery never confessed to raping Penny Beerntsen.

He maintained his steadfast innocence since his arrest by Kenneth Petersen on July 29, 1985. On September 11, 2003, the gates of the Wisconsin Department of Corrections swung wide open as a large contingent of well-wishers shared hugs, kisses, and tears with Avery. Attorney Keith Findley of the Wisconsin Innocence Project had secured a DNA exoneration proving Gregory Allen was the real beachfront rapist, just as the more reputable City of Manitowoc Police Department suspected all along.

Two years later, during October 2005, Avery's tenacious civil lawyers from Milwaukee, Walt Kelly and Stephen Glynn, were pounding away at the tainted Manitowoc County Sheriff's Office. The agency's upper administration was uneasy and uncomfortable. The scrappy civil attorneys were making substantial progress as they assembled their case against Manitowoc County and Sheriff Kocourek, the suspected crook and mastermind of Avery's 1985 frame job.

That month, the following employees got pulled off the job and were paraded into a Manitowoc law office, where they were forced to raise their right hand and be subjected to an uncomfortable videotaped civil rights lawsuit deposition: Sheriff Ken Petersen, Lt. Detective James Lenk, road patrol Sgt. Andrew Colborn, former sheriff's deputy Judy Dvorak, and retired chief investigator Gene Kusche. Dvorak would reveal how she despised Avery, who had no history of any sexual violence but did have a solid alibi to account for his whereabouts during the time of Gregory Allen's rape.

At most of these lawsuit depositions sat a short stubby man who was not dressed in a suit and tie like the room full of lawyers and key members of the sheriff's office such as Petersen and Lenk. Avery's unsightly presence at the same table as members of the Manitowoc County Sheriff's Office had to be sickening to them.

The clock was ticking, ticking closer and closer to the scheduled deposition of the master himself, retired Sheriff Tom Kocourek.

What would he have to say for himself when he found himself seated at the same wooden table, sitting in the very same room, as the unfortunate man from whom he had stolen eighteen years of his life?

CHAPTER TEN

RAV4

One of the most shadowy figures to emerge from the Teresa Halbach murder probe was veteran Manitowoc County classic car buff, Andy Colborn.

Colborn belonged to various classic car clubs around northeastern Wisconsin, and he was fond of the 1950s-era Plymouths. Over the years, Colborn had walked the grounds of Avery Salvage on many occasions to find the right spare parts for his prized collection of old cars. And like so many of the rising stars in the Manitowoc Sheriff's Office, Colborn landed in law enforcement as a last resort. After high school he enlisted in the Air Force, on active duty, serving our country from 1976 until 1988. He was stationed in Nevada for much his time. In his late twenties, he left the Air Force and found work in Las Vegas as an auto transmission mechanic. After three years as a grease monkey, Colborn left Nevada and returned to Wisconsin. That year, 1990, he found employment at the Waupaca Foundry, where he stayed until 1992. But in his early thirties, he set his sights on a new line of work. Manitowoc Sheriff Tom Kocourek offered Colborn a full-time job as a county jailer.

Colborn later gained infamy for his role in Avery's wrongful conviction case. Colborn was the dopey Manitowoc County jailer who spoke with one of the Green Bay area police departments around 1995 regarding the recent arrest of serial rapist Gregory Allen. Colborn was alerted that the police in Brown County had a rapist in custody who had confessed that someone else was imprisoned for a violent assault committed in nearby Manitowoc County.

Many people believe Colborn confided in Sheriff Kocourek about this matter. In the end, Manitowoc County ignored the call, preferring to let Avery rot in prison another eight years for a crime he did not commit. From the moment that Colborn disregarded the call that could have gained Avery his freedom many years sooner, Colborn's career path was on the rise under Kocourek and Petersen. Colborn was moved out of his less desirable job as a jailer and assigned to road patrol. He later was promoted to a shift sergeant. By the fall of 2005, Colborn had delusions of becoming the next sheriff of Manitowoc; Kenny Petersen was nearing retirement and the crooked agency's coveted top spot was opening up.

However, the month of October 2005 was becoming more and more stressful, all thanks to his sheriff's office's arch nemesis. Colborn was being dragged into the civil rights lawsuit of Avery, who was finally freed in September 2003.

Just three weeks before Teresa vanished, Colborn was in uniform when he showed up at the Manitowoc law office to answer a barrage of questions from Avery's civil attorneys of Milwaukee.

Colborn: "I gathered, yes, that they had someone in custody. I don't know if this person had commented directly to the person who contacted me or had commented to other people within that jurisdiction and this eventually got to my caller." (33)

Lawyer: "But the detective had indicated that there was a person in custody who had made a statement about a Manitowoc County offense, correct?"

"Yes."

---

33. Andrew Colborn civil rights lawsuit deposition in Steven Avery case, October 13, 2005

Lawyer: "And what that person in custody had said, was that he had committed an assault in Manitowoc County and someone else was in jail for it. Correct?"

"Yes, sir."

Lawyer: "And that much you're pretty sure of?"

"Yes."

Lawyer: "I mean, that's a significant event?"

Lawyer: "Right, that's what stood out in my mind."

After the newspaper coverage of Avery's exoneration in September 2003, Colborn had realized he was in a hot mess. He needed to confide in someone he trusted about his role in the Gregory Allen episode.

"You brought that up to someone else, correct?" Kelly asked.

"Yes, sir."

"And to whom did you bring that up?"

"To Lieutenant Lenk."

"There was also a conversation that followed that. You spoke to Sheriff Petersen, correct?"

"Yes sir … I remember coming into work and Sheriff Petersen was downstairs where our patrol division is, and I got the impression he was waiting for me to come into work. He initiated the conversation by saying he had spoken with Lieutenant Lenk, and he felt that it would be in the best interest of Lieutenant Lenk and myself and the sheriff's department, I would suppose, that if I was to give him a statement on the gist of our conversation, or what we had discussed. And I asked for clarification on that, you know," Colborn laughed nervously during his deposition.

"And he goes, 'Well what you discussed about a telephone call that you received when you were working in the jail' and I said, 'OK,' and before I went out on patrol I provided this statement."

In the coming days, Colborn realized his lawsuit deposition experience had negative overtones and perhaps lasting consequences that weren't good for him.

Would Avery's lawyers amend their civil rights case to add Deputy Colborn as one of their codefendants? Colborn also had to figure that those who ran the sheriff's office were not going down on a sinking ship. He was emerging as a logical fall guy, a prime scapegoat for Sheriff Petersen and the lawsuit's other codefendants, Kocourek and former District Attorney Denis Vogel.

The continuation and the publicity of Avery's civil rights lawsuit was bad news for Colborn's upcoming sheriff's candidacy. Colborn had been collaborating with Lt. Lenk about his eventual bid for sheriff. A Colborn victory put Lenk in line for a hefty raise and promotion to undersheriff of Manitowoc County.

However, the big election was still a year away but campaign season was just around the corner. But in 2005, there were far more pressing matters. The sheriff's office needed to deal with Avery.

"If we wanted to eliminate Steve, it would have been a whole lot easier to eliminate Steve than it would be to frame Steve, you know?" Sheriff Petersen told Green Bay television station Fox 11 in the days after Avery's arrest.

The Manitowoc sheriff went on to say, "If we wanted him out of the picture like in prison or if we wanted him killed, you know, it would have been much easier just to kill him."

***

One of the most dramatic moments from Avery's murder trial came when Colborn, then forty-eight, was on the witness stand during Avery's trial and defense attorney Dean Strang had a chance to cross-examine him.

"One of the things that road patrol officers frequently do is call into dispatch and give the dispatcher the license plate number of a car they've stopped or a car that looks out of place for some reason?"(34)

"Correct, yes, sir," Colborn answered.

"And the dispatcher can get information about to whom the license plate is registered?"

"Yes, sir."

"And if a car is abandoned, or there's nobody in the car, registration tells you who the owner presumably is?"

"Yes, sir."

"I'm going to ask you to listen, if you would, to a short phone call."

Manitowoc County Sheriff's Department this is Lynn.

Lynn.

Hi Andy.

Can you run Sam William Henry 5-8-2. See if comes back to (Inaudible.)

OK. Shows that she's a missing person. And it lists to Teresa Halbach.

All set.

OK. Is that what you're looking for, Andy?

'99 Toyota?

Yup.

Ok. Thank you.

You're so welcome. Bye. Bye.

When the call ended, Strang resumed his line of uncomfortable questions for Andy Colborn.

"And then you tell the dispatcher, oh, ''99 Toyota?'"

"No, I thought she told me that."

Strang replayed the audio for the jury and Sgt. Colborn to hear again.

OK. Shows that she's a missing person. And it lists to Teresa Halbach.

All set.

---

34. Feb. 20, 2007 cross examination of Andy Colborn by attorney Dean Strang

OK. Is that what you're looking for, Andy?
'99 Toyota?
Yup.
Ok. Thank you.
You're so welcome. Bye. Bye.

Colborn ducked his head toward the courtroom microphone. He avoided eye contact with Strang.

"Were you looking at these plates when you called them in?" Strang asked.

"No, sir."

Then he lifted his head, grimaced, and cracked his knuckles two times.

"Do you have any recollection of making that phone call?"

Colborn buried his head. He paused a few seconds before answering that he guessed he made the call on November 3, 2005.

"Probably after I received a phone call from Investigator Wiegert letting me know that there was a missing person."

November 3 was when Calumet and Manitowoc County first learned of Teresa's disappearance.

Strang followed up with another excellent question.

"Investigator Wiegert, did he give you the license plate number for Teresa Halbach when he called you?"

Colborn would not look up and answer Strang's question.

He was in his comfort zone keeping his head down and looking straight toward his microphone.

"You know, I just don't remember the exact content of our conversation. But he had to have given it to me because I wouldn't have had the number any other way," Colborn testified as he let out another nervous laugh.

"Well," Strang began, "you can understand how someone listening to that might think that you were calling in a license plate that you were looking at on the back end of a 1999 Toyota?"

"Yes," Colborn looked up and shrugged his shoulders.

"But there's no way you should have been looking at Teresa Halbach's license plate on November 3 on the back end of a 1999 Toyota?"

"I shouldn't have been, and I was not looking at the license plate."

"Because you're aware now, that the first time that Toyota was reported found was on November 5?"

"Yes, sir."

The turnabout near the Old Mishicot Dam along State Highway 147 is where several people saw abandoned Teresa Halbach's RAV4 in the days after her disappearance.

***

After the *Making a Murderer* hysteria, many fans presumed Colborn made his cryptic call after snooping around late at night, on his way home from work on November 3, the first night of the missing person's investigation.

That evening, Colborn spoke with Avery in person at Avery Salvage between 6:30 and 7 p.m. to get a statement from Avery about the missing woman's whereabouts. And later that night, Colborn met with Lenk, Manitowoc County Detective Dennis Jacobs, County Detective Dave Remiker, and Calumet County Investigator Dedering. The five men focused on Avery and another Manitowoc County residence Teresa visited on her last day of life, the property on County Road B belonging to George Zipperer. Colborn joined Dedering and Remiker at that house around 9:40 p.m. They made entry at 9:53 p.m. (35)

"I did review voice mail messages left on the answering machine and caller ID. I did locate a caller ID entry on October 31, 2005, at 2:12 p.m. from phone number 920-737-4731. I recognized this as being the cellular phone number of Teresa Halbach."

By all accounts, the Manitowoc County Sheriff's entourage called it a night around 10:30 p.m. No additional work was done to locate Teresa or her missing SUV during the overnight shift.

It's been established that Colborn drove home from sheriff's headquarters in downtown Manitowoc using his personal vehicle.

He testified he fell asleep on his living room couch at his home near Whitelaw. His work schedule had him off the next day, Friday, November 4. But there were other factors at play. Given Teresa's alarming disappearance and the zeal to pin the crime on Avery, Colborn had a lot on his mind.

But if Colborn chose to cross the line from good cop to bad, he had to reconcile these inner demons with his own conscience. After all, Colborn was a God-fearing man who was deeply involved in his Christian church. On one hand, a young woman from a good farm family was suddenly missing. Her worried family deserved the best effort from him and other police. On the other hand, Colborn considered

---

35. John Dedering report, Nov. 3, 2005 contact with George, Jason and Jo Ellen Zipperer

Avery a filthy no-good swine, a glory hound who was leveraging the Wisconsin media to undermine the reputation of the Manitowoc County Sheriff's Office with his constant press coverage regarding his wrongful conviction lawsuit. The lawsuit gnawed at Manitowoc County because it kept giving everyone a black eye. And get this: Avery was now on the verge of becoming one of the biggest millionaires in Manitowoc County. Would he use his exoneration lawsuit money to buy up the city's downtown businesses, own the local pool halls, and maybe a tavern or a strip tease club?

The idea of Avery being rich, filthy rich, was downright repulsive to the community's leaders. And if Manitowoc County's lawyers reached a large settlement as payment to Avery as reparation for all of his injustices, Colborn was a logical fall guy for the screw-up. The footsteps were getting louder and louder. Then, all of a sudden, there came along a golden opportunity for Colborn and others to restore their careers and destroy Avery's life once and for all.

"Just three weeks before Teresa Halbach's disappearance, both Lenk and Colborn were deposed in Avery's civil lawsuit about their own involvement in the failure to follow up an exculpatory lead which contributed to Steven Avery spending another eight years in prison before his eventual exoneration. Curiously, although Lenk and Colborn were aware that authority for the investigation of the Halbach disappearance was transferred to the Calumet County Sheriff's Department because of the conflict of interest arising from Avery's lawsuit, both officers volunteered to search Avery's personal residence and did not inform the Calumet County authorities that they had direct contact with the civil case or that they had themselves been deposed and had their conduct as to Avery called into question in the case a mere three weeks earlier." (36)

---

36. Zellner post-conviction motion 2016

Colborn's cryptic phone call to dispatch remained one of the biggest mysteries associated with Teresa's killing.

But new evidence Zellner uncovered in 2018 strongly suggests Sgt. Colborn, who by all accounts was conscientious about his job, was ambitiously working off the clock, so to speak, on Friday, November 4, because he did not want to let his comrades down.

Former Mishicot resident Kevin Rahmlow positively identified Colborn as the sheriff's deputy whom he alerted to the abandoned RAV4 being parked near the State Highway 147 turnabout.

"In the series, I recognized the officer who I talked to at the Cenex station on November 4, 2005," Rahmlow testified with confidence. "Having watched *Making a Murderer*, I now know that his name is Andrew Colborn."(37)

Zellner's filings from October 2017 reveal, "The eyewitness was also sure he shared his observation with the Manitowoc County deputy. But in that instance, Sgt. Colborn never made a report of this conversation."

During an August 2018 interview for this book, Zellner told the author, "I went to the old dam with Mr. Rahmlow and my investigator. He is absolutely telling the truth about seeing the Halbach vehicle. He is also telling the truth about the Cenex station missing poster in the window regarding Ms. Halbach and her vehicle."

When Colborn made his highly suspicious call into Manitowoc County radio dispatch, he was not utilizing his squad car's CB radio.

"Sgt. Colborn placed this call from his personal cell phone, not his squad car's radio," Zellner said. "Sgt. Colborn testified that, after completing contact with the Zipperers, he signed off at Manitowoc County Sheriff's Department, which would have included leaving his cruiser in the secure (police) lot and drove his personal vehicle home.

37. Kevin Rahmlow affidavit July 15, 2017

"If Sgt. Colborn was on duty and in his squad car, it would be reasonable to expect transmissions to and from Manitowoc County Sheriff's Department dispatch to come over the radio. Because Sgt. Colborn called dispatch from his personal phone, it is reasonable to conclude that he made the call on Friday, November 4, 2005, his day off."(38)

Kevin Rahmlow now believes he encountered Colborn at the gas station around 12:30 p.m. to let him know about the missing woman's vehicle.

"Sgt. Colborn confirmed the identity of Ms. Halbach's vehicle by calling ... dispatch on his cell phone around 7:30 p.m. on November 4 ... Realizing such a call would be recorded, Sgt. Colborn removed the license plates from Ms. Halbach's vehicle to conceal that he had actually located the vehicle at the point in time when he made the call about the license plates."

In the background of Colborn's call to Lynn, the Manitowoc County dispatcher, someone else's voice can be heard.

"Audible in a recording of Sgt. Colborn's call to Manitowoc dispatch regarding the victim's license plate number, a third-party states, 'It's hers.'"

Zellner also realized Colborn's license plate call was tendered to Avery's original trial lawyers Buting and Strang on a CD containing a total of thirty tracks of other dispatch calls in relation to the investigation.

"It is apparent that the recordings are organized chronologically on the CD. Sgt. Colborn's dispatch call was titled 'Track 3.' The preceding, 'Track 2,' is a call to Manitowoc dispatch from an unnamed officer regarding George Zipperer. The officer requested a criminal records check of George Zipperer from the dispatcher.

"It is reasonable to conclude that this call was placed by one of the Manitowoc County Sheriff's Office deputies

---

38. Motion for Post-Conviction Relief filed June 7, 2017

who were with Calumet County Sheriff's Office Detective Dedering before they proceeded to the Zipperer's on November 3, 2005. Therefore it follows that Sgt. Colborn's call to dispatch occurred after he responded to the Avery property to make contact with Mr. Avery and after he drove back to the Manitowoc County Sheriff's Office about his contact with Mr. Avery.

"Sgt. Colborn's explanation that he called Manitowoc County Sheriff's Office dispatch to confirm information obtained from Calumet County Sheriff's Office Investigator Wiegert is contradicted by the chronological order of the ... dispatch calls as produced to trial defense counsel. Sgt. Colborn testified that he placed this call to dispatch after speaking with Investigator Wiegert while he was driving from the Avery property to Manitowoc County Sheriff's Office after making contact with Mr. Avery. However, based upon the chronological organization of the Manitowoc County Sheriff's Office dispatch calls as produced to trial defense counsel, Sgt. Colborn called dispatch after meeting the assembled officers at Manitowoc County Sheriff's Office, long after leaving the Avery property and speaking with Investigator Wiegert," Zellner stated.

Given the uncontroverted facts dug up by Zellner, Colborn's murder trial testimony now appears seriously flawed.

"After departing the Manitowoc County Sheriff's Office for the Zipperers' property, Sgt. Colborn had no viable reason to call Manitowoc County Sheriff's Office dispatch regarding Ms. Halbach's vehicle," Zellner argues. "From the time Sgt. Colborn arrived at the Manitowoc County Sheriff's Office to the time he checked out and returned home, Sgt. Colborn was with at least Detective Remiker and Investigator Dedering, both of whom could have confirmed information regarding Ms. Halbach's vehicle."

A month before Avery's huge trial got under way, Strang and Buting informed Manitowoc County Judge Patrick

Willis of their client's frame-up defense in the murder trial. The lawyers for Avery planned to build their defense on the premise that Lenk and Colborn had falsified several pieces of evidence, namely blood, to secure Avery's arrest and conviction for Teresa's murder.

But Strang and Buting tried to stretch their theory like a rubber band and it never panned out as they envisioned.

They accused Lenk and Colborn of having planted an old vial of Avery's blood, a vial kept inside a cardboard box of files from Avery's wrongful conviction rape case, at the Manitowoc County Courthouse, which was next door to the sheriff's building.

With the trial looming, the prosecution team realized it needed to defuse this argument. In the days before Avery's February 2007 murder trial began, Calumet County Investigator Gary Steier was tapped to speak with Lenk and Colborn regarding their whereabouts during the week leading up to the discovery of Teresa's RAV4 by Pamela Sturm.

Steier's interviews of Lenk and Colborn were non-accusatory and consisted of softball questions that did not include any follow ups. This is understandable because Steier knew that his own head would be dished up like the head of John the Baptist if Wiegert and others discovered he was attempting to grill the two Manitowoc County sheriff's deputies and finding flaws with their interview statements.

Lenk and Colborn were questioned separately about their schedules for Sunday, October 30, 2005, through Saturday, November 5.

"Sgt. Colborn indicates he can recall where he was because his routine is fairly rigid. On Sundays, Sgt. Colborn indicates at 10:30 a.m. he would have left his house and went to his mother-in-law's house to check on her. Sgt. Colborn indicates every Sunday, prior to the start of his shift, he goes over to his mother-in-law's to make sure she is OK. Sgt.

Colborn says he would leave her house about 11:45 a.m. to go to work."(39)

Monday was Halloween, the date when Halbach met her end.

"Sgt. Colborn indicated he had worked a nine-and-one-half-hour workday and was done around 11:18 p.m.," Colborn "would generally go home after his shift is over and watch TV, fall asleep on the couch, and then go to bed."

For Tuesday, November 1 and Wednesday, November 2, Colborn remembered he worked regular eight-hour shifts, finishing at 8 p.m.

"Colborn indicated generally he would have returned home or he would have watched TV and then gone to bed."

Thursday, November 3 was the start of the missing person investigation for Teresa. Colborn was the first officer to interview Avery, a face-to-face interview in which Colborn did not see any noticeable gashes or wounds to Avery's hands. "Sgt. Colborn indicated he had started at 11:45 a.m. where he had worked his eight-hour shift, plus three hours of overtime, assisting Calumet County Investigator John Dedering in speaking to the Zipperers about Teresa Halbach. Sgt. Colborn also remembers he was called to go check the Avery residence. Sgt. Colborn indicated he had concluded his shift around 10:50 p.m."

Next, it was time to ask Colborn about his whereabouts and movements for the next day, Friday, November 4. This time, Colborn claimed he had a foggy memory. He portrayed himself as having what's known in police circles as cop amnesia.

"On Friday, November 4, 2005, Sgt. Colborn indicated he was off. He could not recall what he had done on his off day."

---

39. Interview of Sgt. Andrew Colborn, Investigator Gary Steier, January 11, 2007

Colborn was just one day removed from the biggest day of police work in his career, and he was allowed to answer with a straight face that he simply could not remember anything about his activities and whereabouts the following day, on an open missing person's case, where the victim had not been found, her car was still gone, and the attacker remained at large.

It's also a little-known fact that Colborn was intricately involved in two other very strange discoveries of physical evidence surrounding Teresa's murder. Not far from the location where the eyewitnesses saw Teresa's RAV4 being hidden off Highway 147 at the turnabout, civilian searches also found a silver cellular phone in the ditch. And it wasn't an ordinary phone, either. The phone is commonly known as a burner phone. Burner phones are often used by two groups: people on a limited budget who use them to avoid the expensive entanglements with mobile companies, and the other element of people who use burner phones are criminals. There's a degree of privacy that make it nearly impossible for police to hunt down the caller's activities. A burner phone would be ideal for a drug dealer, a phone harasser, and for a stalker.

On Wednesday, November 9, ten days after Teresa vanished, a search party of Manitowoc County residents notified the police that they had made a suspicious discovery at 2:50 p.m. The find occurred along State Highway 147, just east of Ridge Road. Three police officers were called to the spot: Colborn, Lenk, and Calumet County Deputy Craig Wendling. "In the north ditch right along the gravel line was an Audiovox phone, silver in color. That item was found by a person searching, his name being John Campion … After collecting the phone, we did return to the command post and all the evidence was kept in my exclusive possession in my squad. I then transported all the evidence to the Calumet County Sheriff's Office." (40)

The burner phone became an afterthought as the murder investigation focused squarely on Avery, who was also taken into custody that same day, November 9.

Incidentally, three days earlier, Colborn was also involved in the mysterious find at the creepy Maribel Caves Park. The secluded site is off-the-beaten path but it was located in the same general area where Teresa may have encountered her attacker. It was another example of Colborn being called outside the comfort zone of Avery Road to an off-site location to collect suspicious evidence that would quickly fade into oblivion as far as the police investigators were concerned.

"I was approached by Sgt. Colborn ... and informed he had left the crime scene to meet with a citizen at the Maribel Caves Park. Sgt. Colborn reported that the citizen found a piece of, what appeared to be, woman's blue jeans, and also found a plastic baggie containing a lubrication box ... I informed Sgt. Colborn he should get me all the information on the citizen and I would do an evidence sheet on that showing the exchange of custody." (41)

These mysterious blue jeans belonged to a female. Eerily, they had cut marks on them and bore a similar resemblance to the Daisy Fuentes clothing brand.

---

40. Deputy Craig Wendling, evidence collection from November 9, 2005, along with Manitowoc County's Sgt. Andy Colborn and Lt. Jim Lenk

41. Calumet County Sgt. Bill Tyson, November 6, 2005, supplemental report

*Pieces of torn blue jeans belonging to an unidentified female
were recovered from the creepy Maribel Caves Park property.
It's the same general area where Teresa Halbach vanished.*

CHAPTER ELEVEN

BATHROOM SINK

When Colborn interviewed Avery face to face on the evening of Thursday, November 3, one thing stood out. Colborn did not notice any gash or open wound on Avery's hand. The wound did not bust open until after Colborn left and went on his way back to the sheriff's office. If Colborn had noticed a bloody gash, he would have made a notation of such when he finally wrote up his first incident report of the event, eight months later.

"I, Sgt. Colborn attended a pretrial conference ... I mentioned that I had made initial contact with Steven Avery on Thursday, November 3, 2005. It was suggested to this sergeant on June 29, 2006, that I make an entry on this case narrative describing my initial contact with Steven on November 3, 2005."(42)

Colborn was the noon to 8 p.m. shift commander.

"I personally responded to Avery Auto Salvage initially to make contact with Charles 'Chuck' Avery in an attempt to locate the missing person. The Calumet Sheriff's Office had provided me with a (registered plate) which corresponds with a Toyota RAV4 registered to the missing person, as well as the name of the missing person, that being Teresa Halbach."

When he got to Avery Road, Colborn went to the main business office near Al and Dolores' trailer.

---

42. Manitowoc County Sheriff's Office summary, Sgt. Colborn entry, dated June 29, 2006

"As I exited my squad, again my intention was to walk to Chuck's trailer and make contact with him, however, as soon as I exited my squad, Steven Avery exited Allan and Dolores' trailer from the garage area and made contact with me. Steven inquired as to what I was at the property for. I asked Steven if a girl from Auto Trader Magazine had been on the property that day taking pictures of a vehicle they were selling. Steven replied that the female had indeed been on the Avery property and that she had been photographing a van which his sister was selling."

Even though Avery consistently told everyone that Teresa came between 2 and 2:30 p.m., Colborn chose to write down "it was somewhere around 3 p.m."

"He informed me that he did not speak with her and she had only been on the property five to ten minutes at the most … Steven stated that he did not speak with her and therefore would not know where she was going when she left the Avery property. Steven did volunteer the information that he glanced out the window of his residence and had observed her photographing the van. That is how he knew she was on the property."

When Colborn left the Avery compound, no evidence pointed to Avery as the abductor. Oddly, Colborn never went and spoke with Chuck Avery even though his report indicated visiting with Chuck was his main intention.

"As far as making contact with the Avery family or returning to the Avery property, no further action was taken on November 3, 2005, by this sergeant."

Here's what Avery remembers happened.

"After that conversation, I drove my Pontiac Grand Am from my parents' residence to its usual parking spot outside my garage. I got out of my car and walked to my sister's trailer, which was right next to mine. There, I broke open a cut on the outside of the middle finger of my right hand as I was attempting to unhitch my sister Barb's trailer. Before going to my trailer to put masking tape on my finger, I went into my Pontiac to grab my phone charger. I dripped blood in my Pontiac on the gearshift and other places. Anyone who looked through the windows of my Pontiac could have seen the blood on the gearshift and known there was a cut on my hand. I left my Pontiac unlocked."(43)

Shortly thereafter, Avery, along with his brother Chuck, drove into Manitowoc to buy supplies at Menards. Video surveillance from the store confirms this event.

"I remembered that I went to Barb's door to see if any of her sons wanted to go with me to Menards. Bobby and Blaine were home. I asked Bobby and Blaine if they wanted to go with me and my brother to Menards. I told both of them that a law enforcement officer had just left the property after asking me questions about Ms. Halbach's visit to photograph Barb's van on October 31, 2005. I noticed that Bobby was immediately nervous after I mentioned the visit by the officer. He said that he could not go with me to Menards and that he had 'things to do.' My memory is that Blaine said that he wanted to go to Menards and he went with Chuck and me."

But Avery had just split open his finger. That was troublesome and painful.

"Prior to leaving for Menards, I returned to my trailer to put tape on my bleeding finger. I entered my trailer through the south door because it was closest to the bathroom. I did not lock the south door of my trailer after I entered through it. A large amount of blood dripped onto the rim and sink and the floor of the bathroom. I did not wash away or wipe up because Chuck was waiting for me to go to Menards in Manitowoc with him. I quickly wrapped my finger in duct tape and left the trailer to meet Chuck. I left through the front door of my trailer."

The time they left was between 7:15 and 7:30 p.m. The skies were dark.

---

43. Affidavit of Steven Avery, November 23, 2016

"While we were leaving Avery property, driving a flatbed to Menards in Manitowoc, I saw taillights in front of my trailer," Avery remembers. "The taillights were further apart and higher off the ground than sedan taillights. I told my brother, who was driving, about the taillights. We turned around and drove to my trailer, but the vehicle was gone."

All told, Avery and his older brother were gone about three hours. They didn't make it back to Avery Road until 10 p.m. to 10:30 p.m.

"By the time we got home ... I was real tired. I went into my trailer through the front door and went straight to bed. I did not go back into my bathroom on November 3."

On Friday, November 4, Avery got up around 6 a.m. He walked down the hall to his bathroom to take a shower but was befuddled when he noticed his sink. "I saw that most of the blood on my sink, which I had not cleaned up the previous night, was gone. It seemed to me that the blood had been cleaned up. After reviewing more case documents and thinking about what happened on November 3, 2005, I do not believe that law enforcement broke into my trailer and took blood from my sink and planted it in Ms. Halbach's vehicle."

In retrospect, Avery now suspects the following events occurred after he went to Menards that night.

"I believe that Bobby removed the blood from my sink and planted it in the RAV4. Law enforcement would not remove the blood from the sink because they would not know that the blood belonged to me and would believe that it belonged to Ms. Halbach. Only the killer would know that the blood did not belong to Ms. Halbach and only someone who saw my finger bleeding would know that the blood was mine, so, I think that the only person who was there and knew my finger was bleeding and could have gotten into my trailer was Bobby. He would have taken the blood to frame me and save himself.

DEC 1 2016 19:21:32

Steven Avery has always maintained that someone went into his trailer to remove blood from his bathroom sink shortly after him and his brother Chuck drove to Menards on Nov. 3, 2005.

"Bobby drove his Blazer to the front of my trailer and it was his Blazer taillights that I observed as Chuck turned on State Highway 147. I do not believe that the vehicle could have come from any other location than the Dassey-Janda place because the vehicle was gone in the two minutes it took Chuck, Blaine, and I to return to the trailer." (44)

Avery also pointed out, "the vehicle had to already be on the property when we left and Bobby's vehicle was the only vehicle that was present at the time we left. I believe that my trailer door was unlocked but even if it were locked, the Dasseys had a key to my trailer at their place."

By sheer coincidence, Zellner retained the services of Stuart James, one of the country's foremost experts on blood spatter and blood stain analysis. Earlier in this book, there was mention of the 2006 Omaha murder of Jessica O'Grady, the college coed who disappeared after telling her

---

44. Supplemental affidavit Steven Avery, June 29, 2018

apartment roommates she was heading over to the home of her boyfriend, who lived with his aunt. Although O'Grady's body was never found, the police in Omaha arrested Edwards and charged him with her murder. The prosecution's leading witness was James, the world renowned expert from Fort Lauderdale, Florida. His testimony left the jury from Omaha convinced of the boyfriend's guilt. This was the case where authorities found the defendant's mattress was saturated with blood from Jessica O'Grady. Tiny spatters of blood were found on the ceiling as well as the bedroom posts and nearby clock. Prior to being charged, Edwards was seen on store surveillance camera visiting Walgreens buying cleaning supplies to conceal some of the blood stains rampant throughout his basement bedroom at his aunt's home.

A decade later, James was putting his skills to use researching Teresa's slaying. One of his first experiments concerned the blood stains in Teresa's vehicle.

"Mr. James oversaw experiments that conclusively refute Mr. Kratz's argument that the 'sheer volume, the sheer number of places rule out that the blood in the RAV4 was planted.' The experiments demonstrated that it was actually a small amount of blood that was planted in the RAV4, and it was selectively dripped and one stain most probably was applied with an applicator. (45)

"Mr. James opines that the most likely source of Mr. Avery's planted blood was the blood deposited by Mr. Avery in his sink on November 3, 2005, and not blood from the 1996 blood vial. Mr. James, because of his familiarity with EDTA blood vials, opines that the hole in the top of the 1996 blood vial tube was made at the time Mr. Avery's blood was put in the tube, and the blood around the stopper is a common occurrence and does not indicate that the tube was tampered with."

---

45. Zellner post-conviction filings

Regarding the blood spatter in the RAV4, "Mr. James, based upon the experiments that he oversaw, opines that the blood spatter found in the RAV4 was selectively planted because the experiments demonstrated that if the State's theory that Mr. Avery was actively bleeding from the cut on his right middle finger was true, then blood would have been deposited in many more places in the RAV4 than where it was deposited.

"The blood spatter experiments conducted with actual blood on the subject's middle finger conclusively demonstrate that the blood would have been deposited on the RAV4's outside door handle, key, key ring, steering wheel, the gear shift lever, brake lever, battery cables and hood prop. The blood found in the RAV4 was only deposited in six places, not fifteen, and consisted of small drops of blood in the front of Ms. Halbach's RAV4 on the driver and passenger seats, driver's floor, and rear passenger door jamb."

At Avery's trial, Kratz speculated the blood in the back resulted when Avery picked up and tossed Teresa's dead body into the cargo area of her vehicle.

Stuart James' re-creation of the crime concluded Kratz got it wrong.

"Mr. James opines that the blood spatter on the inside of the rear cargo door was the result of Ms. Halbach being struck with an object consistent with a hammer or mallet while she was lying on her back on the ground behind the vehicle after the rear cargo door was opened."

"Mr. James opines that the State expert, Mr. (Nick) Stahlke, mistakenly described the blood on the rear cargo door as having been projected from Ms. Halbach's bloodied hair after she had been shot and as she was thrown into the cargo area of the vehicle. Mr. James, by overseeing a series of experiments, opines that the State's description of the cause of the blood spatter on the rear cargo door resulting from Ms. Halbach being thrown into the cargo area and blood being projected from her bloodied hair on the cargo door is demonstrably false.

"The erroneous blood spatter testimony of the State's expert Mr. Stahlke resulted in the State presenting a false narrative to the jury about the sequence of events surrounding the attack on Ms. Halbach. The State presented a scenario where Ms. Halbach was already fatally injured in Mr. Avery's garage prior to being thrown in the back of the RAV4. The experiments overseen by Mr. James demonstrate Ms. Halbach was struck on the head after she opened the rear cargo door. She fell to the ground next to the rear bumper on the driver's side where she was struck repeatedly by an object similar to a mallet or hammer."

Stuart James oversaw several blood spatter experiments to demonstrate why special prosecutor Ken Kratz's theory about Teresa Halbach's attack had to be untrue.

After Avery was arrested and charged, he insisted to his lawyers, Strang and Buting, that his blood was planted in the RAV4, coming from his bathroom sink.

However, they ended up settling on a far more salacious theory. They decided to make Colborn and Lenk the culprits of their blood-planting defense.

In fact the following time sequence makes it virtually impossible for Sgt. Colborn to be the blood planter, according to Zellner's fact-finding probe.

"After Sergeant Colborn came to the Avery property on November 3 to speak with Mr. Avery around 7 p.m. he attended a meeting at the Manitowoc County Sheriff's Office at 8 p.m." Zellner explained.

It takes twenty-three minutes to drive from Avery's to the Manitowoc Sheriff's Office headquarters next to the downtown courthouse.

If Avery, Chuck, and Blaine Dassey left for Menards at 7:15 p.m., Colborn only had twenty-two minutes to pull it off.

If they left at 7:20 p.m., then Colborn only had seventeen minutes.

If the Averys left at 7:25 p.m., then Colborn only had twelve minutes.

If they did not leave until 7:30 p.m., then Colborn only had seven minutes.

"It is therefore extremely improbable that Sgt. Colborn planted Mr. Avery's blood in Ms. Halbach's vehicle on November 3, 2005.

After devoting nearly three years to studying the psychology of Teresa's murder, Zellner surmises the killer realized there was a limited window to frame Avery. "The killer was familiar with the Radandt and Manitowoc County pits. He devised a plan to bring the RAV4 from the murder scene to the Avery property.

"He knew that he needed to put something with the DNA of Mr. Avery in the RAV4."(46)

When Steven left for Menards, his south door to the red trailer was unlocked because he didn't expect anybody to break in.

---

46. Post-Conviction Relief Motion, June 7, 2017

"The killer entered the trailer, intent on finding an item of Mr. Avery's with his DNA that he could use to plant DNA in the RAV4 to connect Mr. Avery to Ms. Halbach's murder. In the small trailer, the killer noticed fresh blood in the bathroom sink. The killer quickly collected the blood from the sink in Mr. Avery's bathroom and deposited the blood in several spots throughout the RAV4. The killer recognized that the blood had to be planted quickly, within fifteen to twenty-eight minutes and before it coagulated."

If Teresa's RAV4 was being stashed near the old dam, off Highway 147, it would only take Bobby one to two minutes to get there from Avery Road, do the deed, and get back home before his brother and two uncles returned from the Manitowoc Menards.

But if Bobby did the deed, the next logical question to ask is, how?

CHAPTER TWELVE

BLOOD DOCTOR

Born in 1941 in New York City, Stuart James obtained his bachelor's in biology and chemistry from Hobart College in New York in 1962. He later went on to graduate school at Elmira College where he studied bloodstain evidence, homicide investigations, and forensic microscopy. Among his many accolades, James became certified in 1997 as a competent forensic expert in the discipline of bloodstain pattern interpretation, and he was elected as a distinguished member of the International Association of Bloodstain Pattern Analysts in 2004. James has given consultation and testimony in the following places: Alaska, Arkansas, California, Connecticut, Delaware, District of Columbia, Florida, Georgia, Hawaii, Idaho, Illinois, Indiana, Kansas, Louisiana, Maryland, Massachusetts, Michigan, Missouri, Nebraska, Nevada, New Jersey, New Mexico, New York, North Carolina, Ohio, Pennsylvania, Tennessee, Utah, Vermont, Virginia, Washington, Wisconsin, Republic of South Korea, Toronto, Canada, St. Croix, U.S. Virgin Islands, and Mannheim, Germany.

The person's work he was asked to critique was that of Kratz, who had limited prior experience trying a murder case in Calumet County, according to a review of Westlaw filings.

Before conducting their analysis in Teresa's murder, James and Associates Forensic Consultants studied photos of the RAV4, bone fragments, the burn area behind Avery's garage, burn barrel contents, the burned cell phone, the garage and its contents, and blood stains on Avery's bathroom floor. Additionally, James reviewed the DNA reports, trial testimony, and arguments, including that from Kratz, anthropologist Leslie Eisenberg, and forensic scientist Stahlke. He also gave his undivided attention to the photographs of Teresa's cargo door, portions of the plastic dashboard of the RAV4, and chapters from Kratz's book, *Avery: The Case Against Steven Avery and what 'Making a Murderer' Gets Wrong.*

*Stuart James is regarded as one of the country's
most prolific blood-spatter analysis experts.*

James found it noteworthy to mention how "Kevin Heimerl, special agent with the Wisconsin Division of Criminal Investigation, described there being no blood spatter in Mr. Avery's garage."

"I have reviewed the trial testimony of John Ertl, field response technician for the Wisconsin State Crime Lab. Ertl testified he had some experience as a bloodstain pattern analyst and that he saw no bloodstain patterns whatsoever in Mr. Avery's garage," James said. (47)

"To a reasonable degree of scientific certainty," James continued, "the absence of bloodstain patterns from a gunshot in Mr. Avery's garage is inconsistent with Ms. Halbach being shot in the head in that location."

As for Avery's red trailer, James found it telling that Ertl "found no evidence of bloodstain patterns in Mr. Avery's trailer. To a reasonable degree of scientific certainty, the absence of bloodstain patterns in Mr. Avery's trailer is inconsistent with a brutal attack occurring in that location. Further, the complete absence of Ms. Halbach's blood in Mr. Avery's trailer is inconsistent with her being stabbed or otherwise having sustained a significant blood-letting injury in Mr. Avery's trailer."

But didn't Kratz have a comeback for that? Didn't Manitowoc County's special prosecutor speculate that perhaps the empty jugs of bleach around the Avery property proved Avery and Brendan teamed up to saturate the concrete surface of Avery's garage to get rid of all Teresa's blood and they were masters at it, leaving no blood behind?

"In my professional experiences, it is extremely difficult to clean blood stains with heavy applications of bleach and paint thinner," James said.

At Avery's murder trial, his defense was handicapped and severely undermined because his lawyers chose not to hire a bloodstain pattern expert. The effect was disastrous because, as a result, the defense wasn't able to put forth a compelling argument against the persuasive prosecutor.

"The prosecutor, Ken Kratz, argued that Ms. Halbach was thrown into the rear cargo area of the RAV4 and that her blood was in motion when it struck the interior panel of the cargo door. The cargo door of the RAV4 opens with hinges on the passenger side of the vehicle to create a ninety-degree

---

47. Affidavit of Stuart James, May 3, 2017

angle with the threshold of the cargo area," James said. "If the bloodstain pattern observed on the interior cargo door had been created when Ms. Halbach was thrown into the cargo area and while the cargo door was open, it would likely produce elongated stains that indicate a right-to-left direction of travel relative to the cargo door. No such pattern was observed on the interior of the cargo door. In fact, Stahlke accurately described the bloodstains on the rear cargo area as being 'circular or near-circular.'"

Additionally, there was something else striking about the blood on the cargo door. It was concentrated at the bottom in the left corner.

"The bottom of the cargo door is seventeen inches from the ground. The concentration of bloodstains in this area is not consistent with blood being deposited as a result of Ms. Halbach's body being thrown into the rear cargo area … The pattern on the rear cargo door is consistent with a stationary blood source being struck with a bloodied object and creating a cast-off pattern where the blood droplets have traveled from left to right relative to the rear of the vehicle and onto the open cargo door. I have directed experiments where similar cast-off patterns were created using a hammer swung at a low angle to deposit blood onto the rear cargo door of a 1999 RAV4."

James carried out a first of its kind scientific experiment relative to Teresa's slaying. Kratz didn't do one and neither did Avery's defense team of Strang and Buting.

"For one experiment," James said, "a mannequin was obtained to reenact the scenario presented to the jury by the prosecution. Weights were attached to the mannequin to achieve a weight of approximately 135 pounds to replicate Ms. Halbach at the time of her death."

James worked with staff members of Kathleen T. Zellner & Associates who participated in his series of blood spatter experiments. The mannequin's hair was soaked with EDTA preserved blood and the vehicle used for the experiment was

Zellner's 1999 Toyota RAV4. The volunteer participant was 5-foot-10, 185 pounds and 36 years old. Avery was listed as being 5-foot-6, 218 pounds and he was 43 years old.

"The goal of the experiment was to replicate the prosecution's version of events. First, one of the volunteers attempted to create a bloodstain pattern on the cargo door by flinging the mannequin, but he was not able to do so. Then two volunteers threw the mannequin into the cargo area. They could not create a bloodstain pattern similar to what was observed on the rear cargo door of Ms. Halbach's vehicle."

Finally, James had the volunteers bind the mannequin's hands and feet with rope "in an effort to replicate the scenario described by Brendan Dassey in his confession. The addition of the rope had no effect on the experiment. After I concluded that no blood was being deposited on the cargo door when the mannequin was being thrown into the cargo area, the weights were removed from the mannequin to see what, if any, pattern was created when the weight of the mannequin was reduced to a fraction of Ms. Halbach's body weight. Without the added weight, the mannequin weighed approximately 15 pounds. Even still, we were unable to create a bloodstain pattern that resembled the cast-off pattern observed on the interior of the cargo door."

Stuart James has determined the actual sequence
of events of Teresa Halbach's attack.

Eventually, another blood-spatter experiment involved the RAV4 cargo door being kept wide open.

"When completely open, the cargo door sits perpendicular to the threshold of the cargo area. A volunteer from Kathleen T. Zellner & Associates created cast-off bloodstain patterns on the cargo door by wetting the head of a mason's hammer with EDTA preserved blood and swinging. Cast-off bloodstains are created when blood is flung from a bloodied object."

It was this blood experiment that left James certain as to how Teresa met her end.

"To a reasonable degree of scientific certainty, the bloodstain pattern observed on the rear cargo door of Ms. Halbach's RAV4 was a cast-off pattern created by a blunt instrument. This bloodstain was not consistent with a knife because the blood droplets cast off by the blade of a knife are usually smaller than those observed on the rear cargo door. This bloodstain was not consistent with a gunshot because droplets of blood resulting from a gunshot are smaller than those observed on the rear cargo door. The bloodstain patterns that were most similar to the pattern observed on Ms. Halbach's rear cargo door were consistent with when the victim's body was in a prone position on her back on the ground with her head near the driver's side of the rear bumper and the attacker was kneeling over her, striking her with a bloodied object, consistent with a hammer or mallet while the rear cargo door was open.

"It is my conclusion that the bloodstain pattern on the rear cargo door of Ms. Halbach's RAV4 was not created in the manner described by the prosecution and their experts at Mr. Avery's trial."

Avery's lawyers Buting and Strang theorized Lenk or Colborn doctored the vehicle with a Q-tip of blood once Pam Sturm found the car on Saturday, November 5. Kratz dismissed that scenario. For him, the blood was proof of Avery's guilt.

In July 2017, James offered up his analysis to the ignition stain.

"The prosecution told the jury that all of the blood deposited in the RAV4 was from the cut on the middle finger of Mr. Avery's right hand and that he was actively bleeding. However, there was no blood on the door handle, key, gearshift, interior hood release, hood latch, hood prop and battery cable. It is my opinion that Mr. Avery's blood in the RAV4 is consistent with being randomly distributed from a source because his blood is present in some locations but absent in some reasonably anticipated locations ... The absence of bloodstains in these locations: door handle, key, gearshift, interior hood release, hood latch, hood prop, and battery cable is inconsistent with an active bleeder."

The Avery blood droplets, James interprets, "are consistent with an explanation other than Mr. Avery being in the RAV4 and depositing his blood in those locations with his actively bleeding cut finger. Had Mr. Avery been actively bleeding in the RAV4, it is my opinion that his blood and bloody fingerprints would have been deposited elsewhere in the vehicle."

Once again, James conducted a series of rigorous scientific experiments inside the RAV4 to draw his conclusions. He utilized a pipette to drip blood on the front seats, on a CD case, and on the metal frame by the rear passenger door. Also of note, James used Avery's authentic bathroom sink. It was removed from his Wisconsin trailer and brought to Zellner's suburban Chicago law office about three hours away. Also of note, Zellner's 1999 RAV4 had similar upholstery fabric on the seats of her vehicle. This signified the steering wheel, gear shift, dashboard, and console were probably from the same material.

"An applicator was used to create the stain near the ignition," James said. "For this experiment, I used fresh blood to better represent the time it would take for blood shed by Mr. Avery in his bathroom sink to coagulate and dry.

Blood was drawn from a volunteer and was deposited on the bathroom sink from Mr. Avery's residence. The blood dried on the sink for approximately thirty minutes. Dried flakes of blood were then lifted from the sink using a scalpel."

At that point, James drew even more fresh blood from his volunteer.

"Using a pipette, blood was taken from the sink and transported to Ms. Zellner's 1999 RAV4. Blood was then dripped on the driver's seat, the passenger's seat, between the driver's seat and center console, on a CD case sitting on the passenger seat, and on the door jamb of the rear passenger door. An applicator was used to recreate the stain near the ignition. Depositing blood in this manner and at these locations took less than three minutes."

Moreover, they dripped blood on the carpet floor between the driver's seat and the center console. "The fresh blood absorbed into the carpet and did not form flakes."

In his final analysis, James categorized the blood drops on the driver's seat as a "passive drop." The blood on the passenger seat and CD case also were "passive drops." He classified the blood on the passenger's side door jamb as "passive drop with flow pattern."

The blood near the driver's ignition was produced "with an applicator."

"The stain near the ignition of Ms. Halbach's RAV4 was approximately 2.25 inches from the ignition," James said. "To a reasonable degree of scientific certainty, Mr. Avery would not have deposited blood at that location with his right middle finger while turning the key in the ignition."

It's hard to say whether Avery would have walked free had Strang and Buting directed their suspicions about the planted blood as coming from an alternative suspect instead of trying to blame Lenk and Colborn for any and all shady behavior.

"I told my trial defense lawyers that my blood in the RAV had been taken from my sink," Avery said. "I woke up at 6 a.m. and went into the bathroom to take a shower. I saw that most of the blood on my sink, which I had not cleaned up the previous night, was gone. It seemed to me that the blood had been cleaned up … I tried to tell my trial defense attorneys about the blood in the sink. They did not listen to me and told the jury the blood came from a blood tube at the courthouse."(48)

If the killer methodically planted blood from Avery's sink, the job could be accomplished with a wet sponge and driving to the RAV4 hidden at the Old Dam along Highway 147 in barely five minutes. Dripping the blood inside the RAV4 would take sixty to ninety seconds. Besides a wet sponge, a rag or wet towels would work, James determined.

What does Zellner say about the performance of Buting and Strang regarding their unsuccessful attempt to blame Lenk and Colborn for planting the blood?

"Mr. Avery's trial defense counsel relied exclusively upon a frame-up theory of defense, correctly arguing that all evidence inculpating Mr. Avery was fabricated," Zellner said. "However, they incorrectly argued that Mr. Avery's blood found in Ms. Halbach's vehicle was planted by law enforcement and that it came from a 1996 blood vial held in the Manitowoc County Clerk of Courts Office. Trial defense counsel represented to the jury that the seal of the 1996 blood vial package had been broken and resealed with a strip of Scotch tape. Trial defense counsel would have been aware that this package was opened by members of the Wisconsin Innocence Project in 2002 to examine forensic evidence that could be tested. At that time, Mr. Avery's Wisconsin Innocence Project attorneys broke the seal of the 1996 blood vial package and resealed the enclosed box using only a strip of Scotch tape. There was no credible proof presented to the jury establishing that Lt. Lenk and Sgt. Colborn accessed

48. Affidavit of Steven Avery, November 23, 2016

the Clerk of Court's file to obtain Mr. Avery's blood to plant it in the RAV4."

Zellner has taken Buting and Strang to task for making it appear Lenk and Colborn had prior knowledge of the blood vial's existence in the courthouse vaults.

"However, trial defense counsel failed to present evidence that proved, in any matter, that Lt. Lenk had knowledge of the 1996 blood vial. Trial defense counsel relied on a transmittal form that showed that other evidence from Mr. Avery's 1985 case was sent to the (Wisconsin State Crime Lab) for testing. Simply stated, there is no evidence that Lt. Lenk ever had possession of or even knew about the 1996 blood vial of Mr. Avery's blood stored in the Clerk of Court's office. Despite knowing that there was no provable connection between Lt. Lenk and the 1996 blood vial, trial defense counsel represented to the jury that Lt. Lenk must have inadvertently found the 1996 blood vial in examining the file. This argument was totally lacking in credibility because there was no corroborative evidence to support it.

"Trial defense counsel's theory about the 1996 blood vial was carelessly constructed without corroboration. The blood vial theory was abandoned during the trial and it resulted in no viable theory being presented to the jury about trial defense counsel's claim that the blood in the RAV4 was planted. Trial defense counsel lost credibility with the jury when it was unable to present any evidence that Mr. Avery's blood in the RAV4 was planted.

"Current post-conviction counsel's blood spatter expert has been able to demonstrate that all of Mr. Avery's blood in the RAV4 was selectively planted and that the blood spatter on the rear cargo door was not the result of Ms. Halbach being thrown into the cargo area by her attacker as the State told the jury. The failure of trial defense counsel to have a viable theory supported by expert testimony explaining how Mr. Avery's blood was planted in Ms. Halbach's vehicle all but guaranteed his conviction and life sentence without parole."

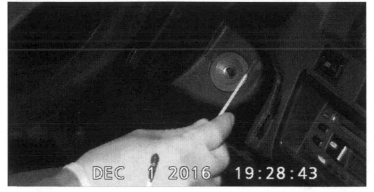

DEC 1 2016 19:28:43

Stuart James is positive that blood was selectively planted into Halbach's auto by the killer, not the Manitowoc County Sheriff's Department, as Avery's original trial lawyers asserted.

***

On Friday, November 4, the Manitowoc County Sheriff's Office decided to revisit Avery. Jim Lenk and his apprentice, Detective Dave Remiker, rode together, arriving around 10:20 a.m. If it wasn't evident the night before, it was now apparent during the daylight hours that Avery Road and Steven Avery were under intense scrutiny. Remiker knocked on the door at Avery's but no one was home. Next, he walked next door to the gray trailer. "This is a residence adjacent to the residence belonging to Steven. I again did not receive any contact from anyone at the residence."

Before Lenk and Remiker went on their way, they saw a golf cart riding through the scrap yard. It was Avery and his mother Dolores. Remiker and Lenk introduced themselves and Avery did not hesitate to answer their questions.

"Steven stated he recalls on Monday, October 31, between 2 and 2:30 p.m., Teresa came to Avery Road and was taking photos of a maroon in color van parked near his residence. Steven stated he had very minimal conversations and contact with Teresa. 'It was just hi, how you doing.' Avery estimated Teresa was gone within five minutes. Steven stated Teresa has been on the Avery property numerous times in the past and occasionally comes to the property to take photos of vehicles to be sold."(49)

At that point, nobody had seen Teresa for four days, Remiker informed Avery. If Avery killed Teresa inside his trailer, would he let the two detectives inside to peek around? Remiker and Lenk decided to pose the question to see how Avery reacted. "I asked Steven if he would be willing to provide me with a verbal consent to search his residence for Teresa," Remiker stated. "Steven immediately provided verbal consent. He stated we could search the interior of his trailer home. I requested Steven to accompany Lt. Lenk and me to his residence to conduct the search. He seemed very surprised. I felt this was the first time that he had knowledge of or was informed that Teresa Halbach is missing."

Remiker searched the trailer. He opened several doors including the bedroom closets and other doorways and closets throughout the trailer. "I did not locate any signs of Teresa inside the residence. Prior to leaving, we thanked Steven for his cooperation."

By 10:38 a.m. the pair of Manitowoc County detectives drove off. If they expected incriminating clues to turn up at Avery's, Lenk and Remiker were both let down. They left empty handed but Avery was definitely not in the clear.

The continued presence of Manitowoc County Sheriff's detectives hovering around Avery Road only served to stoke the rumor mill of Avery's involvement. Several hours after Remiker and Lenk left, Avery made a disturbing observation.

49. Dave Remiker's summary, Manitowoc County Sheriff's Office report on Halbach Investigation

"I smelled cigarette smoke in my trailer on November 4," Avery said. "This was very strange because I did not smoke and Jodi, who lived with me, did not smoke. I thought that someone else had been in my trailer, and I said that in one of my interviews." (50)

Although Bobby does not smoke, Scott Tadych was a heavy cigarette smoker, Zellner observed.

Avery also found signs of forced entry. To document it, he made an entry inside his notebook, the one where he kept Teresa's phone number handy. In his notebook, Avery scribbled the words, "Back to Patio Door."

"Before I left for the family property in Crivitz on November 5, I opened the south door of my trailer and observed pry marks near the door latch."

Not long after the Avery family had cleared out of Avery Road and drove up north to their cottage in Marinette County early that Saturday morning, Teresa's RAV4 was discovered back on the Avery property.

However, just the day before that, on Friday afternoon, an older man, accustomed to minding his own business out in the country along Jambo Creek Road, saw something suspicious from out in his backyard.

What the man saw was central to the still-developing missing person probe of Teresa.

---

50. Steven Avery Affidavit, November 23, 2016

CHAPTER THIRTEEN

TWO CARS

Some Manitowoc County citizens prefer an easy simple way of life. One such person was Wilmer Siebert, now in his eighties. He lives on Jambo Creek Road near the massive Fred Radandt & Sons sand and gravel pits. He's a junk collector. His backyard is littered with cars and car batteries. His two-story white house has seen its better days and looks like it would blow over in a strong windstorm.

A guy like Siebert never expected to be roped into Teresa's murder investigation, and he certainly never figured his wandering, watchful eyes would have a pivotal role in helping Avery's lawyer expose more police corruption than was initially suspected.

"On November 4, 2005, I became aware through the news media that Teresa Halbach was missing and that one of her last stops was at Avery's Auto Salvage. From the media coverage, I learned that Teresa Halbach drove a 1999 Toyota RAV-4 blue-green in color," Siebert said. (51)

On Saturday morning, November 5, the RAV4 turned up double-parked facing in a westerly direction; all the surrounding cars on the outer ridge of Avery Salvage faced east. The persons who decided to dump Teresa's RAV4 there also left it covered with broken tree branches, cardboard boxes, and a rusty car hood. But this was not done to conceal the car as many people who watched *Making a Murderer* mistakenly have said.

---

51. Affidavit of Wilmer Siebert, March 23, 2017

"The tree branches on the RAV show that it was planted by the cops," Zellner told the author. "The branches and random car hood were placed on the vehicle so Kratz could argue that the flyover would not pick up the RAV because it was covered. The other tell that the cops and not the killer planted the RAV is that the vehicle was locked. The killer would not waste time locking the vehicle."

To recap, the following events likely unfolded on Friday, November 4.

Sgt. Colborn was off work, but he would not reveal anything he did that day when asked to do so.

Colborn made a personal phone call into Manitowoc dispatch from a private phone line, reciting Teresa's license plates and seeking confirmation she owned a 1999 Toyota. And then there was the sighting by Wilmer Siebert off Jambo Creek Road.

Zellner said the mid-afternoon sighting by Siebert fits with the time frame of former Mishicot Kevin Rahmlow who maintains he spoke with Sheriff's Sgt. Andy Colborn at the Cenex gas station alerting Colborn to the turnabout on Highway 147 where Rahmlow had seen the abandoned vehicle.

"Sometime before Teresa Halbach's vehicle was discovered, I saw a similar vehicle matching in color, style, and size drive into the Fred Radandt Sons Inc. gravel pit on the access road that is just south of my house. I remember this vehicle had the same spare wheel and cover on the rear cargo door as Ms. Halbach's RAV-4," Siebert said.

But the RAV4 was not the only vehicle that pulled off Jambo Creek Road.

Two vehicles went in, but only one came out.

"I saw a white Jeep closely follow the other vehicle down the access road into the gravel pits. The Jeep looked like an older model and had paint chipping off of the hood," Siebert said.

Two vehicles had sneaked into the far edge of the Avery Salvage property. Siebert, the curious neighbor, watched from his yard. He knew something was up, some mischief.

"A short time after the two vehicles entered the gravel pits, the Jeep exited the gravel pits, again using the access road just south of my house," he said.

In 2007, Ken Kratz told the jury deciding Avery's guilt or innocence how, "Pam Sturm described it as divine intervention ... that it was the hand of God ... as to where we should look at the 4,000 cars that were on this property. Pam Sturm looked in that one place. She never would have gotten through all those cars."

***

Back in 2005, people following Teresa's murder investigation did not have the foggiest clue that the real murder investigation was taking place away from the Avery property.

This was kept hush-hush, a closely guarded secret for a number of reasons. For one, the search and recovery for noteworthy clues of Teresa's murder far away from Avery's red trailer only served to fuel doubts about his role in causing her to die. There was a general consensus within the ranks of Manitowoc County, Calumet County, and the Wisconsin DOJ that Avery needed to be dealt with, this was time to rewrite history and get rid of this persistent, ever-growing public perception problem around Manitowoc County that their local Wisconsin cops were dirty, no good, rotten scoundrels.

During the early stages of the case, the police leaned on Avery's adjoining landowner, Joshua Radandt, who owned and operated Fred C. Radandt Sons quarries. His quarry was directly west and south of Avery's forty-acre tract. Radandt, however, was not the only quarry in the immediate area. There also happened to be a quarry directly south of his land, owned by the government of Manitowoc County. Saturday, November 5, 2005, was a date Josh Radandt would never forget. And neither would people interested in Avery's plight. Late that morning, the SUV of Halbach, without its license plates, was located by volunteer searcher Pam Sturm.

"On November 5, 2005, I was with several friends at the hunting camp," Radandt said. "Law enforcement officers arrived at the hunting camp and asked us if we had seen or heard anything unusual about the Avery property recently … By this time, there was already news media coverage of Teresa Halbach's disappearance that included coverage of the Avery property."(52)

Thinking fast, Radandt remembered how someone at the Avery property was burning a fire a few days earlier. But from his perspective, this was not anything out of the ordinary or suspicious. It went on all the time.

"I told the officers that I saw a fire, orange in color, when I was driving from the Radandt sand and gravel pit to the hunting camp on October 31, 2005, at approximately 5 p.m. I told the officers that I saw the fire from the direction of the Avery property. Because it was dark, or getting dark, when I saw the fire, I was not sure where exactly the fire was located. I did not observe any smoke coming from the fire."

The fire was hardly roaring. There was no thick black smoke or awful stench, such as the foul smell of a young woman's body from being left outside in an open burn pit on a cool autumn night. In fact, there were probably dozens of bonfires set that night throughout Manitowoc and Calumet County out in the country. After all, it was Halloween night.

"The fire did not appear to be spread out and its flames appeared to be two and a half to three feet in height. These characteristics were consistent with my personal knowledge

52. Affidavit of Joshua Radandt, February 10, 2017

of burn barrel fires," Radandt said. "I assumed the fire was contained in a burn barrel. I did not see whether the fire was actually contained in a burn barrel."

Since the overzealous police out to get Avery were desperate for leads, after all, they lacked a body and any physical evidence, the idea of a fire sounded intriguing. The police made Radandt return to their command post headquarters along Avery Road that Saturday evening, hours after the RAV4 had turned up.

"Less than one week after I provided that written statement, two officers, who I believe were from the Wisconsin Department of Justice, met me at the hunting camp to discuss the fire I saw," Radandt said. "I remember them asking me if I was sure what I said I saw. It seemed to me that they weren't satisfied with my statement about the fire. Specifically, it seemed to me that they wanted me to change my story to include a larger fire. Because they were reluctant to accept my story as true, I eventually asked them what they wanted me to say. They told me that all they wanted was the truth. I advised them that I had been telling the truth."

The State investigators made what now appears to be a startling revelation.

"At that time, I was told by the Department of Justice agents that they believed Teresa Halbach's vehicle was driven to the Kuss Road cul-de-sac by driving west through an empty field, then south down the gravel road that ran northeast into the Avery property. They told me that they believed Teresa Halbach's vehicle turned northeast onto that gravel road and entered the Avery property at its southwest corner. It is my understanding that this theory was based on the work of scent tracking dogs," Radandt said.

If Avery killed Teresa, would he hide her vehicle off-site only to move it back onto his family's property knowing the police had the area under siege, thinking he was Teresa's abductor and killer?

Radandt furnished the police the keys to search his three deer camp trailers at his sand and gravel pit behind Avery Salvage. "Later that day, law enforcement called my cell phone again. They informed me that they completed the search of my trailers and that I could use them normally. During the course of this phone conversation, law enforcement informed me that they were going to collect the contents of the burn barrel at the hunting camp at a later time. When I returned to the hunting camp, I observed that they had cordoned off the area surrounding that burn barrel with yellow tape."

But why was one of Radandt's burn barrels at the heart of Teresa's murder mystery? He was never told by police, but he knew something was there.

"To the best of my knowledge, Wisconsin State Patrol assigned officers to watch the burn barrel day and night on a rotating basis until its contents were collected. I was not present when the contents of the burn barrel were collected."

Then Radandt made another observation during that first week of November while Teresa was still being considered a missing person.

He saw the cops on the move. They were far away from the Avery property and working under the cloak of darkness.

"A few days after November 2005, I remember seeing tower lights in the Manitowoc County sand and gravel pit to the south of Radandt's quarry. I remember the lights appeared to illuminate the entire Manitowoc County pit."

Was the real murder investigation taking place in secrecy, far away from Avery's red trailer and his ramshackle detached garage? Radandt began to wonder.

"I understand that there were suspected human pelvic bones recovered from a gravel pit property south of Avery's Auto Salvage. Upon reviewing a map showing the coordinates at which these bones were found, I believe they were found in the Manitowoc County sand and gravel pit."

Back in 2005, the large county-owned sand and gravel pit would have been the perfect place to burn up a body under the cover of darkness. The property along County Road Q was not being used at the time. The land was isolated, far from any immediate homes or commercial businesses. It spanned hundreds of acres.

If someone wanted to trespass at the county quarry or wander through Radandt's sand and gravel pits, back in 2005, it was fairly easy.

There were 'Private Property' trespassing signs posted around the perimeters of the Radandt sand and gravel pits, but that was about it.

"There were locking gates or cables at each access road, but they were rarely used," Radandt said.

During Avery's trial, Kratz did not want to put Joshua Radandt on the witness stand as a prosecution witness. And yet Kratz was keenly interested in learning what information Radandt knew, perhaps so he could spin a yarn for the jury that was simple and easy to follow.

"Approximately one or two months before the start of Mr. Avery's criminal trial in 2007, I was summoned to the courthouse," Radandt remembered. "At the courthouse, I was questioned again about my recollection of seeing a fire in the direction of the Avery property on October 31, 2005. I was not called as a witness to testify at Mr. Avery's criminal trial in 2007."

CHAPTER FOURTEEN

CANINE NOSES

It may have been a night for trick-or-treaters, but Travis Groelle remained steadfast at work for Radandt's gravel pit. He was working near County Highway Q where he was loading and feeding the rock crushing machines. He remembered at least one other employee was working there that night. As Groelle was hard at work, he noticed a strange smell. There was something lowing in the cool autumn breeze and it was unsetting.

"Regarding the smell, he said it was not tires. Said it was a smell that he hadn't experienced before so he could not say what was causing it. (Groelle) said the smell was still in the air when he left and it was coming from east, more towards the middle of the quarry. He did not see any fires." (53)

The surrounding area where Groelle was working is rural, rugged terrain just south of Highway 147. There are hundreds of tall, mature cedar trees planted along both sides of Q. The county gravel pit could be accessed by pulling off Q or by someone wandering in from Josh Radandt's adjacent quarries. To drive to the pits from Avery's takes only a couple minutes.

In November 2005, during the height of the quest to find Teresa, several of Wisconsin's all-around best tracking and cadaver dogs were utilized by law enforcement. The dogs were ushered throughout Avery's red trailer by their handlers and taken near his garage. But those were not the spots that drew the most intrigue. Instead, the action was coming away

53.   Jim Kirby interview of Travis Groelle, August 8, 2016

from Avery's property, about a half-mile away, over toward the spooky stretch of Kuss Road. Kuss Road runs east-west. Avery's place was to the east of Kuss Road.

This was a small, secluded local road flanked by tall cedars on both sides of the street. Less than a dozen acres were nestled along Kuss Road off the woodlands. At the end of Kuss Road was a cul-de-sac overlooking Radandt's quarries; way off in the distance you can see the Avery Salvage Yard. At the cul-de-sac, however, was a winding little conveyor road. The dirt road led into the back of Radandt's deer hunting camp consisting of three mobile trailers.

Prosecutor Kratz theorized that Avery lured Halbach into his red trailer. In reality, the Wisconsin police were concentrating their criminal investigation along a lonely stretch of Kuss Road, about a half mile away.

Monday, November 7, marked the fifth consecutive day of a constant Manitowoc County law enforcement presence around Avery's property. But not everybody who showed up at Avery Road had a stake in the outcome of making sure that Avery went down hard for the crime, notably Kaukauna canine handler Sarah Fauske who showed up with her bloodhound Loof.

"Sheriff Pagel did have two pairs of shoes that belonged to Teresa Halbach. Both were bagged separately in plastic bags. I placed sterile gauze in the toes of all the shoes and removed the insole in a plastic bag with sterile gauze. The shoes were then secured in my personal vehicle," Fauske explained. "When Loof began her task of sniffing for Halbach's scent, it was around 1:30 p.m., 57 degrees, and there was a slight breeze, zero to five m.p.h. blowing from the northwest." (54)

"Find!" Fauske yelled to Loof.

Out near Avery's yard, Loof followed her nose over toward Barb Janda's maroon van where Teresa had snapped a few photos a week earlier.

Eventually, "Loof went up to the south door of the trailer home. The door having a small porch entrance and the door was white in color. K9 Loof wanted to enter the home. K9 Loof continued north along the trailer and went between some pine trees and a burning barrel. K9 Loof smelled a charred area showing some interest then continued west. K9 Loof went west in a picked cornfield. Directly to the south was a gravel pit and in between the two was an area of brush and trees."

The dog became preoccupied with the Kuss Road cul-de-sac.

"K9 Loof worked this area with indications of very strong scent. K9 Loof worked west coming out to a cul-de-sac that was taped off with crime scene tape and two deputies were not allowing access. K9 Loof crossed the tape on one occasion and then was told to not go any further. The

---

54. Exhibit 46, Scent and Cadaver Dog Reports, handler and officer Sarah Fauske

deputies phoned Sheriff Pagel to see if I could continue but were (sic) told to not allow anyone access at this time."

Interestingly, Loof's nose led the bloodhound directly to the same spot that, it just so happens, a small group of men from the Manitowoc County Sheriff's Office were already inspecting that morning. But these men were not about to let a pair of outsiders into their club. As a result, Fauske and Loof were off-limits because it appeared the local police did not want them seeing what they were up to. Was evidence being mishandled or manipulated off Kuss Road? Fauske and her bloodhound weren't allowed access to the closely guarded property, a half mile west from Avery's.

***

Loof was not the only highly specialized dog whose nose steered him away from Avery's. Bob and Julie Cramer of Great Lakes Search and Rescue Canine Group brought along Brutus and Trace, two of their top scent-tracking dogs. Over the weekend, the Cramers were out with the dogs in one of the quarries east of Avery Road, where the dogs alerted. However, when they returned to the gravel piles that Monday, November 7, Brutus and Trace did not alert at the flagged location or the same general area the second time around.

"We then proceeded to a location we were requested to check on Kuss Road where a potential burial site had been located. K9 Brutus checked the area and after passing the area upon entry in the wooded area, he gave a head check returning to the location and gave his bark alert. Alert #12 and seemed particularly interested in a shovel lying next to the disturbed earth." (55)

<hr>

55. Exhibit 46, Scent and Cadaver Dog Reports submitted by Julie Cramer, training director Great Lakes Search and Rescue Canine, Inc.

According to the Cramers, "K9 Trace checked the wooded area first and did not alert, but did show interest, increased animation, and high head checks. Upon returning to the area a second time, K9 Brutus again barked and alerted near the area of disturbed earth."

Later on, the pair of dogs drew a new assignment closer to the Avery compound.

"At the exterior of the home, Brutus again barked at the door and scratched to enter the residence. K9 Trace also barked at the front door. Once inside the trailer, K9 Brutus proceeded to check the interior, alerting inside a bedroom at the bed and pile of clothing. He was very agitated, but no scent source was noticed."

That particular trailer, however, was not Avery's. It belonged to his older brother Chuck.

To reiterate, most of the police focus remained off-site away from Avery's.

"K9 Brutus was then sent to check the berm just west of Steven Avery's property. There was a report of a suspicious looking pile of disturbed earth. Brutus showed no interest in that pile, but did alert on a pile of brush and trash just west of the Avery residence and was very excited along the edge of the berm. This excitement continued as we proceeded south along this ridge and he carefully checked brushy areas west of the Avery yard and along the edge of the salvage yard. His behavior was noted by law enforcement personnel in the area, who indicated that man trailing bloodhounds had also been interested in the same area."

Back at the command post, Julie Cramer compared notes with the others.

"We met with the bloodhound handlers on scene, and it was noted that both live scent dogs and the human remains detection dogs had shown excessive interest in the ridge of land beginning behind Steven Avery's residence and running south to the corner of the salvage yard, where the gravel conveyor is located. This area seems to be of particular interest to the dogs although no scent source has been located in the area."

***

During Avery's trial, any mention of law enforcement's regular presence along Kuss Road during the early stages of the investigation was downplayed.

Kratz tried to avoid the sensitive subject. Just what was Manitowoc County's preoccupation with this area far removed from Avery's trailer? Why were police devoting their utmost time and careful attention to this area if it was of no relevance at all? The answer seems obvious. The police probably uncovered clues and signs of a violent crime. Therefore, they needed to be very secretive and clandestine. Little was written about the efforts to mine the quarry properties for physical evidence related to Teresa's violent death. Along those lines, the police statements that were written down and entered into the official case file were strange.

Some police reports divulge that Calumet Investigator Mark Wiegert had contacted colleague John Dedering at 10:35 a.m. on Monday, November 7.

"He requested that an investigator go to the east end of Kuss Road. I did respond to the area and spoke with retired Deputy Inspector Michael Bushman, Manitowoc County Sheriff's Office. Bushman was leading a team of searchers in the area. It should be noted that the end of Kuss Road is approximately one half mile away from the western edge of the Avery property.

"I arrived at the east end of Kuss Road approximately 10:45 a.m. and spoke with former Deputy Inspector Bushman. He indicated he had found a possible excavation site and did take us to the site. The area was then taped off with crime scene tape and the area was frozen. No one was allowed in or out." (56)

Roughly six hours of time was spent on Kuss Road, the very same spot where the dogs kept finding Teresa's scent. And yet Dedering's report made the following declaration, "At 4:51 p.m., I was notified the excavation area was not pertinent to this case."

The mere fact that Bushman showed up to work Teresa's investigation and then had a leading role in the biggest event of November 7 warrants further scrutiny. Mike Bushman's name is mentioned in only three paragraphs in the entire Calumet County investigative file, which consists of 1,116 pages. Bushman was not even active law enforcement anymore. He was retired, and retired from Manitowoc County, the tarnished agency that already had a direct conflict of interest in spearheading the evidence-gathering efforts against Avery. But Bushman's role in the case went much deeper. As mentioned in Chapter Two, Bushman had a direct role in carrying out the biggest miscarriage of justice in northeastern Wisconsin. Bushman, along with then-Sgt. Kenny Petersen, had implicit orders to arrest Avery for the vicious attack and rape of the candy store owner along the sandy shorelines of Lake Michigan. Now, two decades later, Bushman sprang out of retirement to fulfill another important task, which marked the eighth day of Teresa's disappearance.

As mentioned earlier, much of the preoccupation at Avery's trial by Strang and Buting surrounded evidence planting suppositions, but at that time, a decade ago, nobody was giving much credence to an alternative scenario.

If the sheriff's higher ups at Manitowoc County had no concerns about using fake evidence to nail a guilty suspect or frame somebody they loathed, wouldn't they be just as

---

56. Information Developed Regarding Possible Items of Interest on Kuss Road, Inv. Dedering Report, Nov. 7, 2005

devious about making legitimate evidence and legitimate crime scenes go away or disappear, to seem as if they never existed in the first place?

If that were so, such an assignment was highly sensitive, incredibly covert, and could only be carried out by someone up to the task. A logical candidate would be someone experienced at covering up crime scenes or staging an incident to divert attention away from a criminal suspect to someone else. That person would need to be dependable and someone who would never squeal.

Aside from Teresa's killing, the biggest mystery case at the Manitowoc County Sheriff's Office during the past twenty years concerns the long-suspected police cover-up of the gruesome death of a local teenager, Ricky Hochstetler. He died on a snowy January night in 1999, just six years before Teresa was slain.

The lead investigator assigned to that case by Petersen and Kocourek was a fiercely loyal traffic lieutenant named Mike Bushman.

Under Bushman's direction, the culprit responsible for the Ricky Hochstetler tragedy was never identified, and scores of locals suspect the case remained intentionally unsolved. Other key Manitowoc sheriff's officials assigned to work on that case included Andy Colborn, James Lenk, Dave Remiker, and Jason Jost.

CHAPTER FIFTEEN

COVER UP

The winter of 1998 marked a contentious time for the husband and wife who rented the two-story farmhouse on the far southern outskirts of Manitowoc. Once that winter, the Manitowoc County Sheriff's Office responded for a domestic violence call. The couple was in the midst of a bitter divorce. They had three children, the oldest being a teenage boy named Ricky. He had a part-time job at the Manitowoc Hardees and liked to hang out with fellow teenagers. On Ricky's last night alive, he was dropped off at a house in Manitowoc.

"He was going for a pizza party and movies with his friends," his mother recalled. "On that particular night, I was surprised that he didn't call for a ride home. If he felt that it was too cold or too nasty out, he would always call, 'Mom, can you come and get me?'" (57)

When Debi Hochstetler dropped her son off around 5 p.m. that Saturday, the snow was starting to fall. As the night wore on, a blowing snowstorm kicked up. Winds became nasty and the snow was drifting. It was not a safe night to be out driving, especially for anyone who had consumed too much alcohol at one of the Manitowoc area watering holes.

"When their movies were done, Ricky walked a friend Jennifer home, and then he proceeded to walk home. He was

---

57. 2016 interview with John Ferak for special report published in USA TODAY NETWORK Wisconsin newspapers.

a little past his curfew, so that's probably why he didn't call me. He didn't want to wake me up," his mother said.

Ricky's walk home was about three miles.

Trudging through the snow, Ricky was bundled up in his warm green winter jacket. He began his journey home between 1 and 1:30 a.m.

"He was walking, with traffic, along the edge of the road, three feet off the edge of the road. And they said they could see the vehicle tracks were in and out, in and off the road. Then the vehicle hit Ricky, and he was on the hood of the vehicle and he was dropped down and dragged. And they said that the person made no attempts to stop," his mother said.

Manitowoc County Highway CR is a dark, desolate road out in the country. The posted speed limit is fifty m.p.h. Ricky endured a brutal, agonizing death. He was struck from behind by an intoxicated motorist right around bar closing time.

His broken and battered body separated from the car in the middle of the road.

The drunk driver kept heading south on CR for another two miles until he reached the T-intersection for Newton Road. The hit-and-run motorist had a chance to hop on the interchange for Interstate 43, where heading south goes to Milwaukee and going north ends up in Green Bay.

The fleeing motorist chose to stay on the off-the-beaten-path country roads.

Keep in mind, these were extremely local roads. Only someone who regularly traveled the back roads of southern Manitowoc County would be driving these roads at such a late hour on a weekend after having too much to drink.

There just so happened to be a late-night drinking establishment barely a quarter-mile up the road from where Ricky was run over. The Bil-Mar supper club had been a popular banquet hall and bar for many years around Manitowoc County. Manitowoc's movers and shakers and politically connected wined and dined there. Among them, Manitowoc Sheriff Tom Kocourek had his wedding reception there. There were also a couple of large gatherings at the Bil-Mar that particular Saturday night. One was held for employees and guests of the Manitowoc Ice company and the other affiliated with the Copps Grocery Store. The bar was also open to the general public. A few of the stragglers stayed until the wee hours of the morning, and they pulled out of the parking around the time Ricky was trudging through the drifting snow along the dark road, just minutes away from making it home.

The hit-and-run driver who plowed into Ricky and continued driving was already outside of Manitowoc's city limits, making it highly unlikely the inebriated motorist lived in Manitowoc. Three very small communities were in the general vicinity of the drunken motorist's path, the town of Newton, the village of Cleveland, and the village of Kiel. Based on the travel route, a number of other small Manitowoc County communities such as St. Nazianz, Valders, Whitelaw, and Reedsville were virtually out of the question.

This is known because a Newton resident spotted several broken car parts scattered in the snow the next morning on his way to church. The debris was found one mile to the west of County CR, at the rural intersection of Newton and Center Roads. That intersection was in the middle of nowhere, three or four miles south of the city of Manitowoc, which had a population 35,000.

"I wholeheartedly believe this was an accident," Ricky's mother said. "I know this person didn't mean to do it. But this person also needs to take responsibility, come forward, and help the family."

That Saturday night, Mike Bushman patrolled Manitowoc County's roads as the overnight shift commander. He even saw Ricky's fresh footprints in the snow as he made the rounds along County Highway CR. Five years later, when the Wisconsin Department of Justice opened an investigation into a suspected police cover-up, a state investigator made this notation concerning Bushman: "He was going to check on the condition of the person to make sure they were OK considering the snowstorm. Deputy Inspector Bushman decided to get gas first before following the footprints in the snow."

Bushman's decision to fill up his squad car rather than check on the wandering pedestrian walking home in the fierce snowstorm possibly cost Ricky his life. The seventeen-year-old high school student was hit by a car and his body came to a rest in the road only fifty yards away from his front door.

Around 2:25 a.m., a newspaper delivery driver made the gruesome discovery.

She called 911 and Bushman, Manitowoc County's night patrol commander, learned about the collision as he was filling his tank at the county gas pumps about a half mile away. He made it to the scene at 2:28 a.m.

Around 4 a.m., Bushman and the county coroner Deb Kakatsch knocked on the front door of the Hochstetler white farmhouse. Debi Hochstetler was then rustled out of bed and notified that her only son, the oldest of her three children, was dead in the middle of the road. He had suffered a fractured skull resulting in brain trauma, as well as spinal cord injuries, a fractured neck, internal injuries, and leg injuries.

Many people suspect the cover-up was activated soon after the crime. Off-duty Lt. Rob Hermann, who was working at the time as the Manitowoc County juvenile jail administrator, managed to rush out to the scene.

It's been long suspected by fellow Manitowoc County sheriff's deputies that Rob's younger brother, Todd Hermann, may have been the hit-and-run driver and that Rob showed up at the scene to cover up the crime to ensure the culprit was never identified. The Hermann brothers were untouchables in the sheriff's office, thanks to their father. As a result, Sheriff Kocourek and Undersheriff Kenny Petersen were not about to launch a criminal investigation against one of the Hermann brothers. That would never happen, and Bushman would be tapped to run the investigation to make sure of that.

Even though the banquet hall parking lot was a quarter mile up the road from the hit-and-run tragedy, Undersheriff Petersen told the Manitowoc newspaper within days of the hit-and-run fatality that the Club Bil-Mar was not being probed because "I don't know if the person could have gotten up to a speed that would have caused that kind of injury to the victim or damage to the vehicle," Petersen was quoted as saying to the Manitowoc newspaper in January 1999.

Sheriff Kocourek was also content to let the homicide go cold. He did not want any help from the Wisconsin State Patrol's technical crash reconstruction experts. And he also did not want the Wisconsin Division of Criminal Investigation meddling in the vehicular homicide investigation, either.

Before an autopsy was even done, the local news media was duped by the Manitowoc County Sheriff's Office into believing that Rob Hermann single-handedly had figured out the hit-and-run driver's vehicle. The whole thing was a set up to divert attention away from the real hit-and-run vehicle.

"I determined the vehicle would have to have a gray, painted grill, being a model year from 1985 to 1988," Rob Hermann's reports state. "This vehicle would include Chevrolet pickups, Chevrolet K5 Blazer, and Chevrolet Suburban."

Weeks later, to add to the confusion, Bushman and Rob Hermann alerted the gullible local news media that the broken grill parts may also belong to a 1988 to 1991 full-sized van.

They summoned Manitowoc County Sheriff's deputy Jason Jost to pose for a newspaper photo-op, standing with his back up against a big blue van. The photo, in turn, was seen by thousands of avid newspaper readers in the Manitowoc County area. It served its purpose. It gave the locals the impression that a big full-sized van ran over Ricky Hochstetler, when that was never the case at all.

In fact, no van, no truck, no Suburban, and no Blazer were ever found.

As for Bushman, a dear friend of Kocourek and the Hermann family, who owed both of them for his career in law enforcement after working as a school bus driver, his ambitions of climbing the administrative ladder inside the Manitowoc County Sheriff's Office were also riding on his performance running the hit-and-run probe.

Would he prove himself worthy to Kocourek and Kenny Petersen? That's what this case was about.

As time marched on, though, Bushman recognized that whispers of a police cover-up under his watch were growing louder and louder around Manitowoc County. He decided to take decisive action. He hauled in the father of the hit-and-run victim to the police station for a face-to-face interview.

"I decided to question him about a statement he made reference the opinion that the police may have been involved in the accident and are attempting to cover it up. I wished to catch what type of reaction this would bring," Bushman's reports indicated. "I stated to him that there are over 300 complaints that I worked on and many turned to be just rumors just like the one, for example, that the police were somehow involved in the incident and were intentionally covering it up."

Bushman's decision to confront the victim's poor father by putting the man on the spot had a successful result. "The desired response was received and the redness in his face indicating he was embarrassed at that point indicated he, himself, had been the source of that type of rumor."

Nobody was arrested that year, in 1999, for the vehicular homicide.

Kocourek announced his retirement the following year, enabling Petersen to take over the reins. But it remained to be seen who Petersen would appoint to fill the void inside the culture of corruption at the Manitowoc Sheriff's Office. Because of another retirement and his own promotion to sheriff, Petersen now had to fill the two other top administrative openings at the sheriff's office, both the undersheriff and deputy inspector.

Petersen chose the two men within his ranks who were at the center of the cover-up allegations.

In 2000, Rob Hermann got promoted to undersheriff and Bushman got promoted to deputy inspector. This made Bushman in charge of the entire traffic patrol unit as well as the entire detective bureau even though he had no prior detective experience.

As third-in-command of the entire agency, Bushman decided to hand the sensitive hit-and-run homicide off to someone he trusted, Detective James Lenk, who would not disappoint him. Under Lenk, no progress was made in terms of identifying the killer and the sheriff's office was doing nothing to keep the case in the public spotlight. In 2002, the third anniversary, The Associated Press in Milwaukee tracked down Sheriff Petersen for an interview. He assured reporters that the hit-and-run homicide was not about to be solved.

"What it's going to take to solve the thing would just be luck at this point. I doubt if the truck exists anymore, especially in any kind of evidentiary form," Petersen was quoted as saying.

But why was Sheriff Petersen such a proud pessimist?

Several employees within the Manitowoc County, the ones who had integrity and held their heads high with dignity, suspected their administration had been infiltrated by a number of rats. They believed Ricky's case was a shoddy investigation that arose from incompetence, flat out corruption, or a combination of both.

Bushman and Rob Hermann, the two key promotions given by Petersen, were both responsible for compromising physical evidence, broken vehicle debris found at the snowy scene during the early morning hours of January 10, 1999. Regardless of their motive, their conduct jeopardized any future attempts at prosecuting the culprit.

Even though this was a high-profile vehicular homicide involving the death of a local teenager, the two men at the sheriff's office had not properly tagged, logged, and photographed the broken vehicle parts discovered at the hit and run scene. Most disturbingly, Bushman gave Hermann permission to scoop up the vehicle debris from the scene and to drive around unsupervised with the precious crime scene evidence during the wee hours of the night. Many Manitowoc County residents strongly suspect that the car that hit Ricky Hochstetler ended up at the Hermann family's Cleveland Auto Salvage where it was either repaired or stripped. Cleveland Auto, the family-owned business, was also a perfect place to swap out the evidence.

Considering there was strong sentiment within the local law enforcement community suspecting that Ricky Hochstetler's hit-and-run death was a cover-up, one has to realize the police reports submitted by Rob Hermann may not be reliable. If he was attempting to cover up a crime involving a close family member, there's no telling what was true and what was false. Hermann's overnight report states that he drove around to several Manitowoc area closed auto dealerships and closed businesses during the wee hours of the morning – in his personal vehicle - with the broken grill pieces from the scene of the crime in his possession. There is also no way to verify that anything he wrote actually happened since he did not take photos of any of the businesses and auto dealerships he allegedly visited. Furthermore, nobody else was with him.

"You can get fired for that stuff. That piece of evidence might as well not exist. You have made that evidence have less value or no value at all," noted Brent Turvey, forensic scientist at Forensic Solutions in Alaska. (58)

In Turvey's mind, given Manitowoc County's reputation, there's a strong chance that the police tampered with or swapped out the pieces of evidence from the scene, if they were attempting to cover up the crime for a fellow officer.

"It's all reputation and if Manitowoc County had a good reputation, you don't have to defend it. Because of their bad reputation and continually bad decisions, it's a lifestyle. It's not a mistake. It's who they are."

Before the Teresa Halbach case came along, there were already strong suspicions that the Manitowoc County Sheriff's Office covered up the hit-and-run homicide of Ricky Hochstetler, 17.

58. September 2016 Interview with USA TODAY NETWORK-Wisconsin for three-part series on the Ricky Hochstetler hit and run homicide case of Manitowoc County.

Bushman has said he was under the impression that Rob Hermann took the broken vehicle parts scattered along CR back to his family's "boneyard" in Cleveland, which was about five miles down the road. The Cleveland Auto Sales & Salvage was just a few blocks away from the home of Todd and Shelby Hermann.

Both Rob and Todd Hermann had substantial expertise as auto body technicians and mechanics at Cleveland Auto Sales & Salvage, a rival business of Avery Salvage.

"You don't take parts from a crime scene home with you because you don't know who's going to potentially become a suspect," Turvey added.

At no point during his tenure did Bushman ever once investigate Todd Hermann or Rob Hermann as suspects or co-conspirators in the evidence-mishandling escapade. To this day the question lingers, why did Robby Hermann, the off-duty juvenile jail administrator, respond to the scene of the crime, take charge, and convince everyone to announce later that same morning that the hit-and-run vehicle was a truck, van, or sports utility vehicle - before the autopsy was even done to examine the victim's body and leg injuries?

What motive did Bushman and Rob Hermann have to feed this information to the press, strongly desiring to have it consumed by the public?

In 2004, the Wisconsin Division of Criminal Investigation showed up in Manitowoc to investigate Undersheriff Rob Hermann as the hit-and-run suspect. The DCI agent's reports indicate the victim's mother suspected Bushman "might fear some type of reprisal or professional retaliation from Rob Hermann if the matter was taken seriously."

In August 2004, Wisconsin DCI Agent Eric Szatkowski "informed Hermann that his name had been associated with rumors in the Manitowoc area that he might be involved in the hit-and-run death of Richard Hochstetler. Inspector Hermann said he was called in to work on the case by Deputy

Michael Bushman possibly because Inspector Hermann was experienced in accident reconstruction."(59)

During that same interview, Hermann insisted he was not the hit-and-run driver because he drove his 1998 Chevrolet truck to the scene. "Inspector Hermann stated that he never owned a vehicle matching the description of the suspect vehicle, specifically a Chevrolet truck or van manufactured between 1985 and 1988."

As one might expect, the DCI investigation left more questions than answers. Why didn't the agent probe Todd Hermann, when the same special agent's own reports indicated he heard Todd Hermann was mentioned as a possible suspect?

Foremost, why did the special agent take it at face value that the hit-and-run vehicle was a mid-1980s truck, van, or Blazer given that conclusion was based solely on the word of Rob Hermann, the same sheriff's official under a dark cloud of suspicion for either being the culprit or the ringleader of the cover-up?

In 2006, after being elected sheriff of Manitowoc, one of Rob Hermann's first actions was to appoint his younger brother Todd Hermann to Bushman's former job as third-in-command of the entire Manitowoc Sheriff's Office.

In 2016, I worked as a Wisconsin investigative newspaper reporter re-examining the Ricky Hochstetler case, I tracked down the work cell phone number for Todd Hermann. I called and asked a number of questions about him being a suspect in Ricky's death. Todd Hermann was on vacation that week so I caught him off guard when he answered my call. After I asked my first question, there was a long pause before he responded by saying no comment. He continued to say no comment, suggesting I contact the sheriff, who was his older brother, for any comment pertaining to the case.

---

59. DCI report compiled by Szatkowski from 2004 summarizing his interview of Rob Hermann

At the time of our conversation, Todd Hermann was deputy inspector of operations. He oversaw the entire detective bureau including the lieutenant of his agency's detectives, Andy Colborn.

Despite the best efforts of the Hermann family to keep Ricky's case out of the Wisconsin press and off anybody's radar, the case remains like a smoldering fire which keeps burning. It's an eternal flame for the community around Manitowoc. People in town are mad and frustrated that Ricky's family never got justice and they're more outraged by the belief that the Manitowoc County culture of corruption was responsible for the case going unsolved.

Back in July 2009, five years after closing its initial corruption investigation into the Manitowoc County Sheriff, the Wisconsin DCI revived Ricky's case while Rob Hermann was sheriff and Todd Hermann was third-in-command of the sheriff's office. The decision to reopen the matter came from the top: Craig Klyve, the DCI's director of the bureau for investigative services, noted, "The caller wanted to remain anonymous and would provide no information on the source of the allegations other than the individuals who provided the information were high school friends of the suspect that did not want to get involved in the investigation and did not know the caller was providing information to authorities."

Three months later, a different special agent traveled to Two Rivers to interview the former live-in girlfriend of Rob Hermann, also the mother of his child. She maintained she could not remember if he was actually awakened by a phone call to their house around 3 a.m. back in January 1999. It had been more than ten years since the tragedy. She later urged the DCI to check with the Bil-Mar Club to see if they had any records to verify whether or not Rob Hermann patronized the banquet hall party club that night.

By the time the DCI tracked down the club, the social hall informed the state of Wisconsin investigators that too much time had passed to be of any help.

The Bil-Mar no longer had any records pertaining to the names of their guests on January 9-10, 1999, the night of Ricky's horrible death.

In October 2009, the DCI probe reached a dead end, now a second time.

That same month, the fifty-two-year-old Klyve turned up dead inside his car on a Friday night in Madison at a parking garage. His wife, an assistant attorney general in the Wisconsin Department of Justice, found his body. The Wisconsin State Journal reported Klyve had committed suicide using his service weapon.

"Craig Klyve, our beloved son, brother, husband, father, uncle, and friend, who is cherished by all who knew him, died far too early when he unexpectedly took his life on Friday, October 23, 2009," his obituary notes.

CHAPTER SIXTEEN

NOTHING THERE

If the Manitowoc County Sheriff's Office was never supposed to be investigating Avery because of conflicts of interest, then why was a man in his fifties who was directly involved in Avery's false arrest in 1985, coming out of retirement on the fifth day of Teresa's missing persons case?

That man, designated a team leader for the day, was responsible for the only two events of magnitude that day.

Sign-in logs indicate Mike Bushman, who was at the center of the Ricky Hochstetler hit-and-run cover-up suspicions involving the Manitowoc County's Sheriff's Office, had no prior involvement in the nearly week-old investigation of Teresa. But there he was, showing up on the Avery property, bright and early, around 7:30 a.m. Monday, November 7. He signed in to the command post at the same time as Lt. Todd Hermann, the same man many suspect was responsible for Ricky Hochstetler's death, from six years earlier. Bushman and Todd Hermann signed the command center log at 7:38 a.m.

They were soon joined by fellow deputies Dave Siders, Sgt. Jason Jost, and Sgt. Scott Senglaub. That day, the Manitowoc County Sheriff's group would achieve the most success in turning up previously undiscovered physical evidence as well as mysterious evidence that strongly suggested Teresa had met her gruesome demise about a half mile away from the Avery property.

"The group I was put in was Group A, and the team leader was Deputy M. Bushman," Siders said. "The property which we were assigned to search was a wooded area on White Cedar Road west of Avery's Auto Salvage, in addition to the property north of Steven Avery's residence."(60)

The key word is "assigned." It was a specific assignment and Bushman was brought out of retirement to oversee the very delicate task.

Little was documented in writing by Manitowoc County Sheriff's personnel about the mysterious site on Kuss Road including any interactions between Bushman and Wiegert prior to Bushman heading out to the off-the-beaten-path location. Bushman, the designated Group A team leader, chose not to memorialize any of his activities for that entire day.

Logs show he checked in to the Avery Road command center at 7:38 a.m. There is a second log entry of Bushman re-entering the command post at 4:14 p.m. along with Jason Jost. At 5:33 p.m., Bushman, Jost, and Siders all signed the log showing they were done for the day.

But Bushman's presence during the investigation of the Avery case only begs more questions. By Monday, November 7, Kocourek was just days away from being hauled in to a room full of hostile lawyers ready to grill their co-defendant in Avery's $36 million wrongful conviction lawsuit. Was Bushman someone who was supposed to drop into Teresa's investigation for one day, set the table, and quickly fade into the background before anybody would even notice he was there?

***

In Ricky Hochstetler's horrific hit-and-run death, Bushman's legacy was not bringing the intoxicated and callous hit-and-run driver to justice. Several hours after

---

60. Manitowoc County Sheriff's summary report Halbach investigation, Deputy Siders, Nov. 7, 2005

Ricky's death, after the sun came up, Manitowoc County resident Robert Jeffery saw several broken vehicle parts in the fresh snow at the rural intersection of Center and Newton Roads, the main intersection that led to Cleveland, Wisconsin. This was the same road that led toward Cleveland Auto Sales & Salvage as well as Todd Hermann's house.

Bushman showed up at the intersection, yet did not take any photos or measurements of the vehicle debris. He also did not bring along any trained evidence technicians even though this was a felony vehicular homicide, a serious crime that would have meant prison time for the culprit. Instead, he used a snow shovel to scoop the broken auto parts out of the snow banks and chose not to pursue the fleeing motorist's direction of travel. Bushman was in no mood to pursue the probability that the hit-and-run motorist lived just a few miles down the road around Cleveland. He wrote in his report that the Newton driver "was unable to tell me which direction the suspect vehicle may have went (sic) after the pieces fell off."

It was almost as if the car parts discovered at the seldom-traveled rural intersection never existed. Once Bushman showed up to retrieve them, that intersection became an afterthought as Bushman took enormous measures to steer the case away from Cleveland, Wisconsin.

Bushman had a knack, the record reflects, for making sure critical evidence, which could have aided in finding Ricky's killer, became irrelevant. By the time Ricky's relatives and friends visited the family home on County Road CR, around the date of the funeral services, the large snowbanks started to thaw, thanks to the sunshine. When one of the mourners pulled into the victim's family's driveway, the woman made a startling discovery. She saw numerous broken car parts protruding from the snow. Keep in mind that Ricky was struck just yards up the road and the hit-and-run driver heading south would have passed the house. The damage in the fresh show included a section of headlight lamp with letters and numbers from the manufacturer. The mourners knew the damage surely came from the vehicle that killed Ricky. The witnesses phoned their local sheriff's office, but this would turn into a major letdown once Deputy Jason Jost arrived to investigate.

Besides recovering the main headlight lamp, "I also observed three other pieces of plastic lying just around the corner." In total there were four broken vehicle parts that appeared to be from a newer style car, Jost stated in his reports.

There were no other violent wrecks or collisions reported in front of the Hochstetler rural country farmhouse that winter. Yet the identification of car damage was very problematic for sheriff's officials because, less than seven hours after the crash occurred, Rob Hermann already informed his agency's dispatchers to contact the Wisconsin Department of Transportation to obtain a five-county listing of older model GMC trucks. This was a classic case of misdirection. Hermann wanted to keep the rest of the sheriff's office preoccupied with a never ending pile of busy work over the next several months. More importantly, Hermann's coworkers never got hot on the trail of catching the true villain.

Anyway, Deputy Jost returned to the sheriff's office and, in the days ahead, he huddled with Bushman and the two discussed the fresh car parts found in the snow in front of Ricky's house.

Jost wanted to climb the ladder at the sheriff's office. He was tight with the Hermann brothers. In the end, Jost submitted the following report, "I checked with Lt. Bushman and due to the fact the pieces looked newer, he did not believe they belong to the suspect vehicle on the hit-and-run fatality. At this time, no further follow-up will need to be done."

At no point over the years did Manitowoc County explore the possibility that a car was the type of vehicle that struck Ricky. As far as framing Avery for the crime, that was not possible since Avery remained in prison at that time, still serving out his unjust thirty-two-year prison sentence for Gregory Allen's brutal rape.

In 2004, when the DCI came to Manitowoc asking questions about a cover-up, Bushman responded by saying the state of Wisconsin's registry contained about 25,000 vehicles matching the description of the striking vehicle and Bushman claimed that all 25,000 vehicles were cleared. Overall, the DCI special agent was troubled by Bushman's performance, as noted in his 2004 investigation, but he seemed to view the case more from the angle of incompetence, rather than outright police misconduct on Bushman's part.

"In reviewing the reports, many of the vehicles that were reported do not have detailed descriptions of how they were cleared. This review assumes that every officer did a physical inspection of every vehicle, looking closely for signs of repair/replaced parts in areas that were damaged or could have been damaged. If each officer for each vehicle inspected did not follow that procedure, there is a possibility the striking vehicle was missed."(61)

But how do you pull off a successful police cover-up? Misdirection is critical.

The hit-and-run driver's path of travel home at bar closing time on a Saturday night made it obvious the culprit was headed into far southern Manitowoc County, a largely rural and isolated area. But rather than pursue the most obvious angles, Bushman instructed others, such as Andy Colborn, David Remiker and James Lenk, to waste precious on-duty time running down worthless leads. Assignments given to a number of patrol deputies put them on the road far away in places including Appleton, Fond

61. DCI field report written by special agent Eric Szatkwoski in 2004

du Lac, Green Bay, Kaukauna, Menasha, Neenah, Oconto, Shawano, and Waupaca. Around the one-year anniversary, Sheriff Kocourek informed the local newspaper that he was shipping off the broken grill pieces to the FBI laboratory for analysis. It was unclear why he waited an entire year to do so. Additionally, the FBI was never given access to the broken headlight parts that surfaced in the melting snow near Debi Hochstetler's driveway.

In reviewing the case files, it was obvious Kocourek controlled the investigation and Bushman was there to obey his orders. Under no circumstances were the Hermann brothers, Rob and Todd, to be treated as criminal suspects in the crime or the cover-up. Other members of the sheriff's office have said that Bushman and Kocourek were in agreement, they would prefer to let Ricky's case go cold rather than conduct a rigorous investigation that would lead to one or two outcomes: either clear the brothers of wrongdoing or find evidence showing the brothers had culpability in the crime and or the cover-up.

As it stands, the facts remain the same: Ricky Hochstetler was dragged to his death by a fast car at bar-closing time while walking home. Vehicle parts were located about four miles southwest of the crash scene, at the rural intersection that was the main road toward Cleveland, Wisconsin, home of Cleveland Auto Sales & Salvage. Nobody was ever charged in connection with the gruesome hit-and-run death. What is known is that Mike Bushman spearheaded a sloppy, high-profile homicide investigation that got off to a suspiciously disastrous start and the case floundered from there. Crucial crime scene evidence was mishandled and other noteworthy clues were allowed to fade into oblivion, all thanks to Bushman.

So it stands to reason, in the 2005 disappearance of the Auto Trader photographer, had someone in Manitowoc County called Bushman out of retirement realizing they were at a crossroads and an experienced problem-solver was needed to put the Kuss Road intrigue to a final rest?

That morning, November 7, 2005 only a select number of key law enforcement got to the police command post on Avery Road before Bushman, notably Mark Wiegert at 6:32 a.m., and Bushman's replacement, Deputy Inspector Gregg Schetter, who was a dear friend of the Hermann brothers, at 6:53 a.m., John Dedering at 7:01 a.m., Tom Fassbender at 7:09 a.m., Jim Lenk at 7:15 a.m., and Andy Colborn and Dennis Jacobs at 7:16 a.m. as well as Calumet Sheriff Jerry Pagel and several other Calumet Sheriff's deputies and investigators.

But with no arrests and every day moving closer toward retired Sheriff Tom Kocourek's unsettling federal lawsuit deposition, the discovery of a genuine burial site off Kuss Road was not conducive to an Avery-is-a-guilty-bloodthirsty-psychopathic-killing-machine narrative that Manitowoc Sheriff Kenny Petersen wanted to gin up around the community.

That Monday morning, after Manitowoc County sent a large contingent of loyalists and minions of Sheriff Petersen back to Avery Road, two major events occurred, both involving Manitowoc County's personnel in the search group associated with Bushman.

"While searching land north of Steven Avery's residence, a corn field, I came across a burning barrel which was in my section of area to search. The burning barrel was located out in front of Steven's residence next to the cornfield. I approached the burning barrel and looked inside. I observed a metal vehicle rim and laid it outside the burning barrel. Once I lifted the metal rim, I observed some burnt, melted plastic items … it appeared to me to be a cell phone. I took a closer look at the cell phone and noted there was an 'M' emblem on the front of it. It appeared to be the emblem for a Motorola brand cell phone," Deputy Siders said.

"Deputy Bushman came over and observed the remains of what appeared to be a cell phone. He then contacted the (officer in charge) and informed him that we had some items which needed to be looked at by detectives."

Later that same morning, Bushman was directly involved in the second major incident, arguably the biggest event of the day. As mentioned earlier, Bushman did not document any of his activities that day, including why he was even involved, given that he was already retired, given that he worked for Manitowoc County, and given that he was involved in the 1985 false arrest of Avery.

Calumet County's John Dedering summarized the day-long events at Kuss Road in five short paragraphs. He chose to put few, if any details, in his report. At 10:35 a.m., Wiegert "requested that an investigator go to the east end of Kuss Road. I did respond and spoke with retired deputy inspector Michael Bushman, Manitowoc County Sheriff's Department. Bushman was leading a team of searchers in the area. It should be noted that the end of Kuss Road is approximately one-half mile away from the western edge of the Avery property."

Here's what Sgt. Bill Tyson, one of Dedering's colleagues, wrote in his report. "I received a phone call indicating we needed to leave Barbara Janda's residence and respond to Kuss Road for a suspicious incident. Lt. Lenk, Sgt. Colborn, and I left Barbara Janda's residence at 10:58 a.m. After clearing from the suspicious incident, we did go back to Barbara Janda's residence to finish collecting firearms from the residence."

Tyson added that "search volunteers ... had located an area approximately three feet by three feet that appeared to be disturbed soil."

Dedering got to the dead end road at 10:45 a.m. where he huddled with Bushman, who "indicated he had found a possible excavation site and did take us to the site." What Dedering's report did not point out was the enormous lag time in contacting state forensic scientist John Ertl and his three-person unit from the Wisconsin State Crime Lab that were being used that week to exclusively process potential crime scene in Teresa's disappearance.

Wiegert and Fassbender may not have wanted the state crime lab intimately involved in overseeing the evidence collection efforts, probably because, if evidence was being planted, shifted, or collected to go away, Ertl's unit was likely to blow the lid and unmask somebody's cover. Having a whistleblower as a constant presence could have been disastrous for Manitowoc and Calumet Counties' all-out efforts targeting Avery for Teresa's killing.

Several top-trained police dogs detected Teresa Halbach's scent at the end of Kuss Road, raising the likelihood that she met her demise off-the-beaten path, away from Steven Avery's trailer.

***

Despite the red alert on Kuss Road, Ertl's team remained jettisoned forty-five miles away, toiling away inside an enclosed garage at the Calumet Sheriff's Office. The discovery on Kuss Road remained tight-lipped within the inner circle of Wiegert, Dedering, and Bushman who then chose to notify Colborn, Lenk, and Tyson. At no point that Monday morning was Ertl's three-man crew summoned to Kuss Road to investigate the suspicious possible burial site, near where the bloodhounds and tracking dogs also located Teresa's scent.

While the Manitowoc County-led group huddled and plotted strategy regarding Kuss Road, Ertl's team began combing through four burning barrels that were confiscated the previous day by Lenk, Colborn, Remiker, and Dan Kucharski from the Bobby Dassey property. For reasons never explained, the four deputies had inexplicably chosen to ignore the lone burn barrel of Avery even though it was out in plain view in the front of his yard, and he was their prime suspect. Another twenty-four hours would pass before Deputy Dave Siders, a member of Bushman's Group A, would follow his intuition and not only peer into the Avery barrel, but reach inside and then start pulling out the contents.

"We set up the sifting equipment in the garage and began examining the contents of the barrels beginning with the two of interest to the dog," Ertl said. "These contained a lot of partially burned food and game animal material including chicken, fish, and deer.

"Some hair, metal items, (and) as many unassociated bones as possible were recovered. The first barrel was finished and the second begun." (62)

After a busy morning, Ertl and his crew took a noon lunch break. Back in neighboring Manitowoc County, where the action was heating up, Dedering and Bushman, two men

62. John Ertl's Wisconsin State Crime Lab report of November 7, 2005

about the same age, remained in conversation on Kuss Road. A total of ninety minutes had passed since Dedering learned of the suspicious possible burial site, but there was still no phone call to alert Ertl's team from the state crime lab to the mysterious find.

Ertl's team finished lunch at 12:30 p.m. and resumed their work in the sheriff's office garage. By the time Ertl's crew got to Kuss Road, shortly before 2 p.m., more than three hours had passed since Bushman notified his long-time confidants at neighboring Calumet County about his Kuss Road discovery. The lag time only deepens suspicions about whether incriminating evidence of a crime scene was being hauled away.

In any event, when Ertl's unit arrived at Kuss Road, he saw "white plastic sheeting (that) protruded from the ground on either side of an area 3 feet in diameter, devoid of plants, apparent decomposed wood, or peat-like material. Some moss lay nearby, uprooted, however, there was no sign that soil had been excavated and replaced."

Now that Ertl's group had been called to the scene, there was apparently nothing incriminating there.

"The area devoid of plants appeared to be peat moss and the plastic sheet, the remnants of a peat moss bag as per the label on the underside. Beneath the bag were the decomposing remains of a wooden pallet ... The area was excavated further and no disturbance to the soil layering was evident."

By mid-afternoon, the team of Lenk, Colborn, and Tyson was also summoned back to Kuss Road for a second time. "After the photography by the Wisconsin State Crime Lab was completed, Lt. Lenk, Sgt. Colborn, and I began digging up the area and quickly found out this was not a possible grave or burial site. Upon reporting those findings to Investigator Dedering, the crime scene tape had been removed and the area was reopened," Tyson said.(63)

Ertl's group, summoned to the highly suspicious scene three hours late, finished their assignment at 5:45 p.m. and then returned to the garage in Chilton to continue to process Bobby's four burning barrels. But now another one had been delivered to the sheriff's garage.

"A fifth barrel, reportedly containing remnants of a Motorola cellular phone, had also been transported to the Sheriff's Office in Chilton," Ertl noted.

Between 7:30 and 9:30 p.m., Ertl's crew continued processing Bobby's burn barrels.

"We finished with the second barrel, cleaned up the work area, and departed the sheriff's office. We proceeded to the Best Western motel in Chilton, ate dinner, and retired."

As far as the investigation's paper trail was concerned, the incident at the cul-de-sac off Kuss Road was a big nothing.

"The possible excavation area was processed by Wisconsin State Crime Lab personnel and at 4:51 p.m., I was notified the excavation area was not pertinent to this case," Dedering wrote.

As for Bushman, he faded into the sunset. He never wrote a single report concerning any of his activities on Kuss Road even though he was made a search team leader he was indirectly involved in the recovery of the charred phone at the bottom of Avery's burn barrel, and he was directly responsible for the events that made Kuss Road a day-long police circus.

Had Bushman stumbled upon something on Kuss Road that he should not have? The absence of paperwork only widens the mystery concerning why one of Sheriff Kocourek's most loyal henchmen was suddenly tapped to

---

63. Supplemental report, Sgt. Bill Tyson, November 7, 2005

come out of retirement to help for only one day on the Avery case.

In the end, the police maintained a constant presence on Avery Road for five more days, through Saturday, November 12, 2005. But Bushman's role in the case was now over.

He had done well.

CHAPTER SEVENTEEN

EVIDENCE PILE

On the same day as the Kuss Road controversy, a team of three, two from Manitowoc County and one from Calumet, got the green light to roam the Avery Salvage Yard. They could wander the vast rows of junked and wrecked automobiles, a golden opportunity for one of them to plant evidence, particularly in proximity to Avery's trailer. One man on the assignment seemed less likely to be engaged in planting evidence, though, Sgt. Bill Tyson of Calumet County.

"Upon returning to the crime scene on Monday, November 7, 2005, I was informed that my duty for the morning would be to work with Lt. Lenk and Sgt. Andrew Colborn," Tyson said. "I was informed they did wish for us to open the trunks on all remaining vehicles on the property and after that was completed, enter all the residences and collect all firearms."

Unlike Tyson, Lt. Lenk and Sgt. Andrew Colborn chose not to write any reports to memorialize their activities rechecking the cars around the Avery property that morning.

By the time their day ended, Kuss Road was now off the grid. That following morning, Tuesday, November 8, the generals had realigned their troops squarely back to Avery Road. Wiegert and Fassbender assembled another huge contingent of Wisconsin State Patrol troopers, volunteer firefighters, and area police officers to conduct another all-out blitz canvassing the wrecked vehicles around Avery Salvage. The assignment seemed redundant, considering how the same cars were the subject of a fruitless daylong search two days earlier, on Sunday, November 6.

But this second full-blown search, now called upon the day after Colborn and Lenk went wandering around the salvage yard premises, was sure to bear ripe fruit.

"On Tuesday morning, November 8, 2005, shortly after 9 a.m., we were advised by a trooper that he and his fireman partner had located Teresa's auto license plates along the north border of the salvage yard," Calumet Lt. Kelly Sippel said. "This station wagon would have been parked between the fenced-in compound to the east and an old trailer to the west."(64)

A month later, Wiegert interviewed Brillion firefighter William Brandes Jr. to learn how his evidence harvest was made at 9:15 a.m. "According to William, while searching a car, he noticed some license plates that had been folded twice and were lying on the folded down backseat of an older station wagon ... William reached through the driver's side rear window and picked up the license plates. He indicated he was wearing gloves at that time. William unfolded them so he could read the number on the plate. William stated the registration we were looking for matched the plates he had found."

That same morning of the license plate find, Lenk, Colborn, and Dan Kucharski meandered over to Avery's little red trailer, for the umpteenth time.

"Sgt. Colborn searched the desk area as well as a small cabinet next to the desk for pornographic materials," Lenk said. "I took a three-ring binder from the cabinet which was filled with news clippings of Steven Avery since being released from prison. There were no pornographic materials in the binder. Sgt. Colborn even tipped the cabinet to its side,

---

64. Supplemental Report of Lt. Kelly Sippel

away from the desk, to be sure that no photographs or other materials had fallen between the desk and the cabinet."(65)

Unlike Lenk, Colborn's incident report for his duties that day completely avoided any mention of his activities in Avery's bedroom. He left that up to Lenk.

"When Sgt. Colborn and I were putting magazines and papers back into the cabinet, we were pushing into the cabinet, striking the back of the cabinet as we pushed them in. When I replaced the three-ring binder into the cabinet, I met with some resistance. I pushed it two to three times before it finally went into the cabinet."

At that point, Lenk notified the two others he needed to walk out of the room to make a call to the command post. Then he walked back into the bedroom.

"When I reached the bedroom, I observed a single key laying on the floor," Lenk said. "The key and the key (fob) were laying on the floor just in front of a pair of slippers next to the rear corner of the cabinet ... I informed Deputy Kucharski and Sgt. Colborn that there was a key here and it was not here before.

"We all looked at the key. It appeared to be a key from a Toyota brand vehicle due to the emblem ... We all believe the key was dislodged from the back of the cabinet as we were tipping and banging the magazines and binder in and out of the cabinet."

The license plates and spare key which had surfaced were scooped up that morning. Then in the middle of the afternoon, Manitowoc County Sgt. Jason Jost, the same deputy who worked closely with Bushman on the Ricky Hochstetler hit-and-run case, acted upon his instincts and walked the grounds of Avery's burn pile pit between 1:40 and 2 p.m.

---

65. Manitowoc County Sheriff's Office summary from Lt. Jim Lenk for November 8, 2005.

"Upon returning to the command post, I made contact with Calumet County Sheriff's Office Lt. Kelly Sippel," Jost said. "He responded to the property with me. Without disturbing the area, we walked close to the burn pit to take a further look.

"As we were looking at the ashes laying in the area, it was evident that someone used some type of front end loader to remove ground from this particular location ... as we looked at the ash pile, we observed that there was a bone laying near the south side of the pile, on the east side. Without disturbing the bone, I looked at it as closely as I could. It appeared as though it may have been a vertebrae bone. I could see another bone in the pile." (66)

Jost would also mention that "one piece appeared to be in the shape of a part of a skull."

No forensic anthropologists were summoned to the scene. The Manitowoc County Coroner Deb Kakatsch was kept away from the property. She was not even notified of the bone fragments. Also, the police at the scene, Manitowoc, Calumet, and the Wisconsin DCI, evidently came to a unilateral agreement that photographs and videotaping would not be done showing the bones and where they had been located in Avery's yard.

It was the recovery of the bones on the fourth full day of searching Avery's property that changed the dynamics of the case to Manitowoc County's great satisfaction. One day earlier, the authorities were focused intently on Mike Bushman's find on Kuss Road where the dogs also drew heightened excitement. But law enforcement's three amazing hunches all paid off on Tuesday, November 8. The decision to reprocess all the cars inside the salvage yard now turned up the license plates belonging to Teresa. The return to Avery's bedroom produced Teresa's spare key. The third,

66. Manitowoc County Sheriff's report of Jason Jost's activities of November 8, 2005

the decision to give more scrutiny to the burn pile pit behind Avery's red trailer, turned up charred bones that were later linked to Teresa.

The sudden trove of evidence caused a dramatic shift in the case, just in the nick of time. After all, former Sheriff Tom Kocourek was only two days away from being forced to raise his right hand and give a contentious videotaped sworn statement in Avery's $36 million lawsuit for running a crooked police department. But the work of his former disciples, people who deeply admired him, Lt. Lenk, Sgt. Colborn, and Sgt. Jason Jost, and of course, Mike Bushman, forever put the skids on Avery's federal lawsuit against their former leader.

On November 9, Avery would lose his freedom for good. The scheduled depositions for Kocourek on November 10 and former Avery prosecutor Dennis Vogel, set for November 15, would never happen.

But what would happen is that the tandem of lead investigators, Wiegert and Fassbender, would decide that their top priority on November 9, once they captured Avery, was to drive him to the local Manitowoc hospital to obtain more DNA samples from Avery, even though this was quite unnecessary.

But to them, maybe it was necessary. Perhaps additional clues would be needed down the road, to ensure Avery's guilt.

CHAPTER EIGHTEEN

HOSPITAL STOP

If the murder case brought against Avery was based on fabricated evidence harvested by the cops, then it had to be rock-solid, irrefutable evidence that stood up court. The best evidence to plant nowadays involves DNA, which is risky but rewarding for those who manage to bet away on their wicked misdeeds. Unfortunately for the police profession, there have been a number of crooked cops and CSIs have had their careers implode because they got exposed planting DNA against someone later proven to be innocent. A former friend of mine, the director of the Douglas County Sheriff's Office's crime lab in Omaha, Nebraska, the subject of my first true-crime book, Bloody Lies, was one such cop. In his public corruption case, which was investigated by the Omaha division of the FBI and successfully prosecuted, David Kofoed's downfall that led his eventual imprisonment concerned his ability to gain access to additional blood swabs and blood that he and his CSI team collected from the crimes of at least two high-profile murder cases.

One happened in a garage and another inside a farmhouse. In the first case, the psychopathic killer was guilty and confessed on many occasions to his crime, but although there lacked a body, there was a trail of blood of the killer's murder victim, his 4-year-old son.

In the second case, Kofoed's CSI team collected several extra swabs of blood stains from two middle-aged farmers who were murdered in the middle of the night while they slept in their upstairs bedroom. Kofoed also went into one of the evidence bags and re-examined the bloody shirt of the farmer.

The special prosecutor was able to convict Kofoed by providing that he would plant evidence in cases where his fellow police detectives needed a boost, where they were a wee bit short on having enough solid physical evidence to make an arrest or ensure a guilty verdict. In the first case with the dead little boy, Kofoed dodged a bullet, because the crazed killer pleaded guilty to the crime and did not challenge the strange evidence finds that turned up against him, including blood that was supposedly found inside the bowels of a dirty commercial Dumpster some five months after the boy's body was said to have been put there.

Then, three years later, Kofoed met his downfall because of the brutal farmhouse killings. In that crime, he had fabricated swabs of DNA blood evidence to use against a pair of Nebraska cousins after they were incarcerated by the local police. He mistakenly assumed the small-town police force had arrested the true perpetrators, but he was badly mistaken and ruined his career, making himself into a criminal.

It's safe to say that nobody overseeing Teresa's murder case wanted to have another scenario involving Avery beating the rap. The second time around, in 2005, Sheriff Petersen wanted Avery found guilty and sent away for the rest of his life, punishment for bringing shame and humiliation to himself and other old-timers from the Kocourek administration who were part of Avery's 1985 rape arrest. The sheriff's office endured two years of non-stop embarrassment and ridicule between 2003 and 2005. Avery's arrest for first-degree murder was meant to bring an end to this innocence project wave that so many people and politicians in Wisconsin were beginning to champion.

So on November 9, 2005, the first order of business for Wiegert and Fassbender included a visit to the Aurora Medical Center in Manitowoc with Avery. The two investigators had already made arrangements with a local nurse they trusted to help with their mission. It was around 1:20 p.m. when Wiegert and Fassbender escorted prisoner Avery into an examination room at the hospital.

What was entirely odd about the incident is that Avery was not even under arrest for murder. He was being taken into custody on a gun charge, for having possession of a shotgun that he was not supposed to, as a convicted felon. One of the crimes that Avery was convicted of stemmed from the January 1985 incident where Avery stood along the road and pointed an unloaded shotgun at the wife of the sheriff's deputy because Avery believed the woman was spreading false rumors about him in the community. One of Avery's other crimes during his twenties concerned a 1981 burglary at a local bar where he and a friend stole a couple cases of beer and some sandwiches.

And yet there they were, Fassbender and Wiegert, taking a man being charged with a gun crime over to the local hospital to collect additional samples of his DNA.

"Towards the end of the examination, Nurse Fritsch took two swabs of Mr. Avery's groin area in direct contravention of the search warrant, which specifically restricted that DNA samples were to be taken from Mr. Avery's saliva and blood," Zellner said. "There was no reference to groin swabs in the search warrant. Significantly, Nurse Fritsch's documentation of taking swabs from Mr. Avery excludes any mention of taking groin swabs. A well-qualified nurse following acceptable standards of charting would never fail to document taking the groin swabs unless she were instructed not to document taking the groin swabs by Agent Fassbender or Investigator Wiegert. (67)

"Agent Fassbender and Investigator Wiegert's explanation that they did not realize that the search warrant did not call for taking groin swabs is not credible."

---

67. Zellner motion for post-conviction relief, June 7, 2017

Agent Fassbender's report claims that Nurse Fritsch disposed of the groin swabs.

"Agent Fassbender's report is not credible because Nurse Fritsch never mentions in her charting disposing of the groin swabs. Agent Fassbender's report directly contradicts Mr. Avery's account of his examination as described in his affidavit."

The most reliable witness account of the strange events taking place at the hospital appears to come from Avery himself.

"As Mr. Avery followed Agent Fassbender and Nurse Fritsch out of the examination room, Mr. Avery heard Investigator Wiegert tell Nurse Fritsch to give him the groin swabs, and Mr. Avery observed Investigator Wiegert walk to the examination receptacle as if to discard the groin swabs. Mr. Avery observed that Investigator Wiegert did not drop the groin swabs into the receptacle." (68)

But if Wiegert had pulled a fast one, a well-planned devious scheme to fabricate more evidence against Avery, a golden opportunity presented itself four months into the murder case against Avery.

By February 27, 2006, Wiegert and Fassbender realized the dynamics of Wisconsin's biggest murder case had changed. Avery now had major league criminal defense lawyers, having just hired Strang and Buting. At that point, it appears a decision was made to take out Avery's main alibi witness, Brendan Dassey, and force him to implicate himself and his uncle under a wildly sensational murder plot that had Avery committing premeditated murder inside his back bedroom only to be distracted in the middle of his savagery by the knocking and ringing of his doorbell by his developmentally slow nephew. This distraction apparently caused Avery to take a break from his bedroom rape and torture of Teresa to walk down the hallway to see who might

---

68. Motion for Post-Conviction Relief, June 7, 2017

be at the door. Then, upon realizing it was not his mom or dad, or brothers Earl and Chuck, or his sister Barb, he invited young Brendan to step inside his lair to participate in the evilness.

"It was not until four months after Ms. Halbach's RAV4 was analyzed by the Wisconsin State Crime Lab in Madison that investigators became interested in the hood latch," Zellner said. "The hood latch was first introduced by Agent Fassbender and Investigator Wiegert during their March 1, 2006, interrogation of Brendan."

Here are some questions posed by Wiegert and Fassbender during their interviews with Avery's learning-disabled sixteen-year-old nephew, who ultimately went along with their wishes and implicated himself as the co-conspirator in Teresa's murder.

Fassbender: "OK. Did he go and look at the engine? Did he raise the hood at all or anything like that? To do something to that car?" (69)

Brendan: "Yeah."

Wiegert: "What did he do, Brendan? It's OK. What did he do?"

Fassbender: "What did he do under the hood, if that's what he did?"

Brendan: "I don't know what he did, but I know he went under."

Fassbender: "He did raise the hood?"

Brendan nodded in the affirmative, trying to please his captors.

Fassbender: "You remember that?"

Brendan: "Yeah."

Wiegert: "While he was raising the hood, did you take the license plates off?"

---

69. Interviews of Brendan Dassey by Tom Fassbender and Mark Wiegert, contained in Calumet County investigative reports of Halbach murder case.

Brendan: "No. He did. He took them off. He had them in his house but I don't know after where he put them."

Wiegert: "Where was the knife that he used, you used? Where'd that knife go?"

Brendan: "He left it in the Jeep."

Wiegert: "It's not in the Jeep now. Where do you think it might be?"

Brendan: "I'm sure it was."

Wiegert: "Did you see it in the Jeep?"

Brendan: "Yeah, cuz he set it on the floor, in the middle of the seats."

Wiegert: "Anytime during this, did he get injured?"

Brendan: "Just that scratch, that's all I know; on his finger. It was bleeding a little bit."

Wiegert: "How'd he get that scratch?"

Brendan: "Probably when he was under the hood."

Since Halloween was on a school night, Brendan remembered how his mother Barb called him, reminding him that he needed to be home by 10 p.m.

Wiegert: "When did you clean the place up?"

Brendan: "Like at 9:50. He took the bed sheets outside, and he burnt them."

Fassbender: "Was there blood on the bed sheets?"

Brendan: "Yeah."

Wiegert: "What else did he do?"

Brendan: "That's when he hid the key in the dresser."

Fassbender: "So you and Steven do what at 9:50 p.m. then?"

Brendan: "We cleaned that up and then he told me to throw that on the fire, the clothes, that's full of the blood that was like cleaned up."

When Wiegert asked Brendan to remember the clothes, he drew a blank stare.

Wiegert: "What about the shirt, what color was the shirt?"

Brendan: "Black."

Wiegert: "What about … did you have her bra and panties too? Where were those?"

Brendan: "I don't know."

Wiegert: "So you took it outside and threw it on the fire?"

Brendan: "Yeah."

Wiegert: "Now the shirt, earlier you told us the shirt had blood on it, had a hole in it, was that not true then?"

Brendan: "No."

Wiegert: "Was Steven bleeding?"

Brendan: "On his finger, that's it."

Wiegert: "What did Steven say he was going to do with her car?"

Brendan: "That he was going to crush it."

Wiegert: "Did he say when he was going to try and do that?"

Brendan: "No. He said he would of (sic), actually the sooner, he said, the sooner the better."

Overall, Brendan was doing a terrific job of repeating and regurgitating what Wiegert and Fassbender wanted him to say. In the back of their minds, deep down, these two veteran cops knew his life was over. They were pleased. After all, they wanted to make sure Brendan never saw the daylight outside of a Wisconsin penal institution, at least during their lifetime.

In order to decimate Avery's criminal defense, Fassbender and Wiegert wanted Brendan thinking of them as his father figures, upstanding men Brendan could trust. Under no circumstances was Brendan going to be shown their dark side, their devious side.

Fassbender: "You need a break, any soda or something? I got water here."

Wiegert: "We can get you a soda if you want one. Would you like one?"

Brendan: "Coke."

Since this was going to be Brendan's last day of freedom and the two interrogators knew this, they wanted him to go out with a nice last meal.

Fassbender: "We got some food here, sandwich or anything?"

Brendan shook his head no.

Fassbender: "Are you sure?"

Brendan nodded his head yes.

Fassbender: "Bathroom?"

Brendan shook his head no.

Fassbender: "Just a soda?"

Brendan nodded his head yes.

"All right, Bud, hang in there," Fassbender responded.

A few minutes later, Fassbender returned with the soda for his sixteen-year-old captive.

"Here you go bud."

"Thank you."

"Would you like to have a sandwich or anything?"

Brendan shook his head no.

Fassbender: "You sure?"

Brendan: "Not hungry."

As Brendan was enjoying his refreshing can of Coke, Fassbender remained fixated on Teresa's RAV4.

Perhaps this was because Fassbender knew that a major piece of DNA evidence was still available for evidence planting purposes.

**

March 2, 2006, marked the infamous Ken Kratz press conference where the following ghoulish assertions were not backed up by the facts.

"Sheriff Pagel and I will be releasing to the media the specifics of this case. I will be filing, as I mentioned tomorrow, a criminal complaint by 2 p.m. that will be available for release to all of you.

"We have now determined what occurred sometime between 3:45 p.m. and 10 or 11 p.m. on the 31st of October. Sixteen-year-old Brendan Dassey, who lives next door to Steven Avery's trailer, returned home on the bus from school about 3:45 p.m. He retrieved the mail and noticed one of the letters was for his uncle Steven Avery. As Brendan approaches the trailer, as he actually gets several hundred feet away from the trailer, a long way from the trailer, Brendan already starts to hear the screams.

"As Brendan approaches the trailer, he hears louder screams for help, recognizes it to be of a female individual, and he knocks on Steven Avery's trailer door. Brendan says he knocks at least three times and has to wait until a person he knows as his uncle, who is partially dressed, who is full of sweat, opens the door and greets his sixteen-year-old nephew. Brendan accompanies his sweaty, forty-three-year-old uncle down the hallway to Steven Avery's bedroom, and there they find Teresa Halbach completely naked and shackled to the bed. Teresa Halbach is begging Brendan for her life ... The evidence that we've uncovered establishes that Steven Avery at this point invites his sixteen-year-old nephew to sexually assault this woman that he's had bound to the bed. During the rape, Teresa's begging for help, begging sixteen-year-old Brendan stop, that you can stop this. Sixteen-year-old Brendan, under the instruction of Steven Avery, cuts Teresa Halbach's throat; but she still doesn't die."

Fast forward a month.

Kratz began to realize his twisted sexual fantasy involving a bloody butcher knife, a naked young woman chained to the bed, and two bloodthirsty monsters named Brendan and Avery was not corroborated by any physical evidence. This was not good.

Deep down, Kratz realized this could be troublesome as the biggest criminal case in the state of Wisconsin moved closer toward trial with Strang and Buting now on the case fighting for Avery. Kratz was no longer up against a couple of country bumpkins from the Manitowoc County Public Defender's Office, who were there to get paid to go through the motions of putting forth a defense.

Many people now suspect that Ken Kratz's wild and outrageous press conference claiming that a naked Teresa Halbach was shackled to Steven Avery's bedposts, begging and screaming for her life, was actually a fantasy Kratz came up with based on his own real-life experiences of treating women as his sex slaves, during his time as the Calumet County District Attorney.

"In an effort to corroborate Brendan's confession taken on March 1, Agent Fassbender and Investigator Wiegert ordered that the hood latch be swabbed for DNA evidence," Zellner said. "On April 3, 2006, Agent Fassbender and Investigator Wiegert specifically directed Deputy Jeremy Hawkins and Sgt. Tyson to go into the storage shed where the RAV4 was located to swab the hood latch, battery cables, and interior and exterior door handles."

Actually, how the follow-up search went down only raises more red flags about the dark cloud dangling over the heads of Wiegert and Fassbender.

"The instructions Agent Fassbender and Investigator Fassbender gave Deputy Hawkins and Sgt. Tyson are inconsistent with a good faith effort to recover forensic evidence. If they really thought Mr. Avery had opened the hood and wanted to collect any possible DNA of his from the RAV4, they should have also instructed Sgt. Tyson and Deputy Hawkins to swab the interior hood release lever and hood prop, which, by necessity, Mr. Avery would have handled when opening the hood to disconnect the battery cable," Zellner said.

On the evening of the special task, Tyson gave the hood latch swabs to Hawkins. Hawkins put them into Calumet County's evidence storage. Then the next day, April 4, they were taken out and moved.

"Investigator Wiegert transferred custody of the swab to Wisconsin State Crime Lab personnel, purportedly delivering the swab collected from the hood latch for analysis. However on … custody transmittal documents Deputy Hawkins' name is typed as the submitting officer. Additionally, Deputy Hawkins' name is printed by hand as the submitting officer on the Wisconsin Department of Justice transmittal form … There is no evidence that Deputy Hawkins submitted swabs to the Wisconsin State Crime Lab and all of the evidence establishes that it was Investigator Wiegert who delivered the hood latch swab and printed Deputy Hawkins' name on the transmittal form. It is therefore reasonable to conclude that Investigator Wiegert printed Deputy Hawkins' name by hand in direct violation of all established chain of custody standards and protocols," Zellner said.

During a 2017 NBC Dateline exclusive, Fassbender was reminded how Avery once said, "These guys had it out for me. The whole department was angry at me. This was the perfect opportunity for them to have access to my trailer, plant the key."

"I never actually saw that; never, never saw that from anyone in Manitowoc County," Fassbender told viewers. "I could go on and on about the planting defense and how absurd it is with the multiple agencies we had in there."

At the time of the NBC Dateline interview, however, Fassbender got a free pass. He was not asked whether he had knowledge or a direct role in fabricating evidence or falsifying police reports against Avery. He also was not asked to give an accounting for his appearance in the hospital examination room when the mysterious groin swabs were taken from Avery when they were not supposed to.

As for Wiegert, he remained in the shadows. He did not participate in any on-camera interviews with the NBC anchor. That seems to be his M.O., preferring to lurk in the background. He's the ultimate puppet master, just like he was at Avery Road.

"According to Agent Fassbender's report, the groin swabs taken of Mr. Avery at Aurora Medical Center were discarded ... it is a reasonable probability that they intended to plant DNA from the groin swabs and conceal, from the official medical report, that groin swabs were taken. Investigator Wiegert clearly fabricated the chain of custody form given to Wisconsin State Crime Lab. In light of the new scientific testing done on the hood latch, Investigator Wiegert submitted the groin swabs for the hood latch swabs collected by Sgt. Tyson," Zellner said.

But how would Wiegert have carried this out?

CHAPTER NINETEEN

SECOND TRY

One of the most highly suspicious evidence finds to turn up in the Avery murder case did not result when the independent team of highly trained forensic examiners from the Wisconsin State Crime Laboratory in Madison had their opportunity to inspect, from top to bottom, the interior and exterior of the RAV4. At that period, the car was kept within the confines of their indoor garage, away from any outside interference or skullduggery.

But the Calumet County Sheriff's Office was itching to regain control of Teresa's motor vehicle. Sheriff Jerry Pagel and Investigator Mark Wiegert wanted her SUV back in their property, under their safeguard, sooner rather than later.

Only two days after Avery's arrest, Calumet Corporal Chris Wendorf and Lt. John Byrnes were sent to retrieve a pair of vehicles from Madison. The two summoned Bryan Roehrig and Dan Bangart, who operated Scott's Towing and Dan's Towing, both in Chilton. The two vehicles retrieved on November 11, 2005, were described in police reports as a blue four-door Toyota RAV4 and a 1993 Pontiac Grand Am. "The Toyota RAV4 was loaded on the Scott's Towing flatbed along with the hood of the Rambler strapped to the flatbed underneath the Toyota RAV4. (70)

"Also given to me by (Lucy) Meier was a key the Wisconsin State Crime Lab had made in order to enter the Toyota RAV4 vehicle as the original vehicle key had not been

---

70. Transport of Toyota RAV4 and Pontiac Grand AM, Corporal Chris Wendorf, report Nov. 11, 2005

located at the time they had received the vehicle," Wendorf said. "Also … I had delivered an envelope addressed to the Wisconsin State Crime Lab that had been given to me by Deputy (Jeremy) Hawkins that did contain evidence with a buccal swab from Steven Avery and palm and print cards from Charles Avery, Earl Avery, and Bobby Dassey."

The police entourage left Madison at 1:30 p.m. and made it back to Chilton, their little county seat, at 3:40 p.m. The RAV4 was moved into unit 7 of the Chilton storage units off Mary Avenue.

"I then did tape the vehicle doors with evidence tape, and initial, date, and time stamp such evidence tape," Wendorf said. "The unit was then closed and locked with a fresh, brand new Master Lock key lock that had been removed from its packaging. Evidence bags and property tags, along with evidence, were deposited in Locker 1 of the storage area to wait the property custodian for proper logging."

**

No credible evidence surfaced that Avery ever threw away his bed mattress and box springs, which were surely drenched and saturated with Teresa's blood if the gory killing happened the way Kratz described her death during his wild press conference on March 2, 2006.

But on April 3, 2006, Calumet evidence custodian Jeremy Hawkins and Sgt. Bill Tyson were summoned by their superiors who pulled the strings to refocus on the murder defendant's bedroom material.

"Both Sgt. Tyson and I checked the mattress for any red in color stains on the mattress. The mattress was also checked with ultraviolet light for any stains on the mattress. Presumptive stains were collected and tested. All presumptives on the mattress were negative," Hawkins said. (71)

Nothing of note was found on the headboard, either.

Then, three hours later, for reasons that were never explained in the police reports, Tyson and Hawkins were now being dispatched to the Chilton storage units, the facility housing the RAV4 that was already analyzed by the state crime lab.

But unlike before, the victim's auto was back under the watchful eye of Kratz, Calumet, and Manitowoc Counties. Theoretically, it was now far easier to perpetrate evidence tampering. So, just hours after an inspection upon the bed mattress found no signs of a bloody attack, as Kratz had already declared to the world as fact, Tyson and Hawkins were given new marching orders.

"At 7:25 p.m., Sgt. Tyson and I went to the storage units located at Ann and Frontier Streets. We went to storage unit 7 where the victim Teresa Halbach's RAV4, was located."

Had the time arrived for another improper evidence harvest? Hawkins had specific instructions to start taking DNA swabs inside the car that drew the preoccupation of Fassbender and Wiegert during their interrogation of Brendan.

"At approximately 7:41 p.m., I took a photograph of the hood latch of the Toyota RAV4. At approximately 7:45 p.m., I took a photograph of the left battery cable ... At approximately 7:47 p.m., I took a photograph of the right side battery cable ... After I photographed the right and left battery cable and hood latch, and Sgt. Tyson took DNA swabs of these locations, the storage unit containing the Toyota RAV4 was secured."

Unlike the Hawkins report, Sgt. Tyson made sure to include a noteworthy observation that called into question

71. Processing of evidence, April 3, 2006, Deputy Jeremy Hawkins report

prosecutor Kratz's wild tale about Teresa supposedly being shackled to Avery's bed, fighting for her life.

"It shall be noted that when we analyzed the headboard, we could not see any striations around the spindles of the headboard consistent with that of having handcuffs or leg irons secured to the spindles of the headboard."

When it came time to remove Avery's bed mattress and place it in the evidence training room around 4:30 p.m., "Deputy Hawkins and myself did look at the mattress and did observe numerous stains on the mattress. Deputy Hawkins did numerous presumptive tests on those stains, all of which turned up negative for the presence of blood. The mattress was then returned to the evidence room."

From there, Sgt. Tyson called his boss. "I did place a telephone call to Investigator Wiegert and did inform him of our findings."

Three hours would pass. Wiegert and Fassbender had put their heads together and would have remembered how they were present when the extra pair of unnecessary groin swabs was taken from Avery's body by Manitowoc nurse Faye Fritsch, back on November 9, 2005. These were the swabs Avery said he saw Wiegert pretend to put into the garbage can, but apparently didn't. Had the time finally come to deploy one of these extra Avery DNA specimens?

"Investigator Wiegert and Special Agent Tom Fassbender had informed us they wished for us to do DNA swabs on the interior and exterior of the door handles of Teresa Halbach's vehicle. They also requested DNA swabs done on the hood latch as well as battery cables for the vehicle," Tyson said.

Tyson faithfully carried out the assignment at the storage shed in Chilton. "After the DNA swabs had been collected, the door to the storage locker was secured. Deputy Hawkins and I transported the swabs that were collected to the sheriff's department and the swabs were secured in the Calumet County Sheriff's Office evidence room."

But it was not for long.

Out of nowhere, six months after the car was processed in Madison, Wiegert decided the extra DNA samples were suddenly important to the case. Rather than have the items placed into a sealed FedEx container as is customary for many police agencies, Wiegert assigned himself to personally drive the DNA samples to Madison. He appeared to want to do this alone, without any interference. The records seem to reflect he did not want anybody else looking over his shoulder.

By April 2006, Wiegert's behavior was becoming more bizarre and cryptic. It was as if he were becoming paranoid and obsessive about all of Avery's DNA samples.

Wiegert, the head of the investigation, even authored a strange police report that has no date on it, and yet Wiegert made a point to send a copy of the memo to his friend, and long-time professional colleague, Ken Kratz.

"I had spoken with Detective Remiker in the middle part of April," Wiegert said. "My reason for speaking with Detective Remiker was to request his assistance in determining whether they had any DNA samples, including but not limited to buccal swabs and or blood samples, in their custody from Steven Avery. It should be noted on May 4, 2006, I did receive a copy of Detective Remiker's report detailing any type of DNA evidence, which they have no file."(72)

***

Most people forget, or perhaps they don't realize, but when Avery was arrested by Wiegert and Fassbender on November 9, 2005, his private criminal defense lawyers Dean Strang and Jerry Buting were not yet in the picture.

---

72. Receipt of DNA information from Manitowoc County Sheriff's Department, Inv. Mark Wiegert report

It was not until February 2006, the fourth month of Avery's murder prosecution, that Avery severed ties with the Manitowoc County Public Defender's Office as his legal representation. The Wisconsin Department of Justice and the Manitowoc County Sheriff's Office personnel were surely alarmed and intimidated by the announcement of the new legal team coming on board to represent Avery. After all, Avery continued to insist, over and over, that he was being framed and had nothing to do with Teresa's death.

If the RAV4 was strategically put onto Avery's property to ensure his arrest, and if the spare ignition was strategically dropped onto Avery's bedroom floor on the sixth day of the investigation by a member of the Manitowoc County sheriff's department, you have to step back and ask yourself the following question: Would it be more likely or less likely that the police leading this investigation had another bag of tricks in mind?

The RAV4 was under the control of Wiegert, who put the car into a local police impound lot where he and his cohorts had easy access.

Wiegert, of course, had easy access to the evidence trove taken from the Avery property, as well as to the numerous samples of DNA collected from the bedroom and bathroom of Teresa.

The day after Teresa's RAV4 was found, Wiegert tasked Deputy Craig Wendling with going over to Halbach's house. "Investigator Wiegert wanted me to pick up evidence that would contain Teresa Halbach's DNA in case it would be needed for further identification ... Investigator Wiegert told me a toothbrush, lip Chap Stick, and possibly a vibrator that was located in a dresser would be good items to collect."(73)

---

73. Supplemental report Deputy Craig Wendling, November 6, 2005

Sure enough, all the objects Wiegert had vividly remembered as being inside of Teresa's place, were all still there.

"I did find Teresa's toothbrush … and some Chap Stick … Those items were placed into a plastic bag and sealed."

The deputy also collected "another lip moisturizer that had some hair stuck to it and a hairbrush …" And then in Teresa's first floor bedroom, the deputy carrying out Wiegert's tasks found a cardboard box "containing a reddish maroon case with a zipper. Once I opened that case, I did locate a vibrator or a sexual device. I re-zipped the case, placed it into a plastic bag and sealed it … Investigator Wiegert was notified that the items were obtained and placed into evidence."

Wiegert, of course, was present when the highly questionable two extra DNA samples were collected from Avery, groin swabs that were not necessary, a prisoner who was supposedly being taken into custody on a gun charge, not a first-degree murder charge.

If you believe these cops were crooked and hell-bent on putting Avery in prison to never to come out alive, you have to realize it would only be logical that they would carry out additional dirty tricks in a win-at-all costs mentality, now that Avery had hired Strang and Buting to attempt to prove his innocence.

On the other hand, it's also possible that some of these cops had overestimated the strength and power of Buting and Strang.

CHAPTER TWENTY

GARAGE

Because timing is everything, about a week after Strang and Buting joined the case and championed Avery's defense, people who worked at the Manitowoc County and Calumet County Sheriff's Offices came to a not-so-surprising decision. Sure enough, a follow-up search was needed to go back through Avery's garage.

Why?

There was a feeling in the air that this follow-up garage search, just like the search of Avery's tiny bedroom when the spare key emerged, would not be a failure.

The following line of questioning was posed by Strang to Remiker during Avery's murder trial:

"The search of the garage on November 6, I think that's the first time you actually searched the garage rather than simply sweeping through it to look for Ms. Halbach?"

"Correct."

"You folks found some empty shell casings, looked like .22 caliber rounds?"

"Yes. I think eleven."

"Were you looking for bullets?"

"We were looking for everything."

"Found no bullets in the search on November 6 of the garage?"

"Correct."

"Found no bullets any other time in Steven Avery's garage anytime in November of 2005?"

"Correct."

"It was March 2, 2006, and you were present when bullets or bullet fragments were found in that garage?"

"On March 2, yes, one bullet fragment."

"One bullet fragment?"

"Yes."

During Lenk's testimony, Strang asked the following questions.

"Had Steven Avery actually been sitting there during your deposition?"

"He came in after I had started giving my deposition. Yes, sir."

"And without you telling Mr. Fassbender, and Mr. Wiegert, Sheriff Pagel about the deposition, there's really no way they would have known about it, would they have?"

"No, sir."

"So that's not information they could consider in deciding whether to accept your offer to volunteer to search Mr. Avery's trailer?"

"They didn't have that information, sir."

"Because you didn't give it to them?"

"No, sir, I did not."

"And before you went rummaging through Steven Avery's bedroom once, twice, three times, whatever it was, for hours, would it have been fairer to Steven Avery if someone other than a person who had been deposed in his lawsuit had done that search?"

"No, sir, I don't think it would have been."

"You came back to Mr. Avery's four months later? Not quite four months later?"

"Yes."

"March 1st and March 2nd of 2006?"

"That's correct, sir."

"Much smaller search this time, wasn't it?"

"Yes, sir. I believe it was just the garage."

"A search was going on in the garage?"

"That's correct."

"You came back?"

"Yes, sir."

"Did you participate in that search?"

"No, sir, I did not."

"Why were you back?"

"I came back to see if they needed any, uh, food, any assistance with supplies, see if I could help out. I believe I was there both days, I'm not sure."

During the trial, Calumet County investigator Gary Steier testified he, too, had a critical role in the recovery of the mysterious bullet fragments that turned up in Avery's garage.

"Day 1 of the search warrant, a bullet fragment was located. The item was located by Agent (Kevin) Heimerl and was collected by myself," Steier told the court. "Day 2 of the search warrant, a second bullet fragment was also located by Agent Heimerl and was collected by Detective Remiker."

At the trial, Kratz represented to the jury that the bullet fragments found in the March 2006 garage search were indeed bullet fragments that passed through Teresa's skull.

Fast forward the case a decade.

On May 23, 2017, Christopher Palenik of Microtrace, the company's senior research microscopist, began his analysis upon the questionable bullet fragments used to convict Avery. Microtrace formed in 1992, specializing in the identification of tiny unknown substances and small particles, through chemistry, geology, biology, and materials science. The company became intimately involved in some of the world's most high-profile crimes and disasters including The Unabomber, Oklahoma City Bombing, the Green River serial murders, Jon Benet Ramsey case, Atlanta child murders, the Ivan the Terrible war crimes trial in Jerusalem, and the murder of DEA special agent "Kiki" Camerena in Mexico.

Now, Microtrace had gotten involved in the Avery case.

But first, before conducting any full-blown scientific experiments relative to Teresa's murder trial, four exemplar bullets were fired through bone at the Microtrace laboratory by Lucien Haag, who has authored more than two hundred scientific papers dealing with ballistics. Haag's expertise involves reconstructing shooting scenes and shooting incidents.

Scientist Christopher Palenik works at Microtrace, which is regarded as one of the world's top companies for analyzing trace evidence.

Dr. Lucien Haag of Arizona is regarded as one of the world's top ballistics experts.

Haag's four test bullets all displayed "white translucent particles consistent with the appearance of bone, on the surface of or embedded in each of the four exemplar bullets."

At that point, the test bullets were packaged and sent to the Independent Forensics Laboratory in Lombard, Illinois, where supervisor Liz Kopitke put the four damaged bullets into separate test tubes. She submerged them into what's known as a buffer fluid.

"Ms. Kopitke then shook the test tubes in her hand. The post-extraction exemplar bullets were again examined and photo-documented ... this examination showed that white, translucent particles, morphologically consistent with bone, remained on and embedded in each of the four exemplar bullets." (74)

In other words, the DNA extraction performed by Independent Forensics Laboratory "did not cause the white, translucent particles consistent with bone to fall or become dislodged from the exemplar bullet."

It was now time for the big moment, May 23, 2017.

The Avery case bullet known as evidence tag number #FL was hand-delivered to Microtrace, in Elgin, Illinois, by Wisconsin DOJ Special Agent Jeff Wisch.

After analyzing this bullet under one of the most high-powered microscopes available, Palenik made the following determinations: "There is no evidence to indicate that the bullet passed through bone. In fact, the particulate evidence that is present strongly suggests an alternate hypothesis which is that the trajectory of the fired bullet took it into a wooden object, possibly a manufactured wood product. Furthermore, the presence of red droplets deposited on the bullet suggests that the bullet had picked up additional contamination from its environment at some point after coming to a rest. Based upon these findings, it is our understanding that an investigator was sent by the Zellner

---

74. Affidavit of Dr. Christopher Palenik May 31, 2017

Law Office to the Avery garage to review the area for possible sources of the particulate types described above."

According to Microtrace, two possible sources were recovered around Avery's property. One was particle board in the garage with apparent bullet holes and red painted surfaces including the red painted garage. The other was a ladder in the condemned man's garage.

"Each of the above-listed materials observed on the bullet could be identified specifically if their actual identity is of importance to the investigation. This may provide further constraints or refinement of the hypotheses I have advanced," Palenik said.

Additionally, the law firm of Kathleen Zellner & Associates sought out the expertise of Dr. Lucien "Luke" Haag, a distinguished independent forensic consultant who owns Forensic Science Services Inc. in Carefree, Arizona. Haag has been utilized as an expert witness on firearms identification and firearms evidence across the country.

"The damaged bullet recovered from Steven Avery's garage and purported to yield a full DNA profile of Teresa Halbach shows no evidence of having been shot through Ms. Halbach's skull," Haag said. "The bullet, which was identified as a .22 long rifle bullet, was comprised of such soft metal that there would be detectable bone fragments embedded in the damaged bullet if it had been fired through Ms. Halbach's skull. Because no bone fragments have been identified in the damaged bullet, Item FL, over the course of its examination, including DNA and firearms/tool marks analysis at the Wisconsin State Crime Lab, it is my opinion, to a reasonable degree of certainty in the field of ballistics, that Item FL was not fired through Ms. Halbach's skull." (75)

Haag further explains how he performed a rigorous battery of ballistics testing to illustrate for the court how

75. Affidavit of Dr. Lucien Haag, May 26, 2017

bone fragments would become embedded within .22 long-rifle bullets when fired through human bone.

"I fired two copper-plated lead CCI MiniMag .22 long rifle bullets through one layer of approximately two-millimeter-thick flat bone, then through five inches of soft tissue simulant as a means of recovering the bullet. Bone particles, embedded in the soft lead, were readily visible under a stereo-microscope for both the bullets fired through one thickness of bone and two thicknesses of bone."

Back at Avery's trial, William Newhouse of the Wisconsin State Crime Lab, a firearms examiner, testified as a prosecution witness used by Kratz. "According to Mr. Newhouse's bullet worksheet, Mr. Newhouse identified no trace evidence on the damaged bullet. If there were bone fragments embedded in the damaged bullet, I would expect a reasonably competent firearms examiner to have identified them during their microscopical examination," Haag said.

"Because Mr. Newhouse did not note or describe any bone or bone-like particles embedded in Item FL during his microscopical examination of this damaged bullet, it is my opinion, to a reasonable degree of certainty in the field of forensic ballistics that Item FL was not fired through Ms. Halbach's skull."

Haag's biography notes he is a former criminalist and technical director of the Phoenix Crime Laboratory with more than fifty years of experience in the field as well as having done forensic firearms examinations. He authored the first edition book called *Shooting Incident Reconstruction*. Haag was born in 1940 in Springfield, Illinois.

***

Because Avery's jury trial was heralded as Wisconsin's biggest trial since serial killer cannibal Jeffery Dahmer, it made perfect sense for a sly and unsavory prosecutor to represent wild assertions and stories as fact. Most people around the country fail to understand that court trials, notably murder trials, often don't get to the heart of the actual truth, but are often more about the theatrics and drama. The actors, the winners and the losers, are the lawyers. It's about presentation. It's about style. It's about pizazz. Ken Kratz recognized this, and he excelled at it.

Around the time of Avery's trial, Kratz also had a cozy relationship with several members of the Wisconsin press. They were not about to question him about how he came up with his wild stories of Teresa's murder. For them, he was a reliable and trustworthy source for their story tips, even though he was one of the most untrustworthy public office holders in northeastern Wisconsin.

"At trial it was claimed that the defendant's DNA on the listed item of evidence was deposited from sweaty fingers. This is, of course, pure speculation as there is no forensic test for the presence of sweat. Nonetheless, the DNA that generated the profile came from somewhere," Zellner said.

Enter Dr. Karl Reich. He was enlisted to conduct a series of fact-finding experiments surrounding the mysterious so-called hood latch DNA specimen. That item was the late-to-the-game damning piece of DNA evidence used by the special prosecutor to stick the nail in the coffin at Avery's murder trial.

Dr. Reich runs Independent Forensics in Lombard, Illinois. His company in DuPage County focuses on forensic DNA, molecular biology, protein biochemistry, microbial and human functional genomics, and protein purification. A highly distinguished scientist, Dr. Reich has eight years of post-graduate and fifteen years of experience in the pharmaceutical and biotechnology industries.

The chief scientific officer at Independent Forensics since 2002, Reich is a court-qualified expert witness on forensic DNA, forensic biology, and forensic biology and statistics. As of June 2017, Dr. Reich had given court testimony and sworn pretrial depositions in more than eighty cases in state, federal, and international courts for both civil and criminal matters.

Now he needed to determine, once and for all, was the infamous hood latch DNA specimen used to convict Avery legitimate?

"Volunteers were enlisted to open the car hood of this surrogate vehicle using the engine compartment hood latch, the current and identical method used by the Wisconsin State Forensic DNA Laboratory, Madison," Reich said. "This experimental test was repeated fifteen times. The hood latch was, of course, cleaned after each round of hood opening and subsequent swabbing." (76)

Here were his results.

"In eleven of the fifteen replicates, no detectable DNA was recovered from the hood latch ... In other words, in almost three-quarters of the hood opening trials no measurable DNA was left behind by the individual who opened the hood. Put another way, even when DNA was left on the hood latch after opening the hood, the amount of DNA recovered was between twenty and thirty-five times less than that recovered from the item identified as M05-2467.

"To put it yet another way, the Madison laboratory recovered from six to seven times more DNA than all of the DNA recovered from all of the fifteen hood openings combined."

But how could such a phenomenon occur?

"Given the experimental results, both the body fluid detection data and the DNA recovery data from the hood latch opening trials, the question of what sample M05-2467 #ID really might be, becomes a subject for investigation," Dr. Reich said.

---

76. Affidavit of Dr. Karl Reich, June 6, 2017

Dr. Karl Reich now knows why there was an extraordinary amount of Steven Avery's DNA recovered from the hood latch swab and the spare key on Avery's bedroom floor.

In addition to scrutinizing the dubious hood latch DNA sample, Reich also performed a similar experiment related to the highly questionable spare key. This was the key that surfaced on Avery's bedroom carpet, recovered by Lenk and Colborn, to give Manitowoc County its lone item of evidence to tie Teresa's disappearance to the inside of Avery's trailer.

"Similar to the experimental work to replicate the hood latch results an experiment was done to try to replicate the results from the ignition key of the victim's automobile. An exemplar key, reportedly held by Mr. Avery as if to start a car, gripped by ungloved fingers for twelve minutes, was subject to DNA quantification. It was determined that 0.017 nanograms per microliter was recovered. This result was ten times less DNA than reported by the Wisconsin Department of Justice State Crime Laboratory-Madison on the key they analyzed, item M05-2467 #C."

In both instances, Dr. Reich found the DNA experiments quite startling. "An order of magnitude difference is a significant finding," he said.

Regarding the supposed hood latch DNA, Dr. Reich opined "it is an oft-repeated fear heard from many defendants that the evidence in their case has been enhanced, manufactured, or otherwise manipulated to their disadvantage. There is no doubt that evidence tampering occurs, though there is little to support the contention that this is a widespread practice."

But why would some lawmen, people such as Wiegert, Fassbender, Colborn, Lenk, and possibly others, become tempted to take matters into their own hands?

"It is often assumed that creating an item of evidence de novo or enhancing an item of evidence is an effective method of evidence tampering; however, simply relabeling an errant known standard/reference swab as a questioned item/exhibit accomplishes the goal of identifying the defendant far more efficiently. There is sufficient evidence to hypothesize that this approach to evidence tampering occurred for sample M05-2467 #1D, which was the hood-latch swab," Dr. Reich said.

When Avery went on trial, his lawyers portrayed Colborn and Lenk as the prime evidence planters.

Attorney Zellner's research does not completely abandon Lenk and Colborn as being intimately involved in planting evidence, but her investigators strongly suspect Fassbender and Wiegert were involved in facilitating some of the extraordinary evidence harvests.

If you go back and study the many questionable evidence finds, they often happen after Wiegert and Fassbender give one of their underlings a specific assignment or task that comes at an odd or strange time in the case.

In Omaha, Nebraska, CSI Director David Kofoed ruined his career and went to prison after he got exposed for planting blood swabs as a method to shore up a high-profile double murder case. Kofoed believed the case lacked sufficient physical evidence to move forward with a successful criminal prosecution against the jailed suspects.

Suspects that he was under the erroneous impression were guilty. Kofoed fabricated a perfect DNA sample containing the murder victim's blood to make it look like the jailed suspects had transferred blood from the shotgun killings to their supposed getaway car.

Kofoed waited to plant the blood swab only after he had been assured by one of the misguided lead detectives that the pair of codefendants had to be involved in the farmhouse killings of Wayne and Sharmon Stock in Murdock, Nebraska. The badly mistaken detective, however, had obtained a false confession from the murder victim's mentally impaired nephew. That relative, who had no prior criminal history and had been in special education classes throughout his schooling, ultimately broke down under pressure and threats of being hanged from a tall tree and being put in a gas chamber from his two police interrogators.

The mentally impaired man, in his late twenties, had an IQ in the high sixties.

The nephew of the murder victims agreed to implicate himself as the killer and he named another cousin as his accomplice.

Here's an excerpt from his false confession. The questions were being asked by one of the lead detectives on the double murder case.

"And you fired a shot to shut her up? Isn't that right? I need you to say it out loud, buddy?"

"Yes, sir. Yeah, I think I got him in the head."

The detective then asked if Matthew Livers shot his uncle in a part of his body where it would be hard to walk.

"The knee," Livers confessed. "So he is trying to crawl to the office and then (aunt) Sharmon was woke up screaming of course I believe."

After a brief pause, Livers collected his thoughts and blurted out, "Then I just pulled that trigger and shot her and then she screamed more and then I just ..."

"You just what, buddy?" asked Detective Earl Schenck Jr., a legacy police officer whose father was a long-time sheriff in western Nebraska.

"Put the gun to her face and blew her away," Livers claimed. "Then, then as I headed out, I just stuck it to him and blew him away."

About two weeks later, not a shred of physical evidence existed to tie Livers and his cousin Nick Sampson to the farmhouse murders of their relatives. That was when Kofoed decided to save the day. He produced a perfect DNA sample of murder victim Wayne Stock's blood. He claimed he found the blood when he went back inside the impounded car belonging to the codefendants, a vehicle being kept under police safekeeping at Kofoed's sheriff's office in Omaha, Nebraska. He claimed to have found the blood underneath the dashboard, suggesting to others that this was an area of the car that they forgot to check during the initial eight-hour search that he had supervised about a week or so earlier.

Then, months later, overwhelming evidence showed the real getaway vehicle was a red Dodge Ram truck, stolen in Wisconsin, by the real killers, a teenage boyfriend and girlfriend who were psychopathic goths with an itch to kill.

Livers and Sampson were later proven to be innocent. They had been victims of a sloppy small-town police investigation that led to their unjust incarcerations for a double murder they did not commit. Many months later, the righteous Prosecutor Nathan Cox set them free. The fabricated DNA swabs later put CSI commander Dave Kofoed in prison, but only after the Omaha branch of the FBI got involved.

***

Although most people believe the spare key found on Avery's bedroom carpet was put there by Lenk and Colborn,

Avery's original trial lawyers never developed a strong theory to explain why their client's DNA was on that key.

Strang and Buting also could have devoted more research into the hood latch DNA swab touted by Kratz. Even though they knew the evidence was likely phony, Strang and Buting did not have a strong argument or an expert witness to refute this damning piece of unorthodox forensic evidence when it came time for their client's trial.

The lawyers for Avery also didn't spend enough time following up on the two highly irregular groin swabs Wiegert and Fassbender collected from their client at the time of his arrest when Avery was just being arrested on a weapons violation charge.

According to Dr. Reich, "The chain of custody and disposition of two groin swabs taken from the defendant during his arrest is neither complete, accurate, nor transparent. Such a sample, relabeled as taken from the hood latch of the victim's vehicle, would satisfy all of the observed facts: lack of body fluid, sufficient amount of DNA for a profile, and would link the defendant to the victim without all of the messy and complicated effort to actually deposit DNA on a grease and engine grimed engine compartment metal latch.

"But this hypothesis is a better fit to the data, experimental trials, and needs of the investigators for clear and convincing evidence of a link between the defendant and the victim's vehicle. A swab truly taken from the engine compartment hood latch should have been covered in black engine grime and grease as anyone who has ever had to open the hood of a high mileage car can attest. The swab batting in question was merely very lightly discolored; another fact that does not fit with the claimed origin of this sample."

Another major event in Avery's prosecution occurred on the first and second of March, 2006, when the Manitowoc and Calumet County deputies returned back to the Avery property. Kratz called it the "thorough search" of Avery's detached garage.

But the search warrant also afforded police another opportunity to wander back inside Avery's bedroom. Calumet Deputy Rick Riemer, working closely with Investigator Wendy Baldwin, also confiscated evidence item 8359 which was "a left foot slipper near the east wall in the south bedroom" and item 8360 "A right foot slipper."

But why, four months into the murder case, were authorities, all of a sudden removing Avery's slippers from his bedroom?

Dr. Reich wanted to examine whether the police were attempting to extract DNA from Avery's slippers to have it handy against the despised murder defendant.

"Our lab conducted an experiment to examine whether the bedroom slippers recovered from Mr. Avery's residence could have been the source of his DNA detected on the Toyota ignition key, M05-2467 #C, allegedly recovered from Mr. Avery's bedroom. This hypothesis was tested by creating a pair of worn slippers, sockless, nine hours a day for five days and using this worn item as a source of DNA on an exemplar ignition key. The procedure was to prepare the slippers, rub the key, and then measure the DNA that was transferred ... This approach yielded 0.0393 nanograms per microliter, well below the concentration of DNA reported by the Wisconsin Department of Justice State Crime Laboratory-Madison for the key they analyzed ... at 0.17 nanograms per microliter.

"These data do not support the hypothesis that the DNA identified on the Toyota ignition key came from contact with the slippers photographed in and recovered from Mr. Avery's bedroom. If the Toyota ignition key was indeed enhanced, then it is likely that some other personal item of Mr. Avery's was used for this purpose, some possible examples might include a toothbrush or a cigarette butt." (77)

---

77. Karl Reich, affidavit, June 6, 2017

Of course, simple logic dictates that if Wiegert and Fassbender gathered up two perfect DNA samples from Avery's groin, and they were holding on to them for devious purposes, one groin swab may have been substituted as the hood-latch DNA specimen. The other likely got used for the spare key DNA sample.

"It is hypothesized that a rubbed groin swab taken from the defendant was relabeled and thus became evidence from a hood latch," Reich said. "This hypothesis has not been proven, but it fully explains all of the known facts regarding this item. Taken in context with other facts and allegations in the case of *Wisconsin v. Avery*, this hypothesis deserves careful consideration from the trier of fact."

CHAPTER TWENTY-ONE

HEROES OR GOATS?

In the 2018 Super Bowl, backup quarterback Nick Foles led the Philadelphia Eagles to defeat Tom Brady and the New England Patriots. But after the game, you didn't see crazed football fans storming the field hoisting Brady on their shoulders, giving him a hero's victory celebration. Of course not.

In Avery's murder case, his lawyers Jerry Buting and Dean Strang had engineered an unsuccessful defense and their client got convicted and continues to serve a life prison sentence. And yet the world could not get enough of them. They capitalized on the worldwide notoriety that came from the *Making a Murderer* documentary series, and became like a couple of rock stars. They were booked for countless European media tours to talk about their role on the Avery case. They were the darlings of national television shows including Dr. Phil.

"Mr. Avery holds Buting and Strang partly responsible for his guilty verdict despite the Brady violations of the prosecutors," Zellner said.

Those Brady violations have nothing to do with Tom Brady the losing quarterback in the Super Bowl. Rather, it deals with a federal case law decided by the U.S. Supreme Court that forbids prosecutors and police from hiding and concealing what's known as mitigating evidence, evidence that would be helpful or advantageous to the defendant. Under federal law, prosecutors are expected to provide all information in their possession to the criminal defense's counsel for review as part of the pretrial discovery process.

Here's what Zellner has to say about the overall performance of Buting and Strang. "Strang and Buting had a couple of stellar moments in the courtroom but unfortunately those moments were not nearly enough to win Mr. Avery's case," Zellner said.

"They failed to hire the necessary experts in blood spatter, ballistics, fire forensics, pathology, trace and DNA to combat the avalanche of testimony by the State's fourteen experts. They got hopelessly bogged down and sidetracked by the blood vial theory which was easily refuted by the State. They talked a big game about the cops planting evidence but in the end, they were unable to deliver anything but their own speculative theories."

Based on Zellner's real-life practical experience inside the courtroom, "it is always fatal with a jury to promise something and then fail to deliver on the promise. They failed to carefully review the State's discovery disclosures for impeachment evidence to use against the State's witnesses. Their biggest failure, in that regard, was in failing to call Bryan Dassey to impeach his brother Bobby's testimony that Ms. Halbach never left the Avery property. Bobby would have been discredited and the State's case would have collapsed. After *Making a Murderer* aired, Buting and Strang launched a worldwide tour, as if they had won, rather than lost."

During their pretrial preparation, Buting and Strang overlooked the actual swabs that may have been tampered with by police in order to produce the perfect DNA specimens that came from the spare key in Avery's bedroom and the highly dubious hood latch DNA search, another six months later.

"There is compelling evidence, as we have explained in our pleadings, that Wiegert was involved in switching the hood latch swabs with the groin swabs," Zellner said. "A careful examination of the chain of custody forms for the hood latch swabs demonstrates that Wiegert delivered the so-called hood latch swabs to the Wisconsin Crime Lab but identified another officer as having done so."

Zellner contends that Buting and Strang missed a golden opportunity to destroy the credibility of Colborn's trial testimony about his discovery of the spare key to Teresa Halbach's vehicle. The spare key had suddenly turned up on the carpet near Avery's bed on what marked the sixth time that Manitowoc County Sheriff's officials went into Avery's tiny bedroom. The key gave Manitowoc County a noteworthy clue to finally tie their murder suspect to the Auto Trader photographer's mysterious disappearance.

"We tried many times to duplicate Colborn's story about manhandling the bookcase, and we could not get the key and lanyard to fall out of the back of the bookcase and land where it did. Also, all of the items on top of the bookcase fell on the floor during our experiments. Another great failing of Buting and Strang was in not subpoenaing the bookcase for trial and requesting Colborn, during his cross examination, to come off the stand and demonstrate this miraculous event with the actual key, lanyard, and bookcase for the jury. Colborn could have never replicated what he told the jury happened."

Zellner has unbelievably high standards in terms of taking new clients. Her law firm has a rigid screening process when it comes to accepting condemned prisoners who insist that they were wrongfully convicted.

"I took the Avery case because I thought if I could demonstrate all of the forensic evidence was planted, it would be a wakeup call to law enforcement, juries, judges, and lawyers that they must start demanding the replication of the forensic evidence before they rely upon it in seeking a conviction," Zellner said. "We have challenged anyone to attempt to replicate the State's forensic evidence used to convict Mr. Avery and absolutely no one has been able to do so."

***

During Avery's trial, Strang and Buting put up a valiant effort at one point when they tried to put forth an alternative theory regarding the actual crime scene.

But they were up against the mischievous and cocky Ken Kratz, who wanted to make sure that his salacious story about a bedroom sex-crime murder stuck with the jury's minds. Though there were charred pelvic bones that turned up inside the Manitowoc County quarry several hundred yards south of the Avery property, it appears that Kratz did not want to take the risk that these bones were Teresa's, and possibly neither did Wiegert and Fassbender, so they seem to have reached a consensus, that particular item of evidence would simply be classified as bones of undermined origin and that was that.

That tactical move left defense attorney Dean Strang swimming upstream when he had a chance to cross-examine the prosecution's bone expert, Dr. Leslie Eisenberg of the Wisconsin State Historical Society, during the murder trial.

"Now, you found in the material from the quarry pile two fragments that appeared to you, in your experience, to be pelvic bone, is that right?"(78)

"That's correct.

"There were some cuts, appeared to be some cuts on those pelvic bone fragments?"

"Yes."

"But you weren't able to conclude, 100 percent certain, that these were human pelvic bone fragments; do I understand that correctly?"

---

78. Dr. Leslie Eisenberg, forensic anthropologist, February 28-March 1, 2007 Avery trial testimony

"That's correct."

Eisenberg was also asked about the cut marks to the pelvic bones.

"It was a long, linear cut, on either side of those two bones that were still in proximity. They were essentially a slicing cut on one side and a sharp slicing cut on the other side."

"Did it appear to your eyes that these cuts were, if you could draw any conclusion at all, that the cuts on these pelvic bones were from a smooth edged instrument or a toothed instrument?"

"I cannot answer your question ... because of the burning and charring of the bone itself, it was difficult to make any additional observations beyond that ... If I could place those two adjoining fragments in anatomical position, which I was able to do, as part of the right pelvic structure, those cuts were made on either side, in what I would call a north/south direction, an up and down direction."

When Strang asked if evidence tag 8675 contained multiple burned bone fragments, Eisenberg answered, "That is correct, sir."

Then he asked her if there were separate sites where charred bones, all suspected human bones, shared the same charring and calcination.

"That is correct."

"All of them were fragmented, similarly, from the three sites, again, human bone?"

"That's correct."

"You would certainly agree that it would be very strange weather conditions, indeed, that would transport human bone fragments from the Avery garage area into burn barrel number two on the Janda property?"

"In fact, I would submit there would be no weather conditions that could make that happen."

"You would rule that out?"

"I would."

"Likewise, the quarry pile?"

"Yes, sir ... some bone fragments identified as human had been moved, that's correct."

"Now you have no evidence that human bone fragments actually were burned at more than one site, do you?"

"I do not know that."

"But the burnt bone fragments that you saw from the three sites, again, all were roughly similar in their burning, charring, and calcining?"

"That is correct."

When Strang finished, the prosecution had another chance to sweep away the defense theory about the suspicious pelvic bones being those of Teresa.

Assistant Attorney General Tom Fallon, Kratz's trial sidekick, asked their side's witness, "As you sit here today, you cannot tell us that those bones, to a reasonable degree of anthropological or scientific certainty, are human, can you?"

"I cannot."

***

Dr. Steven Symes has a Doctorate Degree in physical anthropology and he worked as a forensic anthropologist at the Department of the Mississippi State Medical Examiner's Office. In 2008-2009, Symes was honored with the 15th T. Dale Stewart Award, a lifetime achievement given by the American Academy of Forensic Sciences for anthropology, recognizing him for his career, scholarship, and remarkable productivity. He served on the board of directors for the American Board of Forensic Anthropology from 2003 through 2009.

His resume also noted that he is presently on call as the outside forensic anthropology consultant for Summit County, Ohio, Singapore Medical Examiner's Office, Detroit Medical Examiner's Office, Polk County Medical

Examiner's Office in Des Moines, Iowa, and the Will County Medical Examiner's office for its disaster plan.

One of the country's leading forensic pathologists, Dr. Steven Symes of Mississippi has concluded the burning of Teresa Halbach's body did not occur at Avery's property.

"I have testified extensively in forensic trauma to bone and surrounding tissues. The principal topic of my research and experience has been trauma injuries to the skeleton, including ballistic, blunt, burning, healing bone with specific focus on sharp force trauma." (79)

Dr. Symes was retained by Zellner to examine whether Eisenberg had sold out her soul to help the prosecution at Avery's murder trial in a win-at-all-costs scenario. Dr. Symes reviewed all known photographs taken of evidence tag 8675 – the suspected human pelvic bones examined by Dr. Leslie Eisenberg. Then he reviewed all the trial testimony

---

79. Affidavit of Dr. Steven Symes, April 19, 2007

regarding the supposed attempts to identify the pelvic bones that were found at the Manitowoc County gravel pit.

"A microscopic examination of the suspected human pelvic bone, performed in 2005, would have determined to a high percentage of accuracy, whether the pelvic bones were human, and histological slides, made in 2005 from the suspected human pelvic bones, would have determined to a high percentage of accuracy whether the pelvic bones in evidence tag number 8675 were human," Dr. Symes concluded.

But did Dr. Eisenberg sell out her soul, her ethics, and her integrity, to make sure the state of Wisconsin achieved a murder conviction against Avery? After all, she knew how critical her testimony was to the success of the prosecution's case.

"It is certainly below the standard of practice for a reasonably well-qualified and competent forensic anthropologist, at this current time and place, to not perform microscopic and histological examinations of the possible human pelvic bones, and it may have been below the standard of practice in 2005 for a reasonably well-qualified and competent forensic anthropologist to not have performed microscopic and histological examinations of the possible human pelvic bones in evidence tag number 8675," Dr. Symes said.

But there was more in his damning assessment of Dr. Eisenberg's performance.

"It was below the standard of practice for a reasonably well-qualified and competent forensic anthropologist to have relied exclusively upon photographs of the pelvic bones to complete the forensic examination."

Third, "it may be below the standard of practice in 2005 for a reasonably well-qualified and competent forensic anthropologist to have performed an examination and interpretation of bone trauma without microscopic assistance."

Besides Symes, Dr. John DeHaan, one of the world's leading fire and burn experts, also examined the entire Avery case files. DeHaan has worked as a forensic scientist and criminalist since 1970. DeHaan served with the Alameda County Sheriff's Office, the California Department of Justice Bureau of Forensic Services, and the U.S. Treasury Department Bureau of Alcohol, Tobacco and Firearms. He also served as president of Fire-Ex Forensics Inc., since it formed in 1999.

"I have been involved with various aspects of fire and explosion investigation since 1971. In the past twelve years, I have testified as an expert witness in over fifty cases," DeHaan said.(80)

Dr. John DeHaan has conducted dozens of scientific experiments burning the bodies of cadavers under different temperature scenarios as well as indoor and outdoor settings.

In 2017, he was retained by Kathleen T. Zellner & Associates to study everything from the trial testimony, police reports, maps, photos, animated reconstructions, and forensic anthropology reports surrounding the discovery of Teresa's skeletal remains around the Avery property.

For DeHaan, studying the lay of the land was critical. Avery's forty-acre square property was rural, surrounded

---

80. John D. DeHaan affidavit, May 25, 2017

by forests and farms. Their land is south of State Highway 147, about five miles east of Interstate 43, less than ten miles northwest of Two Rivers and about twenty-five miles southeast of Green Bay. The northeast corner of the Avery property had four business buildings including an office, garages, and storage spaces. The residence of Al and Dolores Avery was in the northeast corner. A dirt lane led into the salvage yard where the wrecked cars were left. Another dirt lane, to the south, was where Chuck Avery lived. A third dirt lane ran due west of Avery Road and this lane featured two trailers about sixty-five yards apart, each with a detached garage. Steven Avery lived in the northeast corner trailer and his sister Barb lived in the other trailer with her four sons.

"In the southwest corner of the Avery property there was a dirt lane that ran immediately adjacent to an old gravel conveyor. This lane connected the Avery property to the gravel pits to the south. Within the car pit area, there were numerous dirt lanes separating rows of wrecked vehicles," Dr. DeHaan said.

There were also seven burn barrels spread out across the entire Avery parcel. Steven Avery kept one about forty yards northeast of his trailer. Four more burn barrels were clustered just south of his sister Barb's trailer. The parents, Allan and Dolores Avery, had a burn barrel west of their residence. The seventh barrel was west of Chuck's domicile. All seven barrels were regularly used to burn common garbage from the kitchen and bathrooms. Steven Avery's burn pit behind his detached garage burned "household and automotive discards, trash, and animal remains," DeHaan said.

Then, to the south and to the west, the Avery land was bordered by active gravel pits owned by Radandt and Manitowoc County.

One important distinction DeHaan made was that "The Manitowoc County pit did not border the Avery property."

During Avery's trial, Kratz speculated that Teresa's body was incinerated outside under the dark skies of Halloween.

The circular area consisted of a mound of gravel, about one to two feet high. The entire mound of gravel was about thirty feet in diameter. The burn area was rectangular, about six feet long. "On November 8, 2005, Sgt. Jason Jost of the Manitowoc County Sheriff's Office observed what he suspected may be a vertebrae on the grass outside the south edge of the burn pit … The burned remains of vehicle tires, unburned tires, various hand tools, and a vehicle's bench seat were recovered in the vicinity of the burn pit." (81)

Because the Manitowoc County Sheriff's Office had a reputation for sloppy and incompetent work, no examination was ever done on the wire rings from the tires, an unburned tire, a rubber mallet, a fire-damaged claw hammer, a gravel shovel, the burned vehicle seat, and burned/charred metal scraper with a wooden handle.

"Apparently no examination was performed to establish if any trace evidence linked these items to the death of Ms. Halbach or the burning of her body," DeHaan states.

Here's what else the world-famous fire expert noticed:

The burned debris developed a hard crust, perhaps from the heavy rains between Saturday, November 5, and Monday, November 7.

No forensic anthropologist was present during the November 8 police excavation that began around 3 p.m.

"Crime lab personnel, untrained in anthropology, visually examined potential skeletal fragments to determine their evidentiary value. There was no effort to document from where in the burn pit certain bones were recovered or otherwise document the order with which bones were situated in the burn pit. The crime lab personnel excavating the burn pit placed items of potential evidentiary value in a single box and sent it to Dr. Leslie Eisenberg for off-site examination."

---

81. DeHaan affidavit: Discovery of Bones in Steven Avery's burn pit

Puzzlingly, a decision was made by the leadership team of Wiegert and Fassbender to do no further excavation at the Avery burn pit on November 9. That day came and went without any additional digging. Then on November 10, after Avery was jailed, the Wisconsin Department of Justice was summoned to resume the excavation. "Again there was no forensic anthropologist called to the scene to conduct this secondary excavation. The burn pit was first excavated by hand then dug out using Bobcat-type front-loading tractors," Dr. Symes said.

The bone fragments examined by Dr. Eisenberg led her to conclude the bones came from a woman younger than thirty to thirty-five, shot in the head. "She also concluded that a number of bone fragments showed evidence of crushing or cutting with a tool."

Keep in mind that only a portion of the skeletal remains were recovered. The remains Eisenberg examined were only forty to sixty percent of the total mass of someone Teresa's size. In other words, most of Teresa's bones remain hidden. Perhaps they remain hidden underground, buried somewhere around Manitowoc County's maze of quarries and conveyor roads.

"Dr. Eisenberg identified that two bones recovered from the Manitowoc County gravel pit were still articulated, that is, they had maintained anatomical continuity," Dr. Symes said.

Looking back, the manner in which processing of the burn pits was conducted in such a high-profile murder case was an embarrassment to those involved in the effort: people supposedly proficient at their jobs, people employed by the Wisconsin Department of Justice, the Manitowoc County Sheriff's Office, and Calumet County.

"In this case, the minimal photographs taken before the excavation revealed very little useful information as there were few close-up photos taken before or during the recovery/excavation process … In the few photographs of the burn pit, there appeared to be numerous dried leaves that obscured nearly all identifiable detail of the material below. From Sgt. (Jason) Jost and Wisconsin DOJ Special Agent (Tom) Sturdivant's descriptions, it appeared that the remains showed no anatomical relationship to each other. Some remains were found outside the burn pit and no large bones more resistant to fire were visible at all," Dr. John DeHaan said.

From that point forward, Kratz took it from there.

According to John De Haan, "There was no assessment of fuels associated with the fire other than describing the remains of the steel belts and beading of burned vehicle tires."

Unlike the operation that dug up Avery's property, "I have had the opportunity to see some fifty or more unembalmed adult, human cadavers exposed to a variety of real-world fires," DeHaan said. "These range from accidental kitchen fires, to whole room, post-flashover structure fires, to trench and roadside body disposals, to vehicle fires, to dumpster and burn barrel disposals."

In fact, DeHaan works closely with two of the country's foremost forensic anthropologists, Dr. Allison Galloway from the University of California Santa Cruz and Dr. Elayne Pope from the Virginia State Medical Examiner's Office. "We all assist in the preparation of the demonstration fires set as practical exercises for the students, observe the fires, and document the results."

In his 2012 book he co-authored, *Kirk's Fire Investigation*, 7th edition, DeHaan explains the human body's destruction during a fire is progressive. At first, "the skin shrinks, chars, and splits, exposing the subcutaneous fat. The fat renders out to support a flaming fire adjacent to the body. The muscle tissues dehydrate, char, and burn reluctantly ... Extreme exposure to fire results in loss of mechanical strength. Calcined bones are usually white, blue-white, or light gray in color and are brittle and are easily broken or shattered by contact or pressure."

The bone fragments in Dr. Eisenberg's photographs "appear to be coated with a yellow or tan soil or dust. Dr. Eisenberg reported that she rinsed some of the recovered bone fragments to allow detained examination."

Most of the bone fragments she studied were one to four centimeters in length. "Many were completely calcinated with no charring of organic tissue visible," DeHaan said. "Others bore charred residues of organic material in the cancellous or spongy structure within."

What does this mean?

"Such damage can be induced by exposure to an open-air fire of ordinary combustibles for six to eight hours or for shorter times - three to four hours in a well-ventilated fire in a metal enclosure such as a burn barrel or automobile trunk."

DeHaan further explained that there is a huge distinction between fires set inside a metal enclosure and those set outside.

"In open-air field cremations, exposure to the flames is not uniform, there is minimal additional radiant heat, and charred masses of soft tissue will survive even a prolonged fire, particularly around the head or lower torso."

Of particular interest, the heat output generated by a human body is not substantial. It's on par with an office wastebasket fire, according to DeHaan.

"If a body is allowed to burn undisturbed to completion in either an enclosure or a well-fueled and ventilated fire, the large bones will retain their relative anatomical position, head, neck, shoulders, upper arms, spine, hips upper legs The process of stoking a fire with additional lumber or stirring with an implement during its active burning will cause the mechanical destruction of the bones as they are calcined by the flames and often, considerable displacement."

So what was John DeHaan's analysis of the bones in Teresa's slaying?

"The appearance, size, and type of bone fragments documented in Dr. Eisenberg's forensic anthropology reports and photographs exactly mirror the fragments recovered after burn-barrel cremations involving frequent stirring and stoking observed by this author. Such destruction was observed in wood-fueled burn barrel cremations in as short as three and a half hours."

In another recent criminal case where his expert analysis was sought, the accused killer described stoking a large wood-fueled pyre with several adult human bodies over the course of fifteen hours, DeHaan pointed out.

Later, Dr. DeHaan asserted, most of the bones were crushed with rocks and wood clubs. From there, the larger identifiable body parts that survived the fire were transported to a river for disposal.

"The hundreds of small fragments that were recovered from the burn site were very similar in size, shape and condition to the fragments in Dr. Eisenberg's forensic anthropology photos in this case. Note this involved no confinement except for the wood fuel and was accomplished over a span of 15 hours in an open-air burning pit."

Generally, the destruction of a human body in an open pit fire takes at least six hours, probably longer. The burning of a body thrown into a fifty-five-gallon steel drum with wood fuel can be accomplished in "as little as three and one half hours."

DeHaan is willing to put his name and reputation on the line on behalf of Steven Avery. He signed a sworn court affidavit attesting "it is further my opinion that the body was not burned in the burn pit. This is based on the reported lack of anatomical continuity of the remains, the findings of similarly charred/calcined fragments in burn barrels and other locations on the property and the absence of the more massive fragments that normally resist such exposure.

"I disagree with Dr. Eisenberg's opinion that the main destruction of the body took place in that pit based merely on the amounts of remains recovered from the pit compared to the small fragments found elsewhere in two locations, one being a burn barrel from behind Barb Janda's residence and the other, a burn site in the Manitowoc County gravel pit."

Even more noteworthy, "the reported lack of anatomical continuity of the human bones recovered from Steven Avery's burn pit indicates that Teresa Halbach's body was not burned there. Therefore, it is my opinion that someone transferred Teresa Halbach's bones to Steven Avery's burn pit."

DeHaan said the recovery of the victim's bones inside Bobby Dassey's burn barrel ties everything together.

"The finding of human bone fragments with similar degrees of fire damage in numerous other areas including burn barrels on site is also consistent with the dumping of burned remains into the pit, with some rolling away.

"It should be noted that there were numerous steel vessels on the salvage yard and surrounding properties that could have been used to burn a human body. These were not examined. The wood-fueled boiler and smelter were examined … and no residues were detected there."

But now for the true test: was DeHaan, a nationally recognized fire expert, willing to put his professional reputation on the line and go against the conventional wisdom, to speak out against the Wisconsin police and prosecution team that assembled a successful jury verdict against Avery based on their speculation Avery's open backyard burn pit was the scene of the dismemberment?

"The State represented to the jury that Ms. Halbach's body was burned in an open air burn pit behind Steven Avery's garage from around 7 p.m. to 11 p.m. on October 31, 2005, a period of only four hours. Based upon my review of the descriptions and photographs of the bone fragments analyzed by Dr. Eisenberg, the State's theory is not supported by the physical evidence … burning a body in an open-air burn pit takes six to hour eight hours to accomplish thermal destruction to the degree I observed in Dr. Eisenberg's reports and photos. It is my opinion that the burned bones found in Steven Avery's burn pit could not have been burned to the degree I observed after four hours of burning in an open-air pit like the one behind Steven Avery's garage."

Moreover, DeHaan adds, "the State's theory was also incorrect in its assertion that the burned vehicle bench seat was used to fuel the burning of Ms. Halbach's body. The burned remains of the bench seat were not found in the burn pit, but near it. Its involvement as an external fuel to aid the combustion of a body in a burn pit is speculative and unsupported by any documents I have reviewed.

"The State represented to the jury that the bones were fused with the metal belts in a manner that suggested that the tires from which the steel belts came were burned with the body in Mr. Avery's burn pit. Based upon my review of photographs taken on November 8, 2005, and November 10, 2005, on the occasion of the second excavation of Steven Avery's burn pit, the bone fragments appear to simply be mixed among the metal belts."

DeHaan, president of Fire-Ex Forensics Inc., in Vallejo, California, has expert knowledge of steel-belted car tires involved in fires with human bodies.

"During fire exposure, the steel multi-strand wires degrade, break, and fray to form bristles that readily trap any material coming into contact with them, during or after the fire. Small calcined bone fragments are especially easy to trap. This has been observed in test fires where the fires were under or alongside a burned body as well as on tap."

At Avery's trial, Wisconsin Special Agent Tom Sturdivant noted how Avery's guard dog Bear was on a lead "sufficiently long to give him access to at least some of the burn pit. A quantity of the tire wires/belting was observed to be tangled in the dog's lead at one point ... Dragging the tire remains across the burned debris fragments after the fire would result in the accumulation of fragments in the wire.

The burn pit may have been used previously to dispose of tires so there was no evidence that the entrapment of the debris occurred during the fire that consumed the remains. From my review of these photographs and reports generated by law enforcement at the scene and Dr. Eisenberg in later examination, there is nothing to suggest that the tires were, in fact, burned with the human bones recovered in Steven Avery's burn pit in the manner described by the State," Dr. DeHaan concluded.

Would Avery's murder trial have turned out differently if Buting and Strang had hired a highly regarded fire expert? That's entirely possible. In fact, Buting and Strang had DeHaan on their mind, court files show. They contemplated hiring him, but they didn't carry through with it.

"I personally went through the files of Mr. Avery's trial defense counsel, Dean Strang and Jerry Buting, which they gave to our firm when we announced we were taking on Mr. Avery's case. As I went through the files, I noticed a folder marked 'John DeHaan.' This name stuck out to me because Ms. Zellner had consulted with Dr. John DeHaan, a forensic fire expert, in this case," said Lauren Hawthorne, a law clerk for Kathleen T. Zellner & Associates. (82)

"Inside the folder was the curriculum vitae of Dr. DeHaan. There were no other documents in this file folder. Dr. DeHaan did not testify at Mr. Avery's trial. I checked the curriculum vitae of Dr. DeHaan from the trial defense counsel's box against the curriculum vitae provided to our office from Dr. DeHaan in 2017. I determined that the curriculum vitae of Dr. DeHaan in the trial defense counsel's box belonged to the same Dr. DeHaan that Ms. Zellner consulted."

82. Affidavit Lauren Hawthorne May 4, 2017

*If Avery incinerated Halbach's body in the outdoor burn
pit directly behind Avery's garage, the entire building
would have gone up in flames, Dr. DeHaan noted.*

CHAPTER TWENTY-TWO

THE CRIME

The same Manitowoc sheriff's officials involved in Ricky Hochstetler's hit-and-run vehicular homicide in 1999 never came up with an obvious motive for pinning Avery with the Auto Trader photographer's homicide. But these cops knew, collectively, that Avery needed to pay, and pay hard, for his sins of bringing shame and embarrassment to their Manitowoc County Sheriff's Office.

"Because the State did not need to establish motive, it did not spend any time trying to figure out why Ms. Halbach was murdered," Zellner said. "Both Mr. Avery and Ms. Halbach are victims of a justice system whose success depends upon the integrity, competence, and devotion of judges, law enforcement, prosecutors, and defense attorneys.

"Both Ms. Halbach and Mr. Avery have yet to receive justice. Ms. Halbach has been all but forgotten in the rush to judgment to convict and maintain the conviction of Mr. Avery. Mr. Avery has not been forgotten but buried alive because those individuals who were supposed to save him from a second wrongful conviction failed." (83)

Before his prosecutorial career went down in flames and he moved far away from Wisconsin's Fox Valley area in shame, Kratz was able to spin a courtroom tale suggesting that Avery, after raping and killing Teresa with the help of sixteen-year-old Brendan, got behind the wheel of her Toyota RAV4 and then drove to the far back perimeter of the

83. Notice of Motion and Motion for Post-Conviction Relief, Kathleen T. Zellner, June 7, 2017

salvage yard, squatting down to remove the license plates, disconnect the battery cable, then place large pieces of wood and a hood from another wrecked automobile on the RAV4.

"Mr. Kratz's theory of Ms. Halbach's murder is one of the most preposterous tales ever spun in an American courtroom. If Mr. Kratz's theory were true, then Mr. Avery is a true idiot-savant," Zellner said.

"Mr. Kratz, in a barrage of plot errors, creates an incongruent tale in which Mr. Avery, the savant, without wearing gloves, manages to not leave a single fingerprint in Ms. Halbach's RAV4, while Mr. Avery, the idiot, deposits six drops of his blood on the front seats, by the ignition, and on the rear door jamb. Mr. Avery, the savant, trying to save the day, manages not to leave a single drop of blood on the RAV4 door handle, key, and lanyard, hood prop, gear shift, steering wheel, or battery cables."

A total of eight latent fingerprints were recovered by the Wisconsin State Crime Lab from the doors and windows of Teresa's RAV4. However, Wiegert and Fassbender, with input from Kratz, only wanted those fingerprints compared to a small number of potential suspects. They were let down when they learned that Avery's fingerprints were not a match. None of Avery's fingerprints were recovered from the victim's vehicle. What was the significance of the unidentified latent fingerprints? It heightened the possibility that someone other than Avery was involved in the murder or in moving Teresa's RAV4 to the edge of Avery's property on the night of Friday, November 4, 2005.

"To absolutely ensure that his DNA is linked to the vehicle, Mr. Avery, the idiot, locks the car and opens the hood latch so that his 'sweat DNA' will be found on the latch, just in case the jury is smart enough to figure out that his blood in the RAV4 was planted," Zellner said sarcastically.

"Mr. Avery, the savant, burned the body in his burn pit in world-record time of three to four hours to a point where 60 percent of the bones completely disappeared and all but two teeth evaporated. Mr. Avery, the idiot, picked out some of the larger bones and moved them to his sister's burn barrel and the Manitowoc gravel pit."

"As Albert Einstein once said, 'The difference between stupidity and genius is that genius has its limits.' One would never imagine being convicted on such an idiotic theory, but Mr. Avery was. To understand how this happened, one must examine the other side of the coin: the performance of Mr. Avery's trial defense counsel. The State relied upon the following items of forensic evidence that allegedly linked Mr. Avery to the crime: Mr. Avery's blood in the RAV4, Mr. Avery's DNA on the hood latch, the electronic components, camera, palm pilot, and cell phone in Mr. Avery's burn barrel, the bones and remnants of Ms. Halbach's clothing in Mr. Avery's burn pit, the Toyota key in Mr. Avery's bedroom with Mr. Avery's DNA, and Ms. Halbach's DNA on the damaged bullet found in Mr. Avery's garage."

Zellner also realized that Avery's trial lawyers could have been much better prepared for the trial than they were.

"The State convicted Mr. Avery on this ludicrous theory because trial defense counsel only had two experts to combat the State's 14 experts. One of the trial defense counsel's experts performed at a substandard level and the other was not as qualified as the State's expert. Trial defense counsel claimed evidence was planted but failed miserably in proving that assertion by lacking experts in bloodstain pattern analysis, DNA, ballistics, forensic fire, trace, forensic pathology, and police procedure and investigation. Additionally, trial defense counsel failed to conduct a thorough investigation of the victim's background, deleted cell phone calls, potential third party suspects, or to construct an accurate timeline of Ms. Halbach and Mr. Avery's activities on October 31, 2005," Zellner said.

In 2017, Zellner uncovered an egregious potential Brady violation committed by Kratz. It concerned the behavior of

Manitowoc County Sheriff's Detective Dennis Jacobs, who worked closely with Lenk.

Jacobs was instrumental in retrieving the voice-mail message from the house of George and Jolene Zipperer, the property on County Highway B that may have been where Teresa was headed at the time of her death.

The voice mail, however, no longer exists and, quite suspiciously, it was never furnished by Kratz to Buting and Strang for their review as part of the discovery process at the time of Avery's 2007 murder trial.

"Trial defense counsel, by not carefully reviewing the discovery and not having the appropriate experts, failed to realize ... Mr. Avery's groin swab had been substituted for the hood latch swab by law enforcement; the key discovered in Mr. Avery's bedroom was a sub-key and was planted by Lt. Lenk and Sgt. Colborn immediately before its discovery... Ms. Halbach's last appointment was at the Zipperer's, not the Avery's, and the CD of her voicemail left on the Zipperer's answering machine was concealed and or destroyed by the State to mislead the jury into believing Ms. Halbach's last stop was Mr. Avery's," Zellner said.

"Current post-conviction counsel has retained ten experts and two investigators who have developed strong evidence that undermines confidence in Mr. Avery's verdict."

***

And those suspicions point directly to Bobby Dassey and his violent and abusive stepfather, Scott Tadych. "Current post-conviction counsel is providing this court with new evidence which establishes that Ms. Halbach and her vehicle left the Avery property; that Bobby Dassey gave false testimony about Ms. Halbach and her vehicle not leaving the Avery property; that Bobby Dassey and Scott Tadych gave false testimony establishing each other's alibi; that the

Dassey computer contains images of Ms. Halbach, violent pornography and dead bodies of young females viewed by Bobby Dassey at relevant time periods before and after the murder of Ms. Halbach …" (84)

The two men gave themselves alibis at the time of Teresa's disappearance because they had alibied one another.

During his interview with police, Bobby told the police he was driving along State Highway 147, a highway with a fifty-five m.p.h. speed limit, but he somehow remembered seeing Scott Tadych driving the opposite way.

But at the time of Bobby's first police interview with Dedering, Bobby only drew up blanks. He failed to offer up any details of this strange highway encounter which had supposedly occurred just five days earlier. For instance, Bobby could not say precisely when and where on the road he and Tadych saw each other. This raises the likelihood the story was concocted by Tadych.

"Bobby indicated that as he was traveling on State Highway 147 towards the property he hunts deer on, he did observe an individual known to him as Scott Tadych. Bobby indicated that Scott would be able to verify precisely what time he had seen Bobby."(85)

The work of Zellner's investigators, however, has turned up several questions about their possible involvement in the murder and dismemberment.

"At 2:41 p.m., Ms. Halbach forwarded a call from her cell phone to voicemail, indicating she was preoccupied or distracted by another matter. Her cell phone was deactivated after this point in time, leading to the reasonable inference

---

84. Defendant Steven Avery's Motion for Reconsideration Oct. 23, 2017

85. Interview of Bobby Dassey, November 5, 2005, Investigator John Dedering report

that she was assaulted and murdered at approximately 2:45 p.m. (86)

"Further evidentiary support for Ms. Halbach being assaulted and murdered at the cul-de-sac on Kuss Road is that the scent and cadaver dogs detected a suspected burial site immediately south of the Kuss Road cul-de-sac."

In 2007, Avery's lawyers made the decision to keep their client off the witness stand and not let him to testify in his own defense even though he always professed his innocence in the crime.

Steven Avery has always remains steadfast that he is innocent and had no involvement whatsoever in the kidnapping and killing of Teresa Halbach.

"On October 31, 2005, I remember that I called Ms. Halbach once before she got to the Avery property," Avery said. "I called a second time at 2:35 p.m., but hung up immediately because I saw her at the van, photographing it. I have had the opportunity to review my phone records to refresh my memory. Based upon my recent review of my phone records, I know that Ms. Halbach began photographing Barb's van at 2:35 p.m.

---

86. Kathleen Zellner Motion for Reconsideration, October 23, 2017

"It did not take Ms. Halbach longer than a minute to complete the shooting of Barb's van. When I saw her drive up and park, I was looking out my front window. When I went outside to pay Ms. Halbach, I noticed that Bobby's Blazer was parked in a space between my sister's trailer and garage. By the time I got to my sister's van, Ms. Halbach had already finished taking the picture of the van. I handed her $40 for the listing and she walked to her vehicle and got in. She asked if I needed a receipt and I told her that I didn't. She handed me an Auto Trader magazine and I thanked her."

Avery said he returned to his trailer and put the magazine down on his computer "and walked back outside to go and visit my nephew Bobby. I walked to the middle of my driveway and saw Ms. Halbach's vehicle turning left on Highway 147, headed west," Avery said. "I looked to my right and noticed that Bobby's Blazer was gone. Bobby did not leave before Ms. Halbach because I observed his Blazer parked by Barb's residence when I was outside with Ms. Halbach. If Bobby left a few seconds behind Ms. Halbach, I would have seen his Blazer when I saw Ms. Halbach's vehicle leaving the property.

"I believe that Bobby left about left thirty seconds after Ms. Halbach because I could not see his vehicle. If he left thirty seconds after Ms. Halbach, he would have been near the intersection of the gravel drive, which leads to my and Barb's trailers, and Avery Road. It was not possible to see Bobby's Blazer at that location because there was a dip and a bend in the gravel drive as it approached Avery Road and there were buildings that blocked my view. If Bobby had left thirty seconds after Ms. Halbach, his Blazer would have been in a position where I would not have been able to see it."(87)

---

87. Steven Avery supplemental affidavit, November 14, 2017

These days, Avery's lawyer has also gained access to Bobby's cell phone records from around the time of the crime.

"Bobby stated that he would hunt on the property behind Tadych's house at 12764 State Highway 147 which was east of the Salvage Yard. At 3:02 p.m. on October 31, 2005, Bobby hit off Tower 363X, 5.47 miles west of the Dassey residence. Bobby's hunting spot was only 1.5 miles from Tower 370X. If Bobby was hunting where he claimed to be hunting east of the Avery property, there would be no reason that his call at 3:02 p.m. would have bounced off of Tower 363X, west of the Avery property, instead of 370X," Zellner said. (88)

Back in 2007, Kratz duped people into thinking that Brendan Dassey's blue jeans had been bleached as part of a conniving plot by Avery and Brendan to literally clean every single droplet and speck of blood from Avery's garage. But this was a way for Kratz to divert attention away from the behavior of his two deeply troubled witnesses who he needed to help make his case, Bobby and Tadych.

On March 2, 2006, Lisa Novachek, an employee at the Wisconsin Aluminum Foundry, told police "that on the date of Teresa Halbach's homicide, Scott Tadych did not show up for work. She said she did hear him say that he was going to see his mother in the hospital. Lisa said around the time of Steven Avery's arrest, another girl that works with her, by the name of Chris Graff, had taken a phone call from a hysterical young teenage kid asking for Scott Tadych. Scott was paged, took the phone call and left shortly after that. Scott Tadych's foreman, Keith Schaefer, informed Lisa that he was a nervous wreck when he left."

According to fellow Wisconsin Foundry workers, "he had made a comment that there was some blood on one of

---

88. Motion to Supplement Previously Filed Motion for Post-Conviction Relief, July 6, 2018

the boy's clothes and that it had gotten mixed up with his laundry."(89)

The identity of the hysterical teenager who called Tadych at the Wisconsin Aluminum Foundry was never pursued by the police perhaps because they realized it may expose their arrest of Avery as a sham.

One thing is clear. The caller would not have been sixteen-year-old Brendan. He and Tadych didn't even associate with one another. The idea of Brendan having Tadych's phone number and then calling for him at work is preposterous.

Older brother Bobby, on the other hand, had a close relationship with Tadych.

Back in 2005, law enforcement from Manitowoc and Calumet Counties agreed that they would not attempt to obtain a search warrant to obtain any DNA specimens from Scott Tadych in connection with Teresa's disappearance.

A decision was also made not to compare Tadych's fingerprints with any of the fingerprints left on Teresa's RAV4, after the damaged vehicle turned up at Avery's property.

In 2018, Zellner laid out for Wisconsin's judicial system "the evidence supporting that Bobby was a viable third-party suspect and had a realistic ability to engineer the crime."

She also reminded the court that, "Mr. Avery does not have to prove that Bobby committed the crime as long as his theory is based on evidence beyond a possible ground of suspicion."

For the first time, she introduced for the court how Bobby had an unhealthy and dangerous obsession with Teresa.

Like many sadistic psychopathic killers, Bobby's unhealthy obsession with violent pornography was taking over his life. Court documents reveal he was spending more

---

89. Interview of Lisa Novachek, March 2, 2006, by Investigator Wendy Baldwin

and more time on his personal computer when the rest of his family was not around.

Bobby did not have any girlfriends but he was falling into lust with young attractive women who bore the same general characteristics to Teresa.

Whenever Teresa showed up to do her Auto Trader assignments at Avery Salvage, Bobby seemed to know about her presence.

"Bobby had developed an obsession with Ms. Halbach and on a number of occasions, watched her from the window. The following day after her visits, Bobby commented about her, indicating that he was watching her. Because of Bobby's obsessive and compulsive preoccupation with viewing violent pornography of women who resembled Ms. Halbach, he developed violent sexual fantasies about her."(90)

Zellner suspects that Bobby Dassey tricked Teresa Halbach into stopping her vehicle along Kuss Road under the pretense of doing a hustle shot of his vehicle.

In March of 2006, Kratz held his infamous press conference advising minors not to listen to what he was about to reveal. Although Kratz sustained a murder conviction,

90. Defendant's Reply to the State's Response to Supplement Previously Filed Motion, August 3, 2018

most people agree the murder could not possibly have happened the way Kratz described the crime. The scientific evidence does not support his story.

After devoting more than two and a half years to reinvestigating the case, Zellner offered her own theory on how Teresa died to the Manitowoc County Circuit Court in her thirty-page motion for post-conviction relief filed August 3, 2018.

Here it is:

"Upon Ms. Halbach's arrival on October 31, 2005, Bobby watched her from his window, as he had in the past, but denied to the police that he was aware that she was coming to the property. As Ms. Halbach left the property, Bobby followed. Ms. Halbach was persuaded to pull over in the Kuss Road cul-de-sac area and open her rear cargo door to obtain her camera for a photograph. Advances were made, a struggle ensued, and Ms. Halbach was knocked to the ground and hit by a rock, causing blood spatter to land on the inside of the rear cargo door of her RAV4.

"Ms. Halbach was lifted into the rear of the RAV4 and driven to the area of the suspected burial site, assaulted, and then driven back to the Avery property. The hair bloodstain patterns on the inside panel of the rear cargo area of the RAV4 were created by Ms. Halbach's injured head as the car was driven back to the Avery Salvage Yard. The RAV4 was pulled into the Dassey garage and Ms. Halbach was shot twice in the head. The Dassey garage was never luminoled or checked for forensic evidence of any type; blood found between the Dassey garage and residence was never tested."

Another suspicious lead, pointing toward Tadych's possible involvement in Teresa's murder, went by the wayside by the Calumet County Sheriff's Office. On March 31, 2006, Jay Mathes, an employee at the Wisconsin Aluminum Foundry in Manitowoc, told investigator Wendy Baldwin "he has known Scott Tadych for approximately eight years … He said he had been interested in buying a .22

for his kid and had told Scott about it because he was on a forklift and could find out if anyone had a gun for sale. Jay said about a week ago, Scott said he had a .22 Savage for sale that belonged to one of Barbara's kids ... they agreed on a price of $100. Jay said it had a scope on it and figured it was a rifle and not a pistol.

"Scott approached him and told him he could go out to his truck and look at it. Jay told Scott he was not interested in looking at the gun that particular day and told him he was going to wait until the weekend."

Then, when Mathes inquired about the gun later, Tadych acted weird.

"Scott told him he never had the gun and the kid wanted to keep it now and it was not for sale. Jay described Scott as 'not being hooked up right' and has seen him fly off the handle at everyone at work.'"(91)

Zellner believes Teresa Halbach attacked on Kuss Road and rendered unconscious with a heavy object after being struck in the head near the back of her RAV4.

***

---

91. Interview of Jay Mathes, Investigator Wendy Baldwin report, March 31, 2006

Truth be known, Tadych was a familiar name and face around law enforcement circles at the Manitowoc County Sheriff's Office and in Two Rivers, where he grew up. Without any doubt, his propensity toward violence was tenfold compared to Steven Avery. In fact, Tadych's temper makes Avery look like a little lamb. Yet Manitowoc County deputies who knew both men, Tadych and Avery, gave Tadych a free pass when it came to his version of events and his claims of an alibi, but they chose to disregard and not believe Avery in his repeated denials of guilt when it came to Teresa's disappearance.

On December 27, 1997, Tadych, then twenty-nine, had one of his many violent dustups, this one involving his mother, Patricia Tadych. Police who handled that call on Cottage Lane in Two Rivers Township included Manitowoc County Deputy Gregg Schetter, Sgt. James Lenk, and two other county deputies.

"The complainant … is informed by the reports of Deputy Schetter that upon speaking with Patricia Tadych … her son Scott Tadych came to the residence through the front door without knocking or receiving any type of permission. Patricia stated Scott informed her that he came to pick up his fishing equipment … Patricia stated Scott immediately noticed some of the fishing items had been moved and became angry about this. When Scott questioned her about this, Patricia stated she informed Scott that she needed to remove some of the fishing items due to the fact it was blocking a doorway and she needed to get through the door. Scott became very angry that some of his fishing equipment was missing and (began) yelling obscenities such as "Fucker," "Bitch," "A Cunt," and "A Loser" towards (his mother) Patricia …

"When she asked him to calm down, Scott told her he did not have to calm down … Scott came up to her and shoved his weight into the left side of her body which caused her to almost fall. Patricia stated she did have some trouble breathing and did have minor pain to her left side and shoulder area. (92)

"Patricia stated at this time she became extremely upset and continued to be scared that Scott would cause more injury to her ..."

At that point, she asked her other son, William, to come over.

"Get the Hell out of here!" William barked at his brother.

"I'm not leaving all my stuff," Scott Tadych snapped.

A physical altercation ensued.

William pushed his brother, causing Scott Tadych to fall into the pick-up truck parked in the driveway.

When Scott tried to get up, William pushed Scott again. The cowardly brother who had verbally demeaned and attacked his own mother now wanted to get out of Dodge.

"Scott then entered his vehicle and left the area. William stated Scott attempted to push back and fight back during the altercation but he did not injure William in any way."

For that offense, Scott Tadych was charged by Manitowoc County in January 1998 with unlawfully entering the dwelling of another without their consent.

Four years prior, on July 17, 1994, Tadych was charged with unlawfully entering the dwelling of another without their consent and with unlawfully and intentionally causing bodily harm to another. The Two Rivers Police Department criminal complaint states that Tadych struck and injured Martin LeClair.

A Two Rivers Police officer was summoned to the residence of Constance Welnetz on Jackson Street at 3:05 a.m. She told police that "at approximately 3 a.m. she was asleep with Martin LeClair when she heard a hard knock on their bedroom window. Constance stated she believed it was Scott Tadych as he had done this in the past."

---

92. State of Wisconsin vs. Scott Tadych, criminal complaint filed January 12, 1998

Later, she heard another loud knock. It was at the back door.

"Constance stated that Martin decided to go outside to speak with Scott to tell him to stop harassing her. Constance stated she told Martin not to go outside and she was going to call the police. Constance stated she heard some banging and shouting outside and as she was trying to see she lost the connection with the police. Constance stated at this time Scott walked into her residence without her permission and stated, "You will die for this, bitch." (93)

Constance ran outside. She found Martin LeClair laying in the driveway. He had endured a savage beating.

"He was covered in blood and had a cut on his head. Officer Mark Scheld spoke with Martin LeClair who stated at approximately 3:15 a.m. someone was pounding on the bedroom window and then knocking on the door and they believed it was Scott Tadych. Martin stated he got dressed and went outside to confront Scott. Martin stated they began to argue and were pushing each other and Scott swung at Martin and struck him on the left side of the face with a closed fist and Scott struck him with an unidentified object in his head and he believes he was unconscious for a brief time, but he can't remember until he was in the house and the police were there. At no time did he give anyone permission to strike him or cause him injury."

Scott Tadych's rage and his threats of violence did not slow down as he grew older. In January 2001, four years before Teresa vanished, he was the respondent of a restraining order, filed at the Manitowoc County Courthouse. The document reflects that on January 4, 2001, Tadych "called me at work seven times within a twenty-five-minute period. Threatened to 'kick my ass' and turn me over to

---

93. State of Wisconsin versus Scott Tadych, criminal complaint filed August 9, 1994

social services and just plain make my life miserable. Called me a 'Fucking Cunt Bitch.'"

Tadych had summoned a friend named Scotty to call the woman "and ask when I was going to pay him the $42 that I owed him. I told Scotty to stop calling me and not to follow in Scott Tadych's footsteps ... December 30, 2000, Scott Tadych started calling my house at 10:10 a.m. He called five times within a twenty minute period. I kept hanging up on him."(94)

The previous day, December 30, 2000, "I was getting ready to go out and at about 7 p.m. my phone rang. I answered it. It was Scott again. At that time, someone knocked on my back door. Scott asked what I was doing. I said answering the door stop calling here and hung up. I opened the back door. It was Scott and he pushed his way into my house. I told him to leave, he would not and started screaming and yelling and moving about my house, calling me a "Cunt, Slut, Bitch." Finally, I picked up (the) phone and said if he didn't leave, I would call police. He left slamming my back door knocking off the wreath. I then witnessed and heard him beating on my vehicle and saw him try all the doors to get into the vehicle. Then he spit on my vehicle."

Terrified, the woman sneaked over to the gas station, thinking this was a safe place to hide out.

"Scott followed me there and kept driving by all the while I was in Kwik Trip. When I was done, I went to leave. I backed out of the parking space and Scott blocked me from leaving for about two minutes. After he moved, I went directly to Two Rivers Police Department to report what Scott had been doing."

Even while the woman was giving her statement to the police, Tadych continued to call her. "After I was done with police, I went out. Scott started calling my cell phone from

---

94. Restraining order of Constance A. Welnetz versus Scott Tadych, dated January 4, 2001

a number belonging to Joanne LaRose. I answered and Scott said that if I didn't talk to him and give him another chance, he would ruin my life because I was a worthless piece (of) shit and he would hurt me. I hung up ..."

On June 24, 2002, Tadych was charged with causing a disturbance with Constance Welnetz. That May 14, a Two Rivers officer was dispatched to the Tadych house for a disorderly incident. The victim told police she had "just gotten into a verbal and physical altercation with her ex-boyfriend, Scott Tadych ... she tried to kick Tadych out of her residence because he yelled at her son, Ryan, for getting up late for school. According to Welnetz, Tadych then threatened to make their lives a living hell.

"She further stated that Tadych had shoved her up against the wall and struggled with her to take the phone away." (95)

The woman got her son and daughter out of the house and drove them to school. "Welnetz further stated that Tadych returned to the residence and was threatening to kill her and himself. According to Welnetz, Tadych took her keys and threw his watch and keys at her. When Welnetz called 911, Tadych left the residence."

When Two Rivers Police responded, they saw the woman's wrist was cut and a bathroom door yanked off the hinge.

"Welnetz stated that it was the wrist that Tadych was struggling to get the phone from. She also stated that she was punched twice by Tadych in the right shoulder and that he had used a closed fist."

According to court records, here's a summary of Tadych's criminal history in Manitowoc County prior to the disappearance and murder of Teresa:

---

95. State of Wisconsin versus Scott Tadych, criminal complaint, filed June 24, 2002

November 1994: Guilty of battery, thirty days jail time, probation for one year.

July 1997: Physical abuse of a child was downgraded to battery. Probation for eighteen months and sixty days jail. Charges of disorderly conduct and criminal damage to property got dismissed under the plea.

December 1997: Criminal trespass to a building, sentence involved a fine. A disorderly conduct charge was dropped under the plea.

July 2002: Disorderly conduct. Sentence withheld. Tadych got put on probation through the Department of Corrections for eighteen months. He needed to continue with counseling and take his prescribed medications, perform community service, maintain a full-time job, and pay court fines including a domestic violence surcharge. On February 15, 2004, Tadych was discharged from his probation.

Here's what Zellner has to say about Tadych and her contention that he is a suspected accomplice in the dismemberment and disposal of Teresa's remains.

"We have received several tips about Tadych being very careful not to leave anything with his DNA on it so that someone could retrieve it," Zellner told the author. "He refused to give us blood for a DNA methylation experiment. Tadych's reluctance to provide his DNA has only increased our suspicion of him. Mr. Avery's complete willingness to have further testing performed has solidified my view that he is 100 percent innocent."

But not everyone is rooting for Zellner to succeed.

There remain a number of fierce loyalists, mainly people whose family members, relatives, and dear friends either work in Wisconsin law enforcement or had a role in bringing murder charges against Avery. Along with several high-ranking members of Wisconsin's political government, people including Wisconsin Governor Scott Walker and his right-hand man, Attorney General Brad Schimel, who once played in a band with former Manitowoc County special prosecutor Ken Kratz, they have doubled down and put forth a relentless quest to make sure Avery stays a condemned and convicted murderer, just as they have done with Brendan Dassey, who most people are sure is innocent.

"I couldn't care less about the opinions of those who think I am trying to free a murderer," Zellner told the author. "All of the individuals I have exonerated were believed to be guilty until they walked out of the prison gates. I have not read a single article, social media post, or book from a 'guilter' that is not riddled with factual inaccuracies, legal misperceptions, or profound ignorance.

"The Achilles heel of this group is their leader, a discredited and disgraced prosecutor whose unethical behavior has exceeded anything my legal experts have encountered in any other post-conviction case in the country."

CHAPTER TWENTY-THREE

KEN KRATZ

"That same 'ugly picture' depicted in Kratz's offensive sexual misconduct with women appears in Kratz's solicitation of Avery. Kratz acted out of his own self-interest, in an utterly unethical way, abused his professional office, and engaged in conduct prejudicial to be the administration of justice." – Bennett L. Gershman, state of New York, County of Westchester, sworn affidavit of May 10, 2017.

In the legal profession, prosecutors generally abide by the rules of professional conduct inside the courtroom and surrounding the rights of the accused. But every so often an oily person can infiltrate the criminal justice system in a way that does great harm to America's confidence in their public officials who take an oath to uphold the Constitution and protect the civil liberties and rights of the accused.

Every once in a blue moon, someone like Ken Kratz comes around and is able to play the system to his own advantage, because he's confident nobody else will dare challenge him.

Luckily for everyone, the voting public, police officers, and criminal defense lawyers, there are checks and balances in the legal system. That's why, in all likelihood, the same man responsible for obtaining successful murder convictions against Avery and Brendan Dassey, despite presenting two completely different scenarios in their trials of how Teresa's murder happened, will likely be the eventual fall guy, the poster child for the Avery murder case's implosion, when that day comes.

For every Ken Kratz who poisons the criminal justice system and brings shame and embarrassment to other hard-working, noble and conscientious criminal prosecutors, defense lawyers, and judges, there is someone on the opposite spectrum, someone with a sterling reputation such as Bennett L. Gershman, a highly distinguished state of New York lawyer whose credentials are a thousand times stronger than those of Kratz.

New York law professor Bennett Gershman is one of the country's leading experts on the topic of prosecutorial misconduct.

Gershman worked from 1966 to 1972 as an Assistant New York County District Attorney handling homicides, rackets, appeals, and major felonies. "I presented hundreds of cases to grand juries and tried numerous felony cases to verdict."

From 1972 to 1976, Gershman was an Assistant Attorney General in the New York State Special Prosecutor's Office that was charged with investigating official and political corruption in New York City.

"I was chief of the appeals bureau and the Bronx Anti-Corruption Bureau where I investigated cases, presented cases to special grand juries, and prosecuted many public officials including judges, prosecutors, attorneys, police officers and other public officials charged with corrupt, fraudulent, and dishonest conduct." (96)

These days, Gershman serves as a tenured professor of law at the Elizabeth Haub School of Law at Pace University in New York. He has taught there since 1976. He teaches classes on criminal law, criminal procedure, constitutional law, trial practice, and professional ethics.

"During my academic career I have served as a defense attorney representing many persons charged with serious felonies including murder, rape, organized crime, and drug cases," Gershman said. "I have testified as an expert witness in judicial proceedings and before the United States Congress, the New York State Legislature, and various professional and fact-finding commissions."

Gershman also provided a legal opinion on January 6, 2017, for the nomination of Alabama Senator Jeff Sessions for Attorney General of the United States.

Gershman has written a treatise on the ethical duties of prosecutors called *Prosecutorial Misconduct*, 2nd edition Thomson-West, and a treatise on the criminal trial called *Criminal Trial Error and Misconduct*, that delves into errors and misconduct involving a judge, prosecutor, defense attorney, and jury, and what can be done to challenge the misconduct after the fact.

"I often lecture to judges, prosecutors, bar associations, and other professional and civic groups," Gershman said.

One lawyer who never attended one of Gershman's lectures is Ken Kratz.

"For a prosecutor, the press conference is the most powerful forum in which to communicate with the public," Gershman said. "A press conference gives the prosecutor the

---

96. May 10, 2017 affidavit of New York attorney Bennett Gershman

opportunity to express in a dramatic way the results of an investigation, the crimes being charged, and the involvement of the persons accused of committing those crimes. Because there is a risk that the press conference can prejudice the right of an accused to a fair trial, ethics rules strictly circumscribe what a prosecutor can say at a press conference."

According to Gershman, Kratz's back-to-back press conferences held on March 1 and 2, 2006 "constituted professional misconduct. Kratz, an experienced prosecutor, knew that a prosecutor is not allowed to disparage the character and reputation of an accused, disclose the existence of a confession or other physical evidence, discuss any information that is likely to be inadmissible in evidence … and express an opinion on a defendant's guilt.

"Kratz knew that his statements would make it virtually impossible for anyone watching his press conference to keep an open mind about the case and the guilt of the defendants. Kratz knew what he had accomplished."

At the first news conference event, Kratz declared that law enforcement "now has a definitive set of answers as to what happened to Teresa Halbach" and "we know exactly what to look for and where to look for it." The next day, March 2, Kratz claimed, "we have now determined what occurred sometime between 3:45 p.m. and 10 or 11 p.m. on the 31st of October."

But why would someone in Kratz's position step over the line and commit prosecutorial misconduct, as Gershman outlines? For starters, Kratz would have known he was invincible at the time. In other words, there were no higher powers and authority to call him out and hold him accountable. Therefore, there was no misconduct except in the minds of the disenfranchised.

"More than any other government official, a prosecutor is viewed by the public with esteem and trust," Gershman said. "The public looks to the prosecutor as the official most responsible for vindicating the rule of law and punishing wrongdoers. Given Kratz's prestige and prominence as the special prosecutor by the governor to lead the investigation, Kratz's assertions that law enforcement had 'solved' the case would almost certainly be greeted by the public with both relief that the perpetrators had been apprehended and an outcry to punish them."

During the March 2 press conference, Kratz suggested Avery shackled, raped, tortured, and butchered Teresa to death. "Kratz knew at the time of his March 2 press conference that every statement he made accusing Avery of the horrific acts against Teresa Halbach ... was based exclusively on the uncorroborated confession of 16-year-old Brendan Dassey, which has recently been found by a federal court to have been coerced by police," Gershman said.

"Kratz knew that Dassey was of borderline intelligence, attended special education classes, and was known as a mild-mannered, introverted young man who was never before in trouble with the law ... Dassey's confession presented a narrative that was totally different than the version Kratz used in filing the original murder charges against Avery, and Dassey's confession was legally inadmissible against Avery for constitutional and statutory reasons. In short, Kratz had no evidence and therefore no legal basis to support the new charges of sexual assault and torture against Avery contained in the amended complaint and announced at the press conference."

Deep down, Kratz also knew something the general public did not know. And it was something he very much did not want people and the gullible lapdog members of the Wisconsin press to report.

Here's what it was:

"Kratz knew that a four-month police investigation that had conducted at least eight separate searches of Avery's trailer, garage, and every part of the property had yielded no forensic or physical evidence to corroborate Dassey's confession," Gershman said. "A prosecutor engages in professional misconduct when he makes unwarranted claims and brings unwarranted criminal charges.

Gershman determined that Ken Kratz's pretrial press conferences crossed the lines of decency and violated Avery's right to a fair and impair jury trial in America's judicial system.

"Moreover, in bringing charges that are not legally and factually sustainable, Kratz engaged in professional misconduct for another reason. Prosecutors are commanded 'not to prosecute a charge that the prosecutor knows is not supported by probable cause.' Kratz knew that he lacked sufficient evidence to charge Avery with the acts described in Dassey's confession. Dassey's confession, as Kratz surely knew, was inadmissible against Avery under the Sixth Amendment to the U.S. Constitution. Dassey's confession was also inadmissible against Avery because it violated a fundamental rule of evidence barring use of statements that are hearsay."

But what was Kratz's motivation in holding a press conference making inflammatory assertions against Avery knowing what he was saying was not true?

"He lacked probable cause, indeed, any factual basis whatsoever, to file his amended complaint charging Avery with the additional crimes of sexual assault and torture and then publicly announced those new charges to the world. In my opinion, Kratz brought these new charges against Avery in bad faith. He knew that he would not be able to present these facts against Avery to a jury, as demonstrated by his decision to drop the sexual assault and kidnapping charges on February 2, 2007. He disclosed these facts publicly knowing that they would be heard by prospective jurors and used to prejudice Avery ... By charging without a proper factual basis, and then representing in official court documents and in his public statements that those charges were validly brought, Kratz engaged in fraudulent, dishonest, deceitful, and misleading conduct."

In fact, Kratz's behavior in the case was so far over the top that he "thereby violated the 'attorney's oath' by advancing facts prejudicial to the reputation of a party without any legitimate reason by law or justice to do so," Gershman's affidavit notes.

"It is one thing for a codefendant like Dassey to make allegations that implicate himself and others. It is a far different thing for a prosecutor not only to repeat those statements publicly but also to endorse them as the truth, particularly when there is no factual basis to confirm their validity. All of Kratz's references to Avery's alleged heinous acts were gratuitous, without any legitimate basis in fact or law, without any legitimate law enforcement reason, and destroyed Avery's character, his ability to receive a fair trial, and his Constitutional right to the presumption of innocence. Collectively, Kratz's statements were offensive to the fair and proper administration of justice and the integrity of our system of justice and demonstrated Kratz's unfitness as a prosecutor."

Kratz's egregious behavior ensured Avery's life was ruined and he became a pariah in his community, just as Kratz successfully portrayed Avery during his term representing the voters of Calumet County, who kept electing and re-electing Kratz, time and time again as their arbiter of justice.

"Although the prosecutor is allowed to prosecute with earnestness and vigor and 'may strike hard blows' he is not at liberty to strike foul ones," Gershman said. "Constitutional and ethical rules impose a special obligation on prosecutors to serve and vindicate the truth and administer justice. Thus, a prosecutor violates due process and his ethical duty to serve the truth when he presents inconsistent and irreconcilable theories at two different trials against two different defendants. Such conduct is inherently unfair, disserves the truth, and renders any resulting conviction unreliable."

Many people familiar with the plight of Avery and his nephew are totally oblivious to the fact that after Kratz obtained a murder conviction against Avery, Kratz went on to convict Brendan Dassey based on a totally different set of allegations and theories as far as Teresa's murder was concerned. Something crazy and ridiculous like this only happens in Manitowoc County, Wisconsin.

According to Gershman, here were some of the many examples showing how Kratz strayed outside the boundaries of professionalism and credulity:

From Avery's trial: "All of the evidence points to one person. That's the one person being responsible. I'm going to argue at the conclusion of this case who that one person is. I bet you can guess who I'm going to suggest was responsible."

From Dassey's trial: "Kratz claimed that Brendan Dassey killed Teresa Halbach, or at least participated in her killing with Avery. Kratz claimed that she was killed by Avery stabbing her in the stomach, Dassey slitting her throat, Avery manually strangling her and then incidentally adding a gunshot. He argued she was killed in Avery's trailer, not his garage."

But at Avery's trial: "He argued no blood was found in the trailer. But since Teresa wasn't killed in the trailer, there shouldn't be. She was not killed in the trailer. Where was Teresa killed? This is an easy answer or at least it is an answer that is directed by all the physical evidence in this case. She was killed in Steven Avery's garage."

At Avery's trial, Kratz alerted the jury "we will actually be arguing to you that Mr. Avery handled, handled that weapon in his hands when Ms. Halbach was killed. Teresa's death was caused by two gunshot wounds to the head. Teresa's future aspirations were snuffed out by one act and by one act from one person."

But nobody in Wisconsin's judicial system, notably the Manitowoc County presiding judge Jerome Fox for Dassey's trial, called out Kratz's antics as being inappropriate. Kratz's ability to offer completely different theories against codefendants for the same murder drew a free pass from the judge.

"Kratz's inconsistent contentions at the Avery and Dassey trials violate due process as well as a prosecutor's duty to promote the truth and serve justice," Gershman said. "A prosecutor may not advance at separate trials theories of guilt which cannot be reconciled factually. Kratz could not in good faith argue at Avery's trial that Avery was the only killer and then argue at Dassey's trial that Avery along with Dassey killed Teresa Halbach. Kratz could not in good faith argue at Avery's trial that Halbach's death was caused by gunshot wounds and then argue at Dassey's trial that her death was caused by stab wounds to her stomach and throat and manual strangulation as well as gunshots.

"Kratz could not in good faith argue in Avery's trial that Halbach was killed in the garage and then argue in Dassey's trial that she was killed in Avery's trailer. Kratz's theories … negate one another. His claims are inconsistent and irreconcilable. Such flip-flopping conduct by a prosecutor is inherently unfair, legally and ethically, and undermines the very concept of justice and the duty of a prosecutor to serve truth. A prosecutor cannot engage in such gamesmanship, such conduct destroys confidence in the integrity of the system of justice and the constitutional and ethical precept that the prosecutor's goal is to serve justice rather than winning convictions."

But since Kratz was not a man of ethics or integrity, he also had no shame in writing a book intended to sabotage Avery's long-term prospects of ever getting justice and a new trial.

Part of the information that Kratz contained in his 2017 book, *The Case Against Steven Avery and What Making a Murderer Gets Wrong*, came from information that Avery's trial judge, Patrick Willis, had sealed and therefore was not part of the court record at the time of Avery's trial.

"Kratz's book and media appearances describe in vivid detail how he claims Avery sexually assaulted his ex-wife, his former girlfriend, his niece, and his babysitter, his horrific torture of a cat, and a variety of other violent criminal acts," Gershman said. "Indeed, these allegations parallel the inflammatory allegations Kratz made against Avery in his sealed motion to Judge Willis.

"To be sure, the First Amendment protects Kratz's freedom to publish and talk about his book. But as an attorney, and former lead prosecutor in the Avery and Dassey cases, Kratz's free speech rights are constrained by ethical rules … although Judge Willis unsealed the motion after Avery was convicted, the publishing of this information was unnecessary and would certainly be prejudicial to future jurors if Avery was successful in seeking a new trial. Kratz's book is an inaccurate and inflammatory attack on the popular Netflix series, *Making a Murderer*."

From Gershman's perspective, "there appears to be no legitimate reason for Kratz to disseminate this inflammatory information.

"Although the Avery and Dassey cases have attracted widespread interest, and were the subject of a ten-part Netflix series *Making a Murderer*, Kratz was in a unique position that was different from all other journalists and commentators. Kratz was the lead prosecutor against Avery and Dassey. Kratz was privy to considerable confidential information that had not been officially revealed. Ethical standards specifically address the question of the extent to which a former prosecutor is allowed to reveal secret information obtained in confidence while investigating and prosecuting a criminal matter."

But even more appalling behavior by Kratz began in 2013, after he had already been forced to resign from office in shame and disgrace. By that point, he had retreated to far northwestern Wisconsin where he was struggling to make it in private practice as a criminal defense attorney, in Superior, Wisconsin.

Kratz's correspondence to Avery included outlandish requests pressuring Avery to add him to his prisoner list of visitors.

Kratz further badgers Avery in his correspondence of September 6, 2015: "Since I'm the person who probably knows more about your case than anyone else, I hoped that you would choose me to tell your story to. Unfortunately, you only want to continue your nonsense about being set up. That's too bad because you had one opportunity to finally tell all the details, but now that will never happen." (97)

Gershman maintains that in all of his years of practicing law and studying the ethics and misconduct of prosecutors, he has never once witnessed someone like Kratz.

"Kratz's conduct in approaching the man he vilified, brought unsubstantiated charges against, convicted of murder, and sent to prison for life without parole, in order to

---

97. Kratz's letters to Avery are mentioned in Bennett Gershman's May 10, 2017 affidavit

'tell his story' is unlike any conduct of any ex-prosecutor I have ever encountered," Gershman said.

"Kratz's conduct is offensive to the proper administration of justice. His intimidation and manipulation for his own selfish motive of the person he prosecuted impairs the dignity of the legal profession and the ethical responsibility of lawyers to abstain from overreaching, harassing, and manipulative conduct."

In Gershman's purview, Kratz's ploy to convince Avery into believing that Kratz would be inclined to write an honest book from Avery's perspective is another falsehood that erodes at the credibility of the judicial system.

"Kratz's solicitation of Avery is akin to a personal injury lawyer's solicitation of cases from recent accident victims. Dubbed 'ambulance chasing,' such conduct has seriously impaired the reputation of the Bar. Kratz's conduct in my opinion is even more nefarious. Kratz had a personal involvement with Avery, and sought to manipulate that connection under the guise of appearing to act on Avery's behalf to help him tell his 'honest' story so that the public would 'understand both sides.' But of course, Kratz's appeal for Avery's cooperation ostensibly for disinterested motives was a sham. Kratz wanted to write a book and get the person he prosecuted to help him. His solicitation was disingenuous and prejudicial to the administration of justice."

But, here's why things get even more interesting.

"There is an uncanny parallel between Kratz's solicitation of Avery as a private lawyer and Kratz's solicitation of vulnerable women when he was a prosecutor. In 2010, Kratz was investigated by the Wisconsin Division of Criminal Investigation for sending inappropriate text and email messages to women, including victims in active domestic abuse cases Kratz was then prosecuting. There were at least ten women who complained about Kratz's improper sexual overtures to them. The state investigation led the Wisconsin District Attorneys Association to call for Kratz's resignation, for Governor James Doyle to initiate removal proceedings against Kratz, and after Kratz involuntarily resigned, for the Office of Lawyer Regulation in 2011 to bring a disciplinary complaint against Kratz alleging several counts of professional misconduct."

Afterward, Gershman notes, Kratz was suspended from practicing law in Wisconsin for four months.

In one case where Kratz was prosecuting a parental rights termination case, Kratz became lustful toward the woman involved in the case, telling her "I won't cum in your mouth" and later informing her that he was leaving on a wild trip to Las Vegas where he could have "big-boobed women serve me drinks."

"Kratz commented in court to a social worker that the court reporter had 'big, beautiful breasts" and another time he contacted a young woman almost thirty years younger than he was, inquiring if "she was the kind of girl that likes secret contact with an older elected DA ... the riskier the better."

"You may be the tall, young hot nymph, but I am the prize!" Kratz had texted her.

Indeed, Kratz, the three-time divorced Wisconsin lawyer, was in a league of his own. Time after time, women found him repulsive and did not want anything to do with him.

"Kratz tried to defend his appalling behavior towards the women by raising 'incredible' 'inconsistent' 'hyper-technical,' and 'puzzling' arguments," Gershman said. "His claim that he wanted to amicably resolve the disciplinary proceedings, according to the Wisconsin Supreme Court, 'borders on the intellectually insulting.' Kratz's insistence that his conduct resulted from addiction to drugs does not change the 'ugly picture by the record.'"

But, there was also something at play. There was a pattern developing.

"Interestingly, quite similar allegations in the disciplinary proceedings against Kratz are present in Kratz's solicitation of Avery. Thus, in the disciplinary proceeding Kratz was found to have acted with a 'selfish motive,' manipulated a 'vulnerable woman,' engaged in 'exploitative behavior,' engaged in 'harassing behavior,' showed a 'crass placement of his personal interests above those of his client,' and 'crossed the line separating the unprofessional conduct from the acutely offensive and harassing,'" Gershman pointed out.

However, there is no indication Kratz was pursuing Avery for sexual reasons, like the women who were domestic violence victims he tried to seduce.

"But as a matter of professional ethics, Kratz's conduct towards Avery was as intimidating, self-interested, and manipulative as it was to the women Kratz abused. Avery was in a hopeless position and an easy target for Kratz's solicitations. Kratz knew the prison authorities had objected to Avery speaking to Kratz and that Kratz's overtures might hurt Avery. Particularly disingenuous was Kratz's ploy to suggest falsely that Kratz was simply a disinterested person trying to assist Avery to tell his story - his 'honest' story - to the world, but knowing full well that he wanted Avery's story only if Avery told his story in a way that served Kratz's selfish interests in writing a book and promoting himself. Kratz exploited his former status as Avery's prosecutor 'who knows more about your case than anyone.' Kratz disparaged Avery's 'continued nonsense about being set up.' He intimidated Avery as he did with the women he abused, trying to convince Avery to talk to him by the veiled threat that it was 'too bad' that Avery refused to talk to him 'because you had one opportunity to finally tell all the details, but now that will never happen.'"

Gershman's curriculum vitae notes he has authored four books. He has also written about two dozen law review articles including writings on "Litigating Brady v. Maryland," "Reflections on Brady v. Maryland," "Prosecutorial Ethics and Victim Rights," "Witness Coaching By Prosecutors," and "The Prosecutor's Duty to Truth."

As for Kenneth R. Kratz, the Wisconsin Bar Association online directory indicates he graduated from Marquette University's Law School in 1985 and was admitted to practice law in Wisconsin on May 20, 1985. But as of November 2018, the Wisconsin Bar Association listed Kratz's law license as being suspended for three different reasons: dues, CLE: continuing legal education and for OLR Certification; the Office of Lawyer Regulation was an agency within the Wisconsin Supreme Court.

The website domain on file with the Wisconsin Bar Association for the Kratz Law Firm was also for sale.

CHAPTER TWENTY-FOUR

CREEPY KRATZ

"Dear Governor Jim Doyle, I just want to make you aware of some inappropriate questions that Ken Kratz had asked my seventeen-year-old daughter when we had an appointment with him in July 2010 ... My daughter had a relationship with (name blacked out) who we found out is a registered sex offender."
– September 21, 2010

The jury that convicted Avery of murder in 2007 was led to believe the Manitowoc County defendant was a sexual deviant monster. In reality, special prosecutor Ken Kratz, the man who convicted Avery was the real sexual monster in the courtroom, based on a 143-page investigative file compiled in 2010 by the Wisconsin Department of Justice DCI.

For background, Kratz became licensed to practice law in Wisconsin in 1985. He worked as an assistant district attorney in La Crosse before being appointed as the Calumet County District Attorney in 1992. He would remain in that position until his forced resignation under personally humiliating circumstances in October 2010.

When Kratz was in his fifties, he appeared to be sexually aroused by teenagers, the DCI reports show.

"On our meeting with Ken, he had asked my daughter ... the following questions, keep in mind these are not word for word;

Who would usually take off your clothes before sex, referring to my daughter?

Do you know what ejaculate means?
Would he usually ejaculate in you or out?
About how long did the sex last?

"Then he proceeded to ask about other sex acts, oral sex and then he asked her those questions, mouth to penis, mouth to vagina, etc.

"At the time these questions were going on, I did not feel these were appropriate as she is a victim of a sex offender, and I thought it was the D.A.'s job to make this as painless as possible for the victim. My client advocate ... was in the room also and we discussed this after we left. She felt the same way I did about his questioning. This was before the preliminary hearing, and we don't even know if this will go to trial. Some of those questions I would have a hard time believing a defense attorney would even ask a victim." (98)

The parent informed the Wisconsin governor that she now has a good idea why Kratz asked her seventeen-year-old daughter such lurid questions.

"I felt he violated and further victimized my daughter by getting some sick enjoyment out of the answers she gave to his questions. I also felt he was no better than the guy he is trying to put behind bars as a repeat sex offender. I would hope you would remove him from office so that he will not be able to abuse his powers and further victimize anyone else. As my daughter is under the age of eighteen, I would appreciate it if you would not use my name in any press reports so as to protect her privacy."

***

Ken Kratz's recurring and alarming conduct predated Avery's arrest for Teresa's murder back in 2005, though

98. All accounts cited in this chapter are from the DCI report concerning complaints made against Calumet County District Attorney Ken Kratz

Kratz's misbehavior intensified after the Avery case because he wanted to portray himself as if a famous sex symbol.

If Kratz had worked as the local high school janitor or garbage truck driver, it's probably less likely that his constant creepy behavior would have been tolerated, but in a small Wisconsin town like Chilton, Kratz was somebody. As a result, this gave him a great cover to engage in behavior that was unethical and a blemish on the district attorney's office.

One woman, interviewed by the Wisconsin Department of Justice in 2010, told special agents how she "first met Kratz five years ago when she got in trouble for shoplifting. Kratz was the DA on her case and he charged it out. (She) said Kratz never did anything inappropriate to her at that time."

Then in 2009, Kratz called the woman on her cell phone.

The woman told investigators "she has no idea how Kratz had her phone number. Kratz told (her) that he and his wife were getting a divorce and he wanted to talk to her about things."

After that call, Kratz visited the vulnerable woman at her apartment.

"He told her that he knew everything about her, and if she did not listen to him, he could 'get her jammed up.' Kratz talked about how he was into bondage. He said he ties women up, they listen to him, and he is in control. She said he instructed her to give him a blow job and she did."

The woman was afraid. But she went ahead and performed the sex act upon the District Attorney of Calumet County.

"He had said that he knew everything about her and (she) did not know what that meant ... Kratz had such seniority over her and it was said she had not done anything in Calumet County other than the shoplifting five years prior. (She) did not know what Kratz meant. She did not want to take the chance."

The woman later told the Wisconsin DOJ that "the blow job happened on her couch and she was bent over Kratz. She said Kratz held her hands behind her back ... (she) stated that Kratz was very strong."

The woman told the special agents "while Kratz was still at her apartment, she went to the bathroom and puked. After Kratz left, she puked her brains out and stayed in bed for about a week. (She) stated that she had been raped when she was 16 and said this feels a lot like it."

On the day of the sexual tryst, Kratz showed up wearing one of his finest gray suits. When he got to the woman's apartment, he also told her to close the blinds.

"Kratz talked about being submissive and being dominant. He said that the man was dominant and would tell the woman what to do and he asked if she would be willing to be submissive to him. (She) told Kratz she did not think she would be good at being submissive because she talks a lot. Kratz continued to tell (her) what he did with women and how he takes control. He said the women have to listen to him or he hits them. Kratz spoke about a room he has where he ties women up. Kratz called the room something specific but (she) did not recall what he called it."

Prior to driving over to receive the oral pleasure, "Kratz told her I know everything about you. I can make trouble for you ... she stated that she was very ashamed of what she did. He's a pig. What he did was wrong.'"

Although the State's investigative files indicated Kratz forced the woman to perform a sex act upon him, the state of Wisconsin had no interest in making Kratz into a criminal. He was not about to be branded as a sexual criminal or a rapist.

"Kratz gave her an order to give him a blow job," the reports state. "She said he told her to ask his permission to give him a blow job, and she did. Kratz then put his hands behind (her) head ... She had to unzip Kratz's pants. She said he gave her instructions and told her what to do   the whole time … She said she had never known what the term 'crack whore' meant until then, but that is what she felt like."

On that occasion, Kratz also indulged himself in a plethora of alcoholic beverages, pounding down beer after beer before driving himself home.

"While Kratz was at her apartment (she) continued to get him more beers and he had four or five of them. (She) did not drink with Kratz … during the sex act, Kratz called her a bitch. He said 'that's how you do it, bitch.' She said he had all the power and all the control … After the sex act, Kratz stayed at the apartment and drank three more beers. He asked how (she) felt about being submissive and she said she could not do it. Kratz also talked about his wife and how she did not want to be with him anymore."

The woman told state investigators how "he had grabbed her boobs and pulled her hair. (She) said Kratz touched her breasts under her clothing and she was a fool to have let him in."

There was also something else the woman recalled. It involved money.

"When Kratz left her apartment that night, he left $75 on the kitchen counter. (She) did not see the money until after Kratz left. (She) believed the money was given to her for what she did. When (she) was not answering Kratz's phone calls, he asked if she wanted to give the money back to him. … Kratz became angry about the money, stating that it was a lot of money and wanting it back."

In the end, the woman donated the $75 to a local church.

In the following days, Kratz became a stalker.

"Kratz called her forty to fifty times after this incident, but she would not take his calls. She said he came to her apartment a couple of times, but she pretended she was not home."

***

Around the Appleton and Fox Valley area, Kratz regularly preyed upon a number of women, including women more than half his age.

One was Renee Braun, who spoke with the DCI in 2010. The two met through the website Craigslist, but she was reluctant to pursue his advances.

"Kratz questioned why she did not like older men, and he told Braun he had money. Braun told (DCI agents) that Kratz was her father's age and that was kind of creepy to Braun. Braun further stated that Kratz never told Braun he was married."

Braun reckoned they exchanged about ten text messages starting in 2009.

At the time, she was twenty-seven. In some of his texts, Kratz wrote, "I will treat you nice, you can be with an older man, we can be good friends, he texted 'Do you know who I am? I am Kenneth Kratz, the guy who prosecuted Steven Avery.' Braun says she was not impressed and determined that Kratz was weird.

"Braun stopped the contacts with Kratz before they ever met because Braun realized he was too old for her."

Another young woman also contacted the DCI in regards to Kratz.

Maria Ruskiewicz was from Marinette, Wisconsin, and a third-year law student at Oklahoma City University School of Law. Her first bad experience with Kratz happened in 2008, the year after the Avery trial. She was attempting to get a pardon for a previous drug conviction. Kratz and the judge provided her with letters in support of her pardon.

"DA Kratz wrote Ruskiewicz back, telling her that she should make an appointment with his office to meet with him. Ruskiewicz stated that the letters from DA Kratz were very professional."

Not realizing she was being manipulated, she eventually came to Chilton to meet Kratz in person.

"She recalled that he was not wearing a suit but was wearing a black shirt with a deck of cards on it and they talked about playing poker. DA Kratz and Ruskiewicz then talked about what advice he had to give her.

As expected, Kratz steered the conversation toward his favorite topic.

"DA Kratz started asking her questions related to sex, posing different scenarios and asking what she thought of them. For example, he asked her what she thought about a boss and a secretary having sex or a babysitter and child having sex. He also asked what she thought about people of different ages having sex. Ruskiewicz stated that she thought DA Kratz's questions were weird, but she thought he was just trying to see if she was tough enough to be a prosecutor."

Being naïve, she accepted one of Kratz's professional business cards. It contained Kratz's secret cell phone number. She made the mistake of sending him a text, thanking him for making the time to meet with her.

She had inadvertently opened the door into her life for Kratz.

"Ruskiewicz stated that DA Kratz started texting her back about a week later. It was in one of these texts that he asked how she would please him between the sheets."

The young woman got her uncle involved and later wrote a letter informing Kratz he needed to keep their communications on a professional level. Kratz laid low for about three months, and then like a nasty prickly yard weed, he re-emerged.

"He sent her a text stating that now they had to meet in person. Ruskiewicz stated that this text was out of the blue … She compared the situation to a domestic abuser who has been threatening to beat their victim but then suddenly shows up at the victim's door. Ruskiewicz and DA Kratz never did meet again in person."

State investigators asked the Marinette woman whether "there was any type of coercion from Kratz that she should have sex with him in exchange for his support of her pardon. Ruskiewicz stated that DA Kratz never said anything like that but she felt it was implied because of the timing of his texts to her ... She said she thinks he is a dirt bag, and she believes there are plenty more victims out there."

The DOJ documents showed that: "Attorney Kratz has rationalized his poor behavior by confessing to various addictions: to Ambien, to Vicodin, to Xanax, and to sex, though he fails to point to either medical records or expert medical testimony that would explain the exact nature and severity of his conditions or how they may have affected his ability to conform his behavior to ethical rules. But regardless of how we view Attorney Kratz's behavior, as an involuntary byproduct of addiction, or as a willful blindness to professional standards, the ugly picture painted by the record remains the same. The recommended four-month suspension is deserved."

***

Ken Kratz might still be holding down office in Calumet County to this day if not for the bravery of Kaukauna resident Stephanie Van Groll, who had just turned twenty-five around the time she visited the Kaukauna Police Department to file a report, back on October 22, 2009.

"I met with Mr. Ken Kratz the District Attorney who is handling my ex's case," her police statement reads.

"I went to his office ... to decide what was going to be done with Shannon my ex after I left there. He sent me a text saying that it was nice talking to me and that I have such potential. I said thank you and thought that would be it ... since that text I've received at least 20 plus messages. I talked to one of my friends and they told me to do something about it so here I am. I'm afraid that if I don't do what he wants me to do, he will throw out my whole case and who knows what else."

The following are excerpts from some of Kratz's text messages to the young domestic violence victim whose ex-boyfriend had his criminal case pending in Kratz's office.

"I wish you weren't one of this office's clients. You'd be a cool person to know!"

"I hope you feel better soon. Do you need me to bring you some chicken soup?"

"No text yet today? I'm feeling ignored. Are you even up yet?"

"How about a margarita? That has some fruit juice in it!"

"Seriously I hope you feel better soon. Please keep in touch. It's maybe not the wisest thing I can do, but you are awfully sweet. Just don't tell anyone, ok?"

"Are you the kind of girl that likes secret contact with an older married elected DA ... the riskier the better? Or do you want to stop right know (sic) before any issues?"

"I need direction from you. Yes you are a risk taker and can keep your mouth shut and you think this is fun ... or you think a man twice your age is creepy so stop."

"Either way I think you are very nice. I am very smart, but know this is ALL up to you and really does depend how close to the edge you live!"

"Still wondering if I am worth it? Can I help you answer any questions?"

"Why would such a successful, respected attorney be acting like he's in 7th grade? Are you worried about me?"

"Are you serious? OK? That's it? Are you in a board meeting? You are beautiful and would make a great young partner someday. But I won't beg!"

"I'm serious. I'm the atty. I have the $350,000 house. I have the 6-figure career. You may be the tall, young, hot nymph, but I am the prize! Start convincing."

"Finally an opinion. I would not expect you to be the other woman. I would want you to be so hot and treat me so well that you'd be THE woman! R U that good?"

"You forgot to write me for the last time saying you could never give me enough attention to steal me away, and you are so modest that you wouldn't know how to!"

"And that you may look good at first glance, but women that are blonde, 6ft tall, legs and great bodies don't like to be shown off or to please their men!"

Two days earlier, VanGroll met with Kratz at his office to be interviewed about the ongoing prosecution of her ex-boyfriend for trying to choke her to death.

"VanGroll indicated that during the interview she confided in Kratz about the relationship she had with her boyfriend and the abuse her boyfriend bestowed upon her. VanGroll indicated that at the end of the interview, on October 20, she thought it was funny that Kratz asked her if she would mind if he dropped the charge from a felony to a misdemeanor. VanGroll then stated that she told Kratz that strangling someone was a felony in the state of Wisconsin."

About ten minutes later, came the first of a barrage of text messages thumbed out by Kratz. "The text messages continued over a period of the next two days. VanGroll indicated she felt vulnerable because she had just told Kratz the relationship that VanGroll was in, and she felt Kratz was taking advantage of that situation."

By October 30, 2009, the Wisconsin Department of Justice got involved in the case. The DCI's Peter Thelen reached out to an agent he knew had a close long-time professional relationship with Kratz.

It was Tom Fassbender.

"Peter Thelen had contact with Special Agent Thomas J. Fassbender who confirmed (redacted phone number listed in official police report) was a cellular telephone number used by Calumet County District Attorney Kenneth Kratz. Fassbender had prior contacts with Kratz at said number when making telephone contact with Kratz in an official capacity."

Now that the Wisconsin DOJ was involved, however, the criminal case that had been turned over to them was destined to disappear.

Three days after the conversation with Fassbender, the special agent in charge at the Appleton office got a call from Kratz, who is listed on the investigate reports as being "a person of interest."

"Peter Thelen received a telephone call from Calumet County District Attorney Kenneth Kratz regarding this case," reports from November 2, 2009, show. "He inquired as to whether there was still a criminal investigation going on regarding this and SAIC Thelen responded no, that the case was done as far as Special Agent in Charge Thelen was concerned."

Kratz wanted reassurance the case was closed, which is what he got.

"Mr. Kratz then offered to apologize to Stephanie if Special Agent in Charge Thelen were able to mediate this. Thelen told Kratz that he would pass this information along."

Then Kratz made a second request.

"Mr. Kratz mentioned that he would like to keep this out of the media, if possible. Thelen advised Mr. Kratz that the complaint originated from another agency and DCI was obligated to investigate, at which time Mr. Kratz said that he understood."

Two months later, Kratz was up to his old dirty tricks again.

***

Dawn M. King of Green Bay, forty-six, met Kratz through the Match.com dating site in January 2010. It was Kratz who pursued her, rather than the other way around.

"King stated that she had reservations about DA Kratz from the beginning of his contacts with her, starting with the name he used on his Match.com profile, which was 'Exboytoy1.' King stated that she did not know who DA Kratz was when he first started contacting her. She knew he was an attorney because that fact was written in his Match.com profile."

On January 23, 2000, she agreed to meet Kratz for dinner at the Black and Tan Grille in De Pere, which is a nice suburban community along the Fox River next to Green Bay. The Black and Tan was also an upscale restaurant.

"King said that DA Kratz talked about himself during their dinner. He talked about going to Las Vegas, poker, his wife, and his divorce. He also talked about cases he was working on."

During the dinner, a detective called Kratz and Kratz had no qualms about discussing the criminal case in front of her, even though she told him she understood if he needed to step away to take the call and talk in private.

"But he continued to talk in front of her. King gathered from the conversation that she heard that the detectives were searching some place at the time. DA Kratz and the detective were talking about looking for evidence and searching a car and the trunk of a car. The detective wanted to bring the person in for questioning, but DA Kratz told the detective to wait until they found more physical evidence … After the dinner date, she searched the Internet for information and learned that there was a missing woman from Chilton. During dinner, DA Kratz told King that the detectives were at the boyfriend's house searching. DA Kratz made some reference to her about going to the crime scene with him and made a comment about her wearing heels. King said she did not want to be 'traipsing through a crime scene.'"

It turned out that the case involved a murder. A boyfriend was accused of killing his girlfriend and the crime scene apparently crossed county lines.

"King stated that DA Kratz drank a lot the night of their date. She said they had first met in the downstairs bar and had one drink there, and then they shared a bottle of wine with dinner. King stopped drinking after dinner, but DA Kratz continued to drink several more drinks in the bar after dinner while (we) listened to a live band there. King stated that DA Kratz was not worried about drinking and driving, and she felt he thought he was above the law. DA Kratz told King that he would not have a problem if he was stopped while driving home because he had friends."

The next day, the text messages started.

"They found a body," Kratz texted her.

"King said she thought it was weird and absolutely wrong that DA Kratz was telling her this information about his professional work. She said she was surprised and shocked that he would divulge such information being in the position that he was."

If that wasn't weird enough, Kratz informed her about the upcoming autopsy for the victim and invited her to accompany him to the morgue.

"He invited King to go along with him as long as she would wear heels and act as his girlfriend. King stated that she thought this was wrong on so many levels."

But the texts did not stop.

"Bored in court," Kratz kept messaging her.

In her letter she wrote to Governor James Doyle, King added, "If I didn't answer his texts immediately, he would become insecure and question why I hadn't responded and would attack me or my character. He would remind me of who he was, how he had prosecuted the biggest case around here and what a prize he was. After a few days of contact, I finally told him not to contact me anymore. He complied."

Other women who were victims of Kratz were downright terrified he might come back and harm them if their names were publicized by the Wisconsin DOJ. They agreed to be interviewed by police investigators only on the condition their identities remained a secret in any official criminal investigation files.

One such woman was victimized by Kratz in 1999, evidence that Kratz's creepy and dangerous behavior was going on long before he got involved in prosecuting Avery.

One woman was involved in a domestic dispute with her husband in 1999. The Confidential Informant suffered a black eye and a bump on her head from her abusive husband. Kratz was the prosecuting attorney on her husband's case.

"The (Confidential Informant) indicated that shortly after the meetings with Kratz, Kratz would email the CI with comments such as 'a girl like you wouldn't be attracted to a guy like me, bald and overweight.'"

The emails turned into phone calls initiated by Kratz.

"The CI indicated on one occasion Kratz came over to the CI's house, with the CI's approval, and that the CI and Kratz sat on the couch. The CI indicated that Kratz put his hand under the CI's skirt and he caressed the CI ... The CI also indicated that Kratz had not removed any of his clothing ... while the CI and Kratz were seated on the couch, Kratz's girlfriend or fiancée called and the CI learned that it was the girlfriend's or fiancée's birthday. The CI believes that Kratz forgot ... Once Kratz got off the phone with the girlfriend or fiancée, Kratz called a florist to have flowers sent to his girlfriend or fiancée ... the CI indicated that upon Kratz leaving the CI's residence, Kratz got stuck in the snow in the CI's driveway and had to be pulled out by a neighbor."

The woman also gained insight into Kratz's dark mind.

"Very early in the conversations or emails with Kratz, Kratz made it very clear that he liked women to be submissive ... Kratz would call the CI at work and the CI was not allowed to say anything, and that was part of the game. The CI indicated women weren't allowed to say anything or make any noise ... the CI just had to listen to his sexual scenarios on the phone ... Kratz had four or five sexual scenarios and that he would request the CI choose one of the scenarios that the CI would like done to the CI ... Kratz also offered to send the CI to Chicago to learn how to be submissive."

Kratz's contacts with this woman occurred while Kratz was in the midst of a full-blown criminal prosecution of the woman's husband for domestic abuse.

"Kratz also asked ... if the CI liked to be videotaped or if they could be watched by someone else. Kratz indicated this would only be for his private viewing ... Kratz indicated Kratz had a private room at his house and that no one went into the room except Kratz ... the CI was led to believe by Kratz that Kratz had other videotapes of himself or other females being involved in sexual activity."

The woman told Wisconsin special agents that her lawyer had told her upfront that Calumet County had a reputation for usually awarding custody of minor children to the father, not the mother.

"The CI reiterated that the only reason the CI agreed to engaging in the phone conversations and emails, along with one sexual contact with Kratz, was because Kratz was prosecuting the CI's husband and the CI was led to believe that Kratz could influence the decision over the custody of the CI's children."

About five months later, the woman had moved away when she got a phone call at work.

"The CI was surprised that Kratz had tracked the CI down ... Kratz asked if the CI was married or seeing someone ... Kratz indicated that he had relatives in the area where the CI was presently living."

The two special agents from the DIA who interviewed the woman made the following observations in their summations of her interview.

"On several occasions, the CI cried and indicated that the CI had been second guessing the CI's self for a long time regarding the CI not reporting the conduct of Kratz back when it happened ... The CI indicated that the only reason the CI came forward at this time was to let Van Groll know that Van Groll wasn't alone and that Kratz had conducted this type of behavior with other females."

***

In 1998 or early 1999, Menasha resident Connie Palm ran a personal ad in *The Appleton Post-Crescent* newspaper. She was in luck, bad luck. The male suitor who responded to her singles ad happened to be Kratz. During a handful of introductory phone calls, Kratz made it a point to make sure she knew she was conversing with the District Attorney of Calumet County himself.

"Palm and Kratz met for coffee at Burger King in Kaukauna in 1998 or early 1999. After having coffee, Kratz said he would show Palm where he worked, and they left Burger King together in Kratz's car."

But first Kratz wanted to take her by his house so he could change.

"Kratz talked to her about his past marriages and the details of the demise of his second marriage. He then went into a diatribe of dirty talk, going into detail about what he wanted in a wife or girlfriend sexually and about past experiences he had with numerous women."

After visiting Kratz's house for an hour, they drove toward the government municipal building in the area of Darboy and Sherwood. "While they were parked near the municipal building, Kratz touched the back of Palm's hair. Palm said she backed away from his touch and he stopped touching her. Kratz told Palm again that he works with victims and he understands."

Eventually, Kratz drove the woman back to the Burger King so she could retrieve her car.

"Palm said that during the date, Kratz told her a couple times not to talk to Harbor House (domestic violence shelter where she went for services and support) about him and what he was telling her … when he was talking about the personal things that he prefers and about meeting women in hotels.

"Palm stated that she felt almost as if Kratz were confessing to her about what he did with other women and wanting her to 'OK' his actions. Palm said that Kratz talked about a lot of things during their date, but she only wrote in her letters the details that she could truly remember. Palm stated that during the date she was only thinking about how fast she could get home."

Kratz made the mistake of opening up too much about his deviant side.

"She said he told her he met women on the Internet, they talked about what they expected, and they agreed to meet at a hotel. Kratz told Palm he did not tell these women his real name or what he did for a living and he met them in hotels out of town.

"Kratz also told Palm that he looked at pornography and he felt that it was an addiction because he stayed up until the early morning watching it."

On September 22, 2010, Palm sent a letter to Wisconsin Governor Jim Doyle relaying some of her humiliating experiences with Kratz to the governor.

"Once we arrived at his home he offered to give me a tour and made emphasis upon showing his bedroom where he slept. I then sat down in the living room to wait for him to change clothing which he did. He sat down in the living room and began another conversation where he shared information about past marriages. I found he had been married twice then he shared intimate details about why those marriages ended … then he went into details of the second marriage and he was very explicit. He said they had done a threesome with the neighbor guy down the road and his wife felt that the neighbor had more to offer her.

"You have probably heard about my dark side," Kratz told Palm.

"He shared details about many past experiences and said that he met a lot of women on the Internet, then would meet them at hotels 'out of town,' of course, and he did not give them his real name or profession. He gave specifics about liaisons going into great detail about one woman in particular who wanted him so bad and was so turned on that she was dripping on the bed. He said this several times and would not get off that particular sentence or woman."

"Do I make you nervous?" Kratz asked Palm.

"He went on to share further details and that he does different things with the women like role playing, even using a term I had heard before but can't remember now ...but he explained in great detail that it involves hurting each other physically but there is a common word agreed upon ahead of time like Rumpelstiltskin and when one partner says the word the activity is to stop."

In Palm's letter to the governor, she revealed that over the years, it became common knowledge amongst the powerful people who were movers and shakers around Calumet County that Kratz's behaviors were to be tolerated.

"As the years went on and I became employed with Harbor House Domestic Abuse programs in June 2002 and got to know other professionals, I learned of the prevalence of knowledge of Ken Kratz reputation/rumors and what I felt was a sick collective social tolerance/oblivion to look the other way of this type of behavior from a man who holds a highly regarded public office."

But there was one thing Kratz kept saying over and over during his one and only creepy date with the Menasha woman he met at Burger King.

"I am uninhibited, I am uninhibited ... he went on to say that he would pay to take me to a spa and be pampered all day to get a manicure/pedicure, get my hair done and a bikini wax and he would tell the girls at the salon what he would like done to me down there …he asked me a couple of times to share my fantasies with him and I would not … I have to wonder if putting pictures of Ken in the newspapers in various poses, full body, side view of face, front view, or in other attire like jeans, pictures of him over the years with dates or years attached that he served as DA and assistant DA and aged or changed in appearance might trigger the memory of other women throughout the state of Wisconsin and nearby states … I have to think there are many women out there affected by him."

By November 2010, the Wisconsin Department of Justice had seized Kratz's office computer. For the line reading criminal offense, the report indicated "Misconduct in Public Office." On the line marked "suspect," the name listed was Kenneth Kratz. Ten different women were listed in the document as "complainants."

The DCI report indicated Kratz used the following screen names: Exboytoy1, AppletonAtty and Applnatty. The following search terms were sought: bondage, dominant, submissive, role playing.

"Former Calumet County DA Ken Kratz is accused of sending inappropriate text and email messages to women, including victims in active cases he was working on. Currently looking for a preview of text documents, and possibly Internet dating sites and pornography, if excessive," the report stated.

But in the end, criminal charges of misconduct in public office were never filed against Kratz by the Wisconsin DCI.

CHAPTER TWENTY-FIVE

COMPUTER DISK

On the longstanding obligations in the American criminal justice system is the duty of criminal prosecutors to provide a complete inventory of their side's evidence to the defendant and the defendant's lawyer. And that evidence also includes reports and information that is known as exculpatory. In other words, police reports and investigative files that may shed led on other potential perpetrators who were also being investigated for the same crime.

Exculpatory information would consist of investigative details the police officers and lead investigators had in their files.

The notion of police officers and prosecutors hiding files and reports from the criminal defendant, notably a murder defendant, is frowned upon by the American justice system, and there is longstanding judicial precedence and case law that firmly establishes that such negligent and prejudicial behavior by police detectives and district attorneys cannot be tolerated in a court of law.

Oftentimes, however, information and evidence about over-the-top criminal prosecutors who run roughshod over the rights of the accused never sees the light of day. After all, the prosecution is the one-and-only side in complete control of the evidence. Unless the defense gets lucky, or has a mole on the prosecution team feeding them information, outright proof of prosecutors destroying files or hiding evidence that could change the outcome of a criminal defendant's case don't regularly arise in America's judiciary.

In the spring of 2018, Avery's dogged post-conviction lawyer Kathleen Zellner made a discovery that rocked her world. It was a bombshell piece of evidence that she realized Avery's original criminal trial lawyers, Buting and Strang, did not know about. It was evidence that should have been tendered to them back in 2006 long before their client stood trial for Teresa's murder.

It was a crucial item of evidence that special prosecutor Ken Kratz and his loyal lead investigator, Tom Fassbender, did not want Avery's side to gain access to.

***

On April 21, 2006, Fassbender and Mark Wiegert seized the personal computer and a dozen computer disks from Barbara Janda's home. They wrote their reports in such a way to make it appear as if the computer belonged to Brendan Dassey and that their evidence gathering focused on the sixteen-year-old boy. Nothing could be further from the truth, though.

The next day, the computer was delivered to Grand Chute Police Detective Mike Velie by Fassbender. Velie was considered the region's law enforcement expert on computer forensics in criminal investigations. By May 11, 2006, Velie returned the evidence back to Fassbender, who then decided to sit on the information, that way the defense lawyers didn't have it in a timely fashion.

Seven months later, some of the information that was extracted from the Dassey computer was shared with Strang and Buting. The most noteworthy details and evidence from the computer investigation, interestingly, was never to be shared with Avery's trials lawyers.

"On December 14, 2006, 218 days after the completion of the Velie Final Investigative Report, trial defense counsel was first provided with the Fassbender report to Prosecutor Kratz." (99)

"The Kratz letter does not refer to any enclosed CD titled 'Dassey's Computer, Final Report Investigative Copy.'"

The report furnished to Avery's lawyers was misleading in so many ways, Zellner contends.

"The Fassbender report refers to the examination of Brendan Dassey's computer. There is absolutely no proof that the computer belonged to Brendan Dassey and there is proof that it was primarily used by his brother Bobby. The Fassbender report minimizes the number of violent pornographic images, the severity of the violent pornographic images and incriminating word searches that demonstrate an obsession with inflicting pain on young females, dead female bodies and mutilating female bodies. The Fassbender report also ignores the timeline of the images being viewed which excludes other family members and incriminates Bobby."

Instead, the report was designed to ensure Strang and Buting had no clue, no idea, that Bobby was a sexually disturbed deviant, which would have raised strong suspicions that he, not Avery, was involved in Teresa's murder, according to Zellner.

After all, it's an undisputed fact, some of Teresa's charred bones were found inside Bobby Dassey's burn barrels.

"The Fassbender report refers to a few messages of Brendan's about whether he thought Mr. Avery was guilty of the Halbach murder, while ignoring Bobby's prolific, graphic, and sexually aggressive messages to underage girls. The Fassbender report conspicuously omits the date of May 10, 2006, which is when Detective Velie completed the Velie Final Investigate Report and downloaded it onto a CD."

Keep in mind the prosecution side, Fassbender and Kratz, had the Bobby Dassey computer files in May 2006. The two

---

99. Motion to Supplement Previously Filed Motion for Post-Conviction Relief, July 6, 2018

men sat on the evidence in June, July, August, September, October, and November. All of those months passed and nothing was shared with the trial lawyers representing Avery. Then in December, Kratz wrote up his letter and turned over some information to Buting and Strang, but it was not everything, and it left out the most revelatory information.

"On December 15, 2006, Prosecutor Kratz sent Attorney Strang an itemized inventory of our Steven Avery file. In the inventory, Prosecutor Kratz references: '7 DVDs: Contents of Brendan Dassey's Computer.'" Again, this statement is completely misleading to the defense because 7 DVDs were disclosed that could not be opened without the EnCase program, but the CD, which required no specialized software, was not disclosed," Zellner uncovered in 2018.

Back on December 19, 2006, Strang enlisted his paralegal to send the seven DVDs to his partner on the case, Buting. "But no CD is referenced in her letter because trial defense counsel had not been provided with this CD. Because Special Agent Fassbender kept the CD in his possession, trial defense counsel only received the seven DVDs," Zellner said.

Meanwhile, the clock was ticking toward the looming murder trial, the trial Kratz liked to call the biggest murder trial in the history of Wisconsin.

"There was not time for trial defense counsel to retain a forensic computer expert and perform the forensic analysis of the seven DVDs which took Detective Velie 16 days, by the January 10, 2007, due date for trial defense counsel to file their *State v. Denny* motion. Additionally, because they were not provided a CD with the Velie Final Investigative Report, which contained his criteria, word searches, registry, recovered pornography, Internet history, windows registry, and all MSN messages, they could not effectively use this information to impeach Bobby or establish a motive to murder Ms. Halbach, pursuant to Denny."

Then on the eve of Avery's trial, Strang got a document from Kratz called "Stipulation Project."

Kratz mentioned in his January 25, 2007, correspondence there was a computer analysis of Steve, Teresa, and Brendan's computer hard drives and Detective Velie "found nothing of evidentiary value. We may wish to introduce the fact that they looked. This stip(ulation) eliminates Officer Veile (sic) as a witness."

Five days later, Manitowoc County Judge Patrick Willis rejected the effort of Strang and Buting to utilize *State v. Denny* to present an alternative suspect as part of their case to show Avery was innocent.

"On January 30, 2007, Judge Willis denied trial defense counsel's Denny motion because there was no proof of motive for the murder provided by trial defense counsel," Zellner said.

Another week later, jury selection got underway.

Then, a decade later, "On July 15, 2017, a new Brady witness, Kevin Rahmlow, in two affidavits, came forward and described how he had remembered seeing Ms. Halbach's RAV4 on November 3-4, 2005, by the old dam on State Highway 147 and reporting this to Sgt. Andy Colborn. The RAV4 was located within half a mile of Scott Tadych's former and current residences."

Then, on July 31, 2017, Zellner retained forensic computer expert Gary Hunt to analyze the seven DVDs taken from Bobby Dassey's hard drive. "Mr. Hunt examined the seven DVDs and discovered an abundance of violent pornography and created a timeline that linked a majority of the searches for violent pornography to Bobby."

On November 13, 2017, Zellner met with Buting and Strang to get their reaction.

"Attorney Buting states that neither the CD nor the Velie Final Investigative Report were ever disclosed to trial defense counsel. Attorney Buting points out that the CD was never logged into evidence but instead Special Agent

Fassbender kept the CD in his possession. This explains why trial defense counsel never saw the CD when they reviewed all of the evidence in the case at the Calumet County Sheriff's Department."

Over the course of several months, Zellner reached out to one of the former special prosecutors who assisted Kratz in Avery's prosecution, Assistant Wisconsin Attorney General Tom Fallon. She inquired about the missing CD starting on November 14, 2017, then on December 4, 2017, and finally again on March 20, 2018.

Finally, there was a breakthrough. It came on April 17, 2018.

"Attorney Fallon finally produced the CD, which contained 2,449 pages," Zellner said. "On May 25, 2018, current post-conviction counsel filed a motion to supplement the record on appeal with the CD produced by Attorney Fallon."(100)

In turn, Gary Hunt, Zellner's computer expert, determined that Bobby Dassey's computer was manipulated by someone out to destroy and conceal data on that computer. But why would someone do that?

"Mr. Hunt, after his examination of the 7 DVDs and the CD, made the following conclusions … Mr. Hunt detected eight periods in 2005 which are relevant to the murder of Teresa Halbach, when computer records are missing and presumably deleted from the Dassey computer: August 23-26, August 28 - September 11, September 14-15, September 24 - October 22, October 23-24, October 26 - November 2, November 4-13, and November 15 - December 3."

And here's what he extracted from Teresa's last day alive.

---

100. Zellner's Motion to Supplement Previously Filed Motion for Post-Conviction Relief, July 6, 2018

"On October 31, 2005, the Dassey computer was used to access the Internet at 6:05 a.m., 6:28 a.m., 6:31 a.m., 7 a.m., 9:33 a.m., 10:09 a.m., 1:08 p.m., and 1:51 p.m."

As for the CD that was previously withheld from Strang and Buting prior to Avery's trial, it did not require any specialized software, according to Hunt.

The CD turned out 2,632 Internet keyword searches for the following terms: body: 2,083; journal: 106; gun: 75; RAV: 74, MySpace: 61; fire: 51; gas: 50; stab: 32; cement: 23; bullet: 10; DNA: 3; bondage: 3; throat: 2; tires: 2, blood: 1.

"The CD contained 14,099 images recovered from the computer. The CD also contained 1,625 photos categorized as recovered pornography, which means that these images had been deleted and then recovered. A search of the MSN messages reveals communications between Bobby and various individuals who identified themselves as teenage girls in the age range of 14-15. Bobby identified himself as being a 19 year old. The messages have explicit sexual content."

Obviously, Avery's murder trial may have turned out drastically different had Kratz and Fassbender turned over to the defense all of the contents related to Bobby Dassey's computer.

"Bobby's trial testimony about being asleep from 6:30 a.m. to 2 p.m. would have been impeached by the contents of the seven DVDs and one CD, which would have shown that he was awake and on the computer eight times in that time frame," Zellner said in July 2018.

"The vast quantities of child pornography and the violent images of young females being tortured, sexually assaulted and mutilated on the Dassey computer at times when only Bobby was home, in addition to his MSN sexually-explicit conversations with 14 and 15 year olds, as well as the word searches after the murder that indicate an interest in skeletons, dismemberment, knives through skin, fire, handcuffs, guns, bullets and blood, could have been utilized by trial defense counsel to impeach Bobby's credibility with the jury by illustration of his knowledge and preoccupation with unique details of the crime."

The CD in question also "contains conversations between Bobby and 14 and 15 year old girls ... Bobby asks that the girls flash him using a webcam."

But during Avery's trial, Kratz lauded Bobby Dassey. He made sure Bobby was considered a brave, impartial witness the jury could trust and believe, just like Kratz.

"Again, a witness without any bias," Kratz told the jury during closing arguments. "It is an individual that deserves to be given a lot of credit. Because sometime between 2:30 and 2:45 he sees Teresa Halbach. He sees her taking photographs. He sees her finishing the photo shoot. And he sees her walking up towards Uncle Steve's trailer."

Buting and Strang both strongly assert that having access to the hidden CD that was kept from them by Kratz would have altered their defense strategy.

"I accepted without challenge Ken Kratz's assertion in a January 25, 2007, email to me that Velie's analysis of 'Steve, Teresa's, and Brendan's' computers yielded 'nothing much of evidentiary value. With the belated production of the Velie forensic analysis to Mr. Avery's current lawyers in April 2018, it now appears to me from materials that Ms. Zellner and co-counsel have filed that the Velie forensic analysis in fact did include much of evidentiary value, in direct contradiction to Mr. Kratz's claim.

"Given what I know now about the existence and content of the Velie forensic analysis, this looks to me like deceit. It looks like deceit about who used this computer; it looks like deceit about the evidentiary value of the information extracted from the computer. At a minimum, it looks like material information bearing on innocence that the State knowingly possessed, had exclusively in its possession, and withheld from the defense." (101)

What else did Strang point out in his summer 2018 affidavit?

"We would have used the information in the Velie forensic analysis to support our motion by strengthening our showing that Bobby Dassey was an alternate suspect. At a minimum, the information would have gone to Bobby Dassey's availability and opportunity to commit violent crimes against and kill Teresa Halbach on October 31, 2005; to his sexual motive or other deviant motive to do so ... and to the credibility of his alibi. We also would have sought to introduce evidence of incriminating Internet searches that likely were made by Bobby Dassey, and would have confronted him on cross-examination with those searches and other information contained in the Velie forensic analysis."

It's highly probable that if Kratz and Fassbender didn't selectively choose to keep the computer analysis CD from Buting and Strang, the trial would have had a different outcome. If Bobby Dassey's trial testimony was shown to be a complete farce, it is very likely the jury wouldn't have returned a guilty verdict for Avery.

"Information demonstrating a probability that Bobby Dassey used that computer to gain access to the Internet on October 31, 2005, during times that he claimed to be asleep and while Brendan Dassey was known to be at school that day, also would have been used in cross-examination of Bobby Dassey at trial, had we known that information in the Detective Velie and Gary Hunt forensic analyses. I note that, in the end, the jury asked during deliberations for Bobby Dassey's testimony."

---

101. Affidavit of Wisconsin criminal defense lawyer Dean Strang, June 4, 2018

In retrospect, one has to wonder whether Kratz and Fassbender intentionally withheld the CD from Avery's trial lawyers because they suspected Bobby was the killer and realized the case had already reached the point of no return.

"Current post-conviction counsel's expert Mr. Hunt's forensic examination of the seven DVDs revealed 128 violent images of young females being tortured, sexually assaulted and mutilated," Zellner said. "There were dozens of images depicting young females in pain because of having objects and fists forced into their vaginas. The images also depicted dismembered, decapitated, and drowned bodies of young females. Many of the female images, both alive and deceased, bear an uncanny resemblance to Ms. Halbach.

"Two pictures were found in the unallocated space, the first showing Ms. Halbach and Mr. Avery, the second showing only Ms. Halbach. The pictures were in an unallocated space because someone had deleted them. There is no way to know when these images were acquired or deleted. Therefore, prior counsel was deprived of a complete compilation of all the violent images, word searches, timelines, messages, and recovered images that had been deleted during the Halbach murder investigation. The State's forensic examiner was also suppressed. All of this material could have been used to establish Bobby as a third-party Denny suspect."

But, couldn't the prosecution come back and say, hey, wait a minute, there were four boys living under the Dassey roof. Isn't it possible any one of them was the deviant pervert constantly viewing this dirty disgusting smut that was messing with their mind?

When Zellner's expert utilized his 2017 computer forensic tracking software on the computer, Hunt uncovered a total of 667 Internet searches for sexual images "on weekdays when Bobby was the only member of his family at home during the week from 6:30 a.m. to 3:45 p.m. All other Dassey family members who lived at the residence ... were either at work or school during those hours."

Prior to Teresa's disappearance, Barb and her husband Tom Janda had split up and he was no longer staying on Avery Road. "According to Barb, Tom Janda moved out before October 15, 2005, and never looked at pornography on the Dassey computer. Bobby was the only person at the Dassey residence from 6 a.m. to 3:45 p.m. on the weekdays. During the week, Blaine and Brendan were in school until 3:45 p.m. Bryan lived with his girlfriend and worked during the day. Barb also worked a day shift, and Tom Janda no longer lived at the residence." (102)

Zellner also enlisted the expertise of retired FBI behavioral analyst, Gregg McCrary, to weigh in on the matter.

McCrary "opines that these Dassey computer searches demonstrate the obsessively compulsive nature of Bobby Dassey's Internet searches and the fascination with sexual acts that involve the infliction of pain, torture, and humiliation on females and an equally disturbing fascination with viewing dead female bodies.

"Barb hired someone to reformat the Dassey computer prior to law enforcement seizing it. The reformatting resulted in a number of images being removed during the critical period before and after the murder."

But, since Kratz was liable to say and spout out anything, couldn't the special prosecutor now pontificate this was all Steven Avery's doing? Perhaps Avery was sneaking into his sister's trailer during the daytime when she wasn't around to fill his mind with dirty and wicked fantasies that would drive him over the edge and make him murder Teresa?

"The State attempted to convince the jury that Mr. Avery's motive in setting up the appointment with Ms. Halbach on October 31, 2005, was to lure her to his property to sexually assault her," Zellner said. "During the searches of the Avery

102. Motion to Compel Production of Recent Examination of the Dassey Computer, July 3, 2018

property, the State focused on trying to gather pornography from Mr. Avery's residence. However, a forensic analysis performed by the State's examiner of Mr. Avery's computer in 2006 revealed no searches of sexual images, much less violent images and dead bodies. Mr. Avery never accessed the Dassey computer. He did not have the password for the computer, nor did he possess a key to the Dassey residence which was locked when no one was home. Mr. Avery only entered the residence with permission or a Dassey family member."'

Furthermore, Avery would be eliminated as being the deviant culprit on all but fifteen of the 128 computer searches just by the fact that he was thrown in jail on November 9, 2005. "Brendan would be eliminated from all but 26 of the 128 searches at issue by having been arrested on March 1, 2006."

Former FBI stalwart Gregg McCrary maintains that a competent group of police investigators would have considered Bobby Dassey a prime suspect in the death of Teresa Halbach.

CHAPTER TWENTY-SIX

FANTASY LIFE

Ann Wolbert Burgess, Ph. D, has co-authored twenty-four books, thirty book chapters and more than 160 peer-reviewed articles. She teamed up with internationally noted FBI profilers John Douglas and Robert Ressler to co-author the book, *Sexual Homicide: Patterns and Motives*. It was her research on that book in particular that gave her a window into the mind of a murderer, a murderer whose mind is fried by constant visual images of violent X-rated pornography.

"We interviewed 36 sexual murderers and we concluded that, as a group, they had several traits in common: One, they had a longstanding preoccupation and preference for a very active fantasy life. Two, they were preoccupied with violent, sexualized thoughts and fantasies. In my opinion, in reviewing Mr. Hunt's affidavits, the obvious preoccupation with violent pornography, which includes torturing young females and dismembering and or mutilating female bodies, over time would result in a justification for killing.

"My opinion is based, in part, upon a review of sexual images contained in the Dassey CD and seven DVDs, Mr. Gregg McCrary's second supplemental affidavit, and Mr. Hunt's analysis of the Internet searches, including the timing and frequency of the searches as well as description of the violent pornographic images." (103)

Dr. Burgess believes that McCrary's analysis of Teresa's death being a sexually motivated crime was right on the money.

---

103. Affidavit of Dr. Ann Burgess, July 5, 2018

"The Dassey computer examination by Mr. Hunt also revealed that Bobby Dassey was untruthful when he testified that he had been asleep on October 31, 2005, until 2:30 p.m. I also agree with Mr. McCrary that Bobby should have been considered a prime suspect because of his untruthful statements during the investigation, combined with the nature of his Internet searches."

Burgess pointed out that twenty-two search terms described forcing objects into female vaginas; thirty-seven search terms described violent accidents and violent car crashes with images of dead bodies; thirteen searches for drowned, dead, or diseased female bodies; sixty-five searches for describing the infliction of violence on females including fisting and images of females experiencing pain.

Dr. Ann Burgess contends that Bobby Dassey was engaged in a dangerous and obsessive web of violent pornography and death. She said this is all too common in cases of violent sex crimes against young women including many that end in murder.

"Further, Mr. Hunt determined that 562 of the searches were performed on 10 weekdays. Mr. Hunt described folders created on the Dassey computer entitled, 'Teresa Halbach,' 'Steven Avery,' and 'DNA.'"

"The searches speak to the compulsive nature of the offender, specifically the sadism, as the fantasy life translates into the compulsion to act out the sadistic fantasy, example, a sexual homicide," Dr. Burgess said.

"A person obsessed with violence is more likely to commit a murder than someone not so obsessed."

Here's what Dr. Burgess informed the court regarding the computer disk that Kratz chose to hide from Strang and Buting back in 2006.

"The images on the CD also contain blindfolded and bound girls, dismembered bodies, and bestiality. All of these images display a fascination with dominance, control, and mutilation, which is characteristic of many sexual homicides. The mutilation of Ms. Halbach's body is consistent with a fascination with the morbid images found on the Dassey computer of dead and dismembered human bodies."

Dr. Burgess has been recognized by courts as an expert witness on child pornography, crime classification, offender typology, rape victims, rape trauma, and serial offenders.

"All of the opinions offered within this affidavit are based upon a reasonable degree of scientific certainty in the field of psychiatric nursing," she said. Dr. Burgess has been a professor of psychiatric nursing at Boston University since 2001.

"I have also reviewed Steven Avery's second supplemental affidavit in which he describes Bobby commenting on Teresa Halbach after each appointment that she had at the Avery Salvage Yard. Specifically, Mr. Avery says that Bobby would say, 'I see that your girlfriend was here again.' Since Bobby was never present when Ms. Halbach was on the property, Mr. Avery concluded that he must have been watching her from a window. Clearly, Bobby had developed an unhealthy obsession with Ms. Halbach. It is also significant that Bobby has always maintained that he did not know that Ms. Halbach was coming to the property, but there is a conflicting report from the Wisconsin Public

Defender Office dated November 23, 2005, in which Bobby admitted that he knew Ms. Halbach was coming to the property that day."

From her perspective, what was not recovered from Bobby Dassey's home computer during the police investigation into Teresa's murder case is just as important, if not more striking, than what authorities and computer forensic experts did actually find.

"The Dassey computer examination by Mr. Hunt revealed eight significant periods of deletions related to the times that Ms. Halbach visited the Avery property," Burgess said. "It is not unusual ... an organized offender would try to cover up his fantasies by deleting files from a computer. Furthermore, I agree with Mr. McCrary that it is highly significant in any investigation if there is an attempt to delete or destroy records. Clearly, the person deleting or destroying records, has to be considered as a suspect in any homicide investigation."

During the closing arguments in front of the jurors from Manitowoc County, Kratz told them, "We could start with the moment of the visual or with the image of that man, Steven Avery, standing outside of a big bonfire, with flames over the roof, or at least over the garage roof, and the silhouette of Steven Avery, with the bonfire in the background and the observations made by some witnesses. Can you all picture that? Can you picture that as a moment, as a moment in time? And that moment, by the way, although dramatic and although important, should tell the whole story," Kratz told jurors at the end of the five-week-long trial.

"That moment of Steven Avery, after the murder was committed, of Steven Avery tending the fire, of Steven Avery disposing or and mutilating the body of 25-year-old Teresa Halbach. That would be a good place to start. But I'm not going to start there. I'm going to start somewhere else. I'm going to start with the Toyota RAV4. The Toyota RAV4, which was owned by Teresa Halbach, which was discovered

on the fifth of November at the Avery Salvage property …
Because the discovery of that RAV4, the discovery of Teresa
Halbach's vehicle, changed the course of not only this case,
but the clues and the secrets found in that vehicle changed
the lives of everybody in this room. Look around, everybody.
The clues found in that vehicle, on the fifth of November,
changed everybody's lives. Yours included. Your lives will
never be the same, ours won't. Families won't. That moment
is particularly important. And that is where we're going to
begin."

That was vintage Kratz.

As far as her academic background, Burgess obtained
her bachelor's degree from Boston University, her master of
science from the University of Maryland, and her doctorate
of nursing science from Boston University. She also has an
honorary degree from the University of San Diego. Here's
what Dr. Burgess had to say, given her dedication and
expertise in getting to know the psyche of the criminal mind,
the deviant sexual offender who gravitates into the abyss.

"The offender in the Halbach murder would be classified
as an organized offender who plans, thinks things through,
and tries to cover his tracks by deleting incriminating files,
interjecting himself into the investigation as a primary
witness for the State, misleading the investigators about the
timeline and events surrounding the murder, and would be
very likely to attempt to plant evidence and frame another
for the murder," Dr. Burgess concludes.

"The offender would keep secret his commission of the
sadistic murder of Ms. Halbach. The police should have
considered Bobby a prime suspect in the murder of Ms.
Halbach and should not have eliminated him as quickly as
they did."

While finishing this book, the author reached out to
Zellner, the country's leading wrongful conviction lawyer,
to gain her insight into the killing and dismemberment of the

young Auto Trader photographer who never made it home to her family's farm on Halloween 2005.

"Bobby has been described by family members as being a very quiet, socially awkward teenager who never dated," Zellner said. "He spent a great deal of time on the computer, which was in his bedroom. Our experts have developed a profile of the individual doing the computer searches for violence pornography. The individual was obsessed with inflicting sexual violence on young females and displayed a strong interest in viewing deceased, mutilated female bodies. My experts believe the individual is very disturbed and seems to hate women."

Zellner said she has visited with Avery, one on one, about Bobby, since this was his nephew, and he saw him often, from September 2003 until his arrest in November 2005.

"According to Mr. Avery, Bobby became increasingly obsessed with Ms. Halbach in the few months before her death," Zellner said. "Mr. Tadych (Bobby's stepfather) has a history of domestic violence. Bobby and Mr. Tadych have told multiple lies about the events of October 31, 2005. The police reports demonstrate that Bobby and Mr. Tadych went out of his way to try to get the police to charge Steven. As early as November 5, 2005, Bobby tried to implicate Steven in the murder. Mr. Tadych talked obsessively about the case at work during the investigation. Both Bobby and Mr. Tadych changed their stories to fit the State's narrative. I believe Bobby in particular completely duped the cops, planted the bones and blood to frame Mr. Avery and willingly and enthusiastically became the State's star witness."

And the State's star witness was also aided by the dubious testimony from his future stepfather, Scott Tadych, who furnished him with an alibi, actually, an alibi for both men, around the exact time of Teresa's disappearance and killing.

That day, Tadych failed to show up for his work shift. He claimed he made two separate visits to a local hospital to visit his mother who was apparently undergoing back surgery in Green Bay. Keep in mind this was the same woman Tadych tried to beat up and had called several despicable vulgar names during an explosive outburst that led to his arrest by police just a few years earlier.

"That afternoon, or that morning, I was up by my mother," Tadych testified under oath during questioning by Kratz at the murder trial.(104)

"Then I left her and I went to the woods hunting. I went to my trailer and then I went to the woods hunting. Archery hunting, bow hunting, archery."

Next, Kratz asked, "About what time was it that you got out into the woods or that you got to your deer hunting stand?"

"About 3 p.m."

"On your way to deer hunting, that would be just before 3 p.m., did you observe anybody on the roadway?"

"Yes I did. I saw Bobby Dassey on Highway 147. I was going west and he was going east."

"Where is it, Mr. Tadych, that you hunt, or at least that day, where was it that you were going hunting?"

"In Kewaunee."

In the minds of the jurors, Tadych's testimony iced any suspicion toward Bobby as being the more likely killer. At the same time, Tadych helped bury Avery, a man he hated because he resented the fact that Avery was in line to collect a multi-million dollar settlement for the 1985 wrongful conviction case. And because he knew the cops investigating Teresa's death were not street smart individuals, Tadych realized he could essentially say whatever he wanted, and no one would question his statements or question his motives.

"Tadych went on to indicate that Steven has a large amount of control over Brendan as well as the rest of the

---

104. Day 12 jury trial of Avery, Scott Tadych testimony February 27, 2007

Dassey and Avery families. He states he believes this due to the large amount of dollars that Steven was possibly going to be coming into ... He stated he has known Steven approximately two years. Tadych went on to indicate Brendan spends most of his time with Steven and that Steven had taken Brendan up north a lot. Scott went on to indicate his gut feeling is that Steven had some sort of sexual relationship with Brendan but he has nothing to back this feeling up." (105)

During Avery's trial, Tadych made sure that he helped the prosecution nail Avery.

"I saw a big fire," he testified. "It was a big fire. It was bigger than normal ... They were almost as tall as the garage. Eight feet, ten feet. I don't know, ten feet maybe. Ten feet tall the flames were."

"It was a big fire?" Kratz asked his friendly witness.

"It was a big fire," Tadych repeated for the jury.

"Where did you go then, Mr. Tadych?"

"I went back to where I was living at the time, the trailer house on 147. About two miles away."

When Bobby Dassey was initially interviewed by the police, Bobby told them how he and Tadych had crossed paths while driving past one another, around the same time as Teresa's murder, going the opposite directions on Highway 147. Suspiciously, when Bobby was pressed to remember where the two saw one other on the road, just a matter of days earlier, he couldn't offer a definitive answer.

"Bobby indicated that as he was traveling on State Highway 147 towards the property he hunts deer on, he did observe an individual known to him as Scott Tadych. Bobby indicted that Scott would be able to verify precisely what time he had seen Bobby," Dedering's report five days after Teresa disappeared showed.

105. Interview of Scott Tadych, Investigator John Dedering, March 30, 2006

Dedering's report though was hollow. There was a lack of follow-up questioning. The most obvious question was not asked of Bobby, that is, how would Bobby know that Scott Tadych would be able to know the exact time that the two men passed one another?

When Avery stood trial, Dean Strang questioned Tadych about his whereabouts around the time of Teresa's murder as well as the story about Tadych and Bobby seeing one another on the highway.

"It's a 15-minute drive or something like that to your hunting spot?"

"Approximately, yeah."

"And this is when, on your way to hunting, is when you see Bobby Dassey?"

"Correct."

"He's going east in the other direction on Highway 147?"

"Correct."

"Speed limit on 147?"

"Fifty-five."

"And the two of you, obviously, are going in opposite directions?"

"Yes."

"And so you pass each other and you are later able to tell the police that Bobby was going deer hunting?"

"Yes."

"How do you know that?"

"How do I know that is because Bobby Dassey was going to the trailer where I live to hunt behind it."

"Let me understand. He's going to hunt deer right behind your trailer?"

"Yes."

"But you don't hunt deer right behind your trailer?"

"Occasionally, yes."

"And when did he tell you about this hunting trip that he planned right behind your trailer?"

"I don't recall him telling me. He had permission from the landlord to hunt there."

"So you figured since you saw him driving east on Highway 147 he must be going hunting?"

"Yes."

"Anybody else see you going west on 147 to go hunting, so far as you know?"

"Bobby Dassey."

"And had you told him that you were going hunting?"

"No."

"How would he have known that you were going hunting?"

"Because I was in my camouflage clothes."

"You were in your camouflage coat?"

"Yes."

"In your green Ford Ranger?"

"Yup."

"Passing one another at 55 miles an hour?"

"Nope. Where I passed Bobby I probably was only doing maybe 25 miles an hour tops. He was slowing down to turn in my driveway and I was driving up 147."

"I see. And so you surmise that he would have known you were going deer hunting because he would have seen you in your camouflage clothing?"

"Yes."

"Did you go hunting with anybody that day?"

"No."

As it turned out, Tadych, who has a reputation of being a compulsive liar, wound up giving numerous inconsistent statements to the police and in court in regard to Teresa's murder. The size of the fire he saw in Avery's backyard changed dramatically from his initial interviews with police to the point of him serving as a main witness for Kratz. He also told police he went and visited his mother at the Green Bay hospital two separate times on the day of the murder and nobody in the police investigation made any attempt to verify either visit. In addition to the dubious story about seeing Bobby on the highway, Tadych insisted Barb Janda left his place that night after watching Prison Break. Later on, he changed that story and claimed she spent the night with him. The later story gave him a rock solid alibi to refute any allegations he might have been involved in burning and dismembering Teresa's body, along with Bobby Dassey, after the skies grew dark after slaying, perhaps at the Manitowoc County gravel pit where the pelvic bones were later found.

During a tape-recorded interview with Dedering and DCI agent Kevin Heimerl, Bobby admitted that he did not leave to go into work at the Fisher Hamilton Manufacturing plant in Manitowoc until almost two hours later than normal.

"Dassey indicated he stayed home until 11:30 p.m. on October 31, 2005, and then left for work at Hamilton Manufacturing," their reports state. There appeared to be no follow-up questions as to why Dassey didn't go into work as scheduled.

On February 27, 2006, when Bobby underwent a follow-up interview, Dedering asked him again about his activities on the day of the homicide. This time, Bobby told the police "he got up at approximately 9 p.m., got ready for work... Bobby indicated that when he was leaving for work at approximately 9:30 p.m., he noticed that Steven was having a bonfire. He estimated that the flames were five to six feet in height. He stated that it was a good-sized fire and that Steven has had fires there in the past ... He stated he worked from 10 p.m. until 6 a.m. the following day and when he arrived home, he noticed nothing unusual and that the fire was out." (106)

In late 2017, Gregg McCrary filed a second affidavit with Wisconsin's criminal justice system, in reference to Bobby Dassey.

---

106. Interview of Bobby Dassey. Investigator John Dedering, Feb. 27, 2006

"The fact that Bobby Dassey became the key witness for the prosecution and that his testimony placed Teresa Halbach on the property 'walking over to Steven's trailer' after she completed her assignment, interjected him into the prosecution in a way that should have raised the suspicions of reasonably trained detectives if that testimony is untrue. Based upon the affidavit of Bryan Dassey, it appears that Bobby Dassey's testimony was untrue. In my opinion, a prudent investigator would have considered Bobby Dassey a suspect and would have investigated him as such. There is no evidence that authorities ever investigated, much less eliminated, him as a suspect or investigated the discrepancies in his trial testimony." (107)

McCrary also offered the same sentiments regarding Tadych, who had a lengthy history of abusing women and he was at the center of the controversial letter that arrived at the Green Bay post office, the infamous SIKIKEY letter.

The letter made reference to a body being burned up at 3 a.m. at an aluminum smelter, which is where Tadych has worked.

"Mr. Tadych worked the third shift at the Wisconsin Aluminum Foundry. The note, which was never thoroughly investigated by law enforcement, is potentially of great evidentiary value because the note was sent on November 9, 2005, and it was not disclosed to the public until November 11, 2005, that Ms. Halbach had allegedly been burned on the Avery burn pit," Zellner said.

But that's not all.

"Mr. Tadych's nickname at work was 'Skinny' and, according to a current employee, many of the shift workers are not totally literate. It is a reasonable inference that a semi-literate employee might have misspelled the word 'Skinny' in the note."

107. Supplemental Affidavit of Gregg McCrary, October 20, 2017

At no point during Teresa's murder probe, did anybody in Wisconsin law enforcement attempt to get the fingerprints or DNA samples from Tadych to compare with the evidence in the case, including the eight fingerprints that were recovered from the RAV4 that did not belong to Avery, Brendan Dassey, or Bobby Dassey, among others in the family.

"At a minimum, Mr. Tadych should have been asked to provide his DNA and fingerprints so that they could be compared to crime scene evidence," Zellner said. "Mr. Tadych's failure to respond to Kevin Rahmlow's text about seeing the RAV4 at the turnaround by the old dam on November 3 and 4, 2005, before the discovery of the Halbach vehicle on the Avery property, is also suspicious."

Rahmlow, of course, is the man who came forward in 2017, providing a sworn affidavit about his first-hand experience of seeing the RAV4 abandoned after Teresa's disappearance, but not on the Avery property, as Kratz represented.

"I went to the old dam with Mr. Rahmlow and my investigator," Zellner said. "He is absolutely telling the truth about seeing the Halbach vehicle. He is also telling the truth about the Cenex station missing poster in the window regarding Ms. Halbach and her vehicle. Some people think he is mistaken about speaking to Colborn being it was Colborn's day off and he would not have been in uniform. I find that point to be unpersuasive because Colborn was involved in the biggest investigation of his life. I do not believe that he would take a day off in the middle of the investigation. He wanted to run for sheriff. I believe he would have worn his uniform on his day off because it would have given him a little bit of authority.

"No cop or witness has come forward giving Colborn an alibi for Mr. Rahmlow's claim, nor does anyone say they saw him in plain clothes on November 4, 2005. This is a cop who absolutely does not write up reports, if at all, until years later.

"Mr. Rahmlow's timeline of seeing Ms. Halbach's vehicle on the early afternoon of November 4, 2005, and Mr. Siebert's timeline of seeing her vehicle drive onto Mr. Avery's property shortly thereafter, match. Mr. Rahmlow has no motive to lie and had moved from Wisconsin to Michigan years before."

Rahmlow was hardly the only person who remembered seeing the RAV4 concealed off State Highway 147 in the days prior to its startling appearance on the back end of Avery's property.

CHAPTER TWENTY-SEVEN

DAMAGED

When former Mishicot resident Kevin Rahmlow came forward in 2017, he made it abundantly clear that he saw Teresa's RAV4 being concealed at the Highway 147 turnabout near the old dam toward Mishicot. It turns out Rahmlow was hardly the only person in Manitowoc County who remembered seeing Teresa's vehicle being concealed off the road near the Old Dam.

"I lived in Mishicot in 2005. On October 31, 2005, I was driving east on Highway 147 toward Mishicot when I saw a vehicle by the old dam on the north side of the road. It was around dusk, but there was enough light for me to make out its shape and color," said Paul Burdick, a long-time resident of Mishicot.

"It was a small SUV, greenish in color. It was facing northwest and parked facing a tree."(108)

However, when Burdick drove past the old dam another time, in the coming days, he made another observation.

"Several days later, the vehicle was gone," he said. "I did not report what I saw to the police. The talk around town was that some people in the community called in the vehicle to the police."

However, at the Manitowoc County Sheriff's Office, there are no written documents indicating anybody responded to a call of an abandoned vehicle, Teresa's RAV4, being dumped near the old dam.

---

108.   June 28, 2018 sworn affidavit of Paul Burdick

Interestingly, Zellner also discovered Manitowoc County's radio transmissions concerning calls and efforts to find Teresa or her RAV4 on Friday, November 4, 2005, no longer exist.

"Ms. Halbach's vehicle was observed parked by a tree at the old dam by witness Paul Burdick on October 31, 2005," Zellner said. Then, over the next few days, Zellner noted, "Ms. Halbach's vehicle was observed parked in the same location at the old dam by witness Kevin Rahmlow. (109)

The sightings of Teresa's RAV4, dumped behind the tall trees and wild brush along the state highway, also point to the suspected involvement of Tadych in the murder, according to Zellner. The distance between where Tadych lived in November 2005 and the location of the abandoned vehicle, was roughly a half mile.

Provided this was the murder victim's vehicle, then how did it get to Avery's property and why did it sustain front-end damage? There is no denying the fact that Teresa's RAV4 was damaged after she visited Avery Salvage. But nobody in Wisconsin law enforcement made much of an effort to find out why her vehicle was damaged.

What caused the driver's side blinker light to get knocked out? Where did this occur? Why did the culprit make it a point to stop what he was doing, get out of the vehicle and pick up the broken vehicle debris, and place it into the cargo area?

Photos of the vehicle also make it clear the front bumper was torn as well.

A few logical scenarios remain. The killer may have struck an object driving the victim's vehicle after dark, panicked, and retrieved the blinker light. The other scenario is that the police, and perhaps one of the searchers such as

109. Defendant's Reply to the State's Response to Defense's Motion to Supplement Previously Filed Post-Conviction Motion for Relief, August 3, 2018

Ryan Hillegas, the ex-boyfriend of Teresa, were involved in the car mess up.

Zellner suspects that the RAV4 may have been moved from the Old Dam Turnabout to the Radandt Sand & Gravel pit that Friday afternoon of November 4, and then after dark, it got towed onto the Avery property where it was spotted the next morning.

Steven Avery has told his lawyer he believes the RAV4 had to be towed onto the perimeter of the Salvage Yard property at some point in time because the vehicle was facing west, meaning it may have been unhitched at that point because the tow driver could not turn it around.

"Also the RAV, according to Steven, is parked too close to the vehicle next to it so that there is not room to exit the driver's door of the RAV for a man to exit," Zellner said. "Steven believes the parking light damage was the result of towing."

Zellner has been attempting to gain access to the broken blinker light in order to have to it tested for trace evidence and DNA, but the state of Wisconsin has put up a vigorous fight to thwart her attempts to have the blinker light tested. It is also fighting her efforts to have the pelvic bones undergo testing to confirm whether these charred bones positively belong to Teresa.

"The parking light on Teresa Halbach's car was damaged after she left the Avery property on Halloween 2005. We know the car was not damaged before Halloween," Zellner said.

"The specific damage was located in the area of the driver's side parking light and is consistent with the vehicle being driven through the Radandt Gravel Pit and colliding with one of the metal property stakes on Radandt's property or the red Pinto blocking access to the Avery property.

Over the past couple years Zellner's investigators have tried repeatedly to interview Halbach's ex-boyfriend, Ryan Hillegas, the young man who organized the search party efforts to find Teresa. Hillegas was the individual who met up with Pamela Sturm on the Saturday morning of November 5, 2005. That was the day that Sturm and her daughter showed up late and told Hillegas they wanted to go and search the Avery Salvage yard themselves. In turn, Hillegas and Teresa's roommate, Scott Bloedorn, supplied Sturm with a camera and they also furnished her with the phone number to reach Calumet County Sheriff Jerry Pagel.

However, Zellner's repeated attempts to interview Hillegas about any facets of Teresa's disappearance and the front-end damage to Teresa's RAV4 have been unsuccessful. Hillegas has refused to be interviewed by Zellner's investigators, Kirby & Associates, she said.

"Mr. Hillegas injected himself into the police investigation by taking an active role in the volunteer search," noted police procedural expert witness Gregg McCrary.

"He gave a female volunteer a camera and a direct phone number to the sheriff. It appears that he directed her to the area where the victim's vehicle was located. He also appears to have misled police when he told them that Ms. Halbach had damaged the front driver's side of her vehicle months before her disappearance, had filed an insurance claim for that damage and had taken the cash payout without repairing her vehicle. However, it appears that particular damage was done more contemporaneously with the crime and a check with Ms. Halbach's insurance company revealed that she never filed an insurance claim for the front end damage." (110)

On May 26, 2017, the insurance company for Teresa Halbach responded to the subpoena sent to them by Kathleen T. Zellner & Associates. "Pursuant to your subpoena, ERIE has made a diligent and exhaustive search of its records and finds no such claims to have been presented … between the

---

110. Affidavit of Gregg McCrary, May 8, 2017

years 2003 and 2006 pertaining to Teresa M. Halbach. As such, The ERIE has no records to provide," advised Kevin F. Nelson of the litigation/claims examination department.(111)

***

When Zellner filed her original post-conviction relief on June 7, 2017, the 221-page document outlined a number of explosive Brady violations she said were committed by Kratz. In many cases, the existence of even one Brady violation warrants a conviction reversal and sends the case back for a new trial.

"In *Brady v. Maryland*, the Court held that the State violates an accused's constitutional right to due process of law by failing to disclose evidence. A Brady claim requires a showing that the undisclosed evidence is favorable to the accused because it is either exculpatory or impeaching; the evidence was suppressed by the State either willfully or inadvertently and the accused was prejudiced because the evidence is material to guilt or punishment," Zellner's motion argues.

Zellner's team uncovered a number of key pieces of evidence that were never furnished to Avery's original trial lawyers, Buting and Strang.

One was the voicemail CD taken from George and Jolene Zipperer's home.

"When Ms. Halbach first arrived in the vicinity of the Zipperers' residence, she made a phone call which was answered by the Zipperers' answering machine. Allegedly, Ms. Halbach left a voicemail that she could not locate the Zipperer residence. On November 3, when the Zipperers were interviewed at 9:30 p.m., they told the investigators that Ms. Halbach had left a voice message on their answering

---

111. Exhibit 59, Response to Subpoena to Erie Insurance, May 26, 2017

machine. The voicemail was listened to by Detective Remiker of the Manitowoc County Sheriff's Office and it was copied by Manitowoc County Sheriff's Office Detective Dennis Jacobs onto a CD. The CD of Ms. Halbach's voicemail recording on the Zipperer answering machine was never turned over to trial defense counsel and has allegedly disappeared.

"Mr. Fallon confirmed in a letter to current post-conviction counsel on April 20, 2017, that neither Calumet nor the Manitowoc Sheriff's Offices have been able to locate the CD of Ms. Halbach's voicemail left on the Zipperer answering machine." (112)

The disappearance of the voicemail, however, may have something to do with Kratz's professional misconduct, Zellner contends.

"Suspiciously, Mr. Kratz never played the recording of the 2:12 p.m. voicemail for the jury. It is reasonable to conclude that Mr. Kratz concealed the 2:12 p.m. voicemail because it confirmed that the Zipperers' residence was Ms. Halbach's last stop ... Clearly, the destruction and or concealment of Ms. Halbach's voicemail to the Zipperers leads to the reasonable conclusion that her voicemail refuted Mr. Kratz's timeline and so it was concealed from trial defense counsel. Investigators concealed the voicemail left by Ms. Halbach on the Zipperers' answering machine because it refuted their theory that Ms. Halbach's final appointment was Mr. Avery."

The second Brady violation allegation pertains to Teresa's fuel tank.

"Although the odometer reading from Ms. Halbach's vehicle was noted at the Wisconsin State Crime Lab, no reference was made by law enforcement or the Wisconsin State Crime Lab to the amount of gas remaining in the RAV4's fuel tank, which would have provided vital

---

112. Motion for Post-Conviction Relief, June 7, 2017

information about how far the car had traveled since its tank was filled to capacity on October 29, 2005," Zellner said.

Police obtained Teresa's credit card statements which show that two days before her death, Teresa spent $37.94 to purchase a full tank of gas at the Exxon station in De Pere, a suburb adjacent to Green Bay. Zellner determined her 1999 Toyota RAV4 had a fuel capacity of 15.3 gallons.

"Mr. Fallon has confirmed on April 20, 2017, that the State failed to determine and document the gas level remaining in Ms. Halbach's vehicle when it was discovered on the Avery's property. Clearly, the State did not want the mileage revealed because it would have completely refuted its theory that Ms. Halbach and her car were driven many more miles after she left the Avery property," Zellner said.

A third Brady violation allegation concerns the highly questionable flyover conducted by Calumet Sheriff Jerry Pagel and his investigator, Wendy Baldwin. Their reports showed they were up in the sky for several hours flying over the terrain and specifically over the Avery property under the guise of searching for Teresa's vehicle. But they may have had ulterior motives. Their flyover may have been a shifty way for them to survey the Avery property to find the perfect spot to put Teresa's RAV4. A video of their flyover was provided to Strang and Buting but the video they got was only a few minutes long.

"Wendy Baldwin and Sheriff Pagel were in the air for around four hours yet the State produced only three minutes of footage," Zellner informed Judge Angela Sutkiewicz during the summer of 2017. "Mr. Kratz saw the unedited flyover video and knew that the RAV4 was not there at that time, but knew that the State's case might fail if the RAV4 was not present before 6 p.m. on November 4.

"The video was intentionally edited to conceal the fact that the RAV4 was not present at the time of the flyover on November 4."

Back in 2006, Strang and Buting notified Kratz about the questionable flyover videotape. "We currently have a spliced copy on a DVD which is obviously from several different dates, times, or aircrafts with no separation or designation as to their date and time. Thus I assume there must be a master copy of the complete videos," Buting wrote to Kratz back on July 24, 2006.

The lawyers for Avery asked Kratz to provide a complete copy in 2006, but that never happened.

A fourth Brady violation outlined by Zellner concerned the Wisconsin police investigators maintaining an oath of silence about their knowledge that Teresa's vehicle was driven through the Radandt quarry properties. Zellner has an affidavit from the quarry owner who swears under oath that the criminal investigators from the Wisconsin Department of Justice told him such.

"DOJ investigators never authored a report documenting their conversation with Mr. Radandt about the RAV4 being driven from his property and planted on Mr. Avery's property," Zellner said. "Mr. Kratz did not call Mr. Radandt as a witness at Mr. Avery's trial. The failure to produce this evidence to trial defense counsel was a clear Brady violation because this information could not only have been used to impeach the State's witnesses it also would have provided exculpatory evidence for Mr. Avery that the RAV4 was planted on his property."

One of the biggest pieces of overlooked evidence in Avery's 2007 trial concerned the front-end damage to Halbach's vehicle.

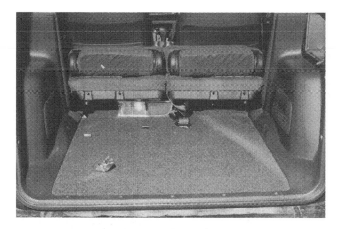

Attorney Kathleen Zellner has offered her theory explaining the date and circumstances for when the murder victim's blinker light got damaged.

CHAPTER TWENTY-EIGHT

AVERY'S BRAIN

Across the Missouri River from Omaha, Nebraska, sits the gateway into Iowa, the city of Council Bluffs. On July 22, 1977, a retired police captain was cruelly murdered by someone brandishing a shotgun. The murder victim was working overnight security at a car dealership. Four months later, two black teenagers, Terry Harrington and Curtis McGhee from Omaha, were rounded up and presented as the ruthless murderers. In August 1978, an all-white jury from Pottawattamie County rejected Terry Harrington's claims of innocence. Harrington insisted he was at a music concert and was later visiting one of his former high school football coaches. The prosecution found a crime lab analyst who testified at Harrington's jury trial that gunshot residue was recovered from a jacket seized from Harrington's home.

The prosecution's case came together after a young man named Kevin Hughes was arrested for involvement in a stolen car ring. After promises of leniency from the police and a $5,000 reward, Hughes agreed to testify that he, Harrington and McGhee tried to steal a car at the lot in Council Bluffs and that Harrington fatally shot the 56-year-old John Schweer, at the dealership. (113)

Harrington served out of his life prison sentence at the Iowa Department of Corrections. The 1980s rolled by, so did the 1990s. Then, in 1999, he had his first encounter with Lawrence Farwell, PhD.

---

113. The National Registry for Exonerations, Curtis McGhee

"I am a Harvard-educated forensic neuroscientist and founder of brain fingerprinting. I have testified in court as an expert witness on brain fingerprinting. I have conducted research on brain fingerprinting at the FBI, the CIA, and the U.S. Navy. TIME magazine named me one of the TIME 100: The Next Wave, the top innovators of this century who may be 'the Picassos of Einsteins of the 21st Century," Farwell said. (114)

In 1991, Farwell published literature on brain fingerprinting and was awarded a patent in 1994 and 1995.

Brain fingerprinting expert Dr. Lawrence Farwell has been honored by TIME magazine as one of the magazine's future Einsteins of the 21st century.

One of Dr. Farwell's brain fingerprinting clients, Terry Harrington of Omaha was in an Iowa prison for decades for the murder of a retired Iowa police officer that Harrington did not commit.

114.　Affidavit of Lawrence Farwell, PhD. April 26, 2017

"The technique has a known and very low error rate. The science underlying brain fingerprinting is well accepted in the scientific community."

"For national security reasons, I was not allowed to publish the details of the research conducted by myself and my colleagues at the FBI, the CIA, and the U.S. Navy until 2012," Farwell said. "Abstracts and brief reports that were published prior to that time did not disclose the specific methods that produced the highly accurate and reliable results reported in these studies."

On March 5, 2001, Farwell presented his brain fingerprinting analysis in the Iowa District Court for Pottawattamie County, in the murder case involving condemned Iowa prisoner Terry Harrington.

So how does this revolutionary testing procedure work?

"Brain fingerprinting detects information stored in the brain. It does not detect how that information got there. Information that the suspect knows from reading a newspaper, from interrogations, or from hearing testimony at a trial is not applicable in a brain fingerprinting test," Farwell said, because, "A finding that an individual knew such information would prove nothing about his participation in the crime. Knowledge of such information could be explained by his having read the newspaper, participated in the trial, etc."

To do the test, Dr. Farwell uses EEG, electro-encephalography, to measure an electrical event starting three hundred milliseconds after the exposure to the stimulus.

"If the person is a witness to or perpetrator of the crime, his response to stimuli that embody accurate details of the crime will evoke a P300 response," Farwell said.

Farwell has used the test on people and their purported alibi statements, but he admits there are some drawbacks in that area.

"However, in the case of an alibi, all that can usually be determined is whether the alibi story has validity as the subject's remembered experience. It is not usually possible to determine whether the exact timing of the alibi experience places the subject away from the crime scene at the time of the crime," he said.

And that's helped Dr. Farwell perfect his patented brain fingerprinting test.

"Brain fingerprinting provides definitive, reliable, valid scientific evidence regarding whether specific information is stored in a particular brain or not. Brain fingerprinting, like other forensic sciences, does not make a scientific determination of guilty or not guilty. That is a legal decision to be made by the judge and or jury," Farwell said.

In 2000, Terry Harrington attempted to overturn his 1978 Council Bluffs, Iowa, murder conviction for killing the retired police captain by arguing the Farwell brain fingerprinting test amounted to newly discovered evidence. "In the Harrington case, I developed a series of probes for the crime scene and a separate series of probes for the petitioner's alibi, from previously undisclosed police files, interviews with witnesses, examination of the location where the crime took place, and other evidence," Farwell said.

"I administered the test of Harrington in May 2000, and in October 2000 I rendered a report to the Iowa District Court analyzing the P300-MERMER responses. I supplemented the report with a separate analysis based solely on P300 brainwave responses on November 10, 2000. Both analyses produced a result of 'information absent' regarding the crime scene probes and 'information present' regarding the alibi probes, with a high degree of statistical confidence, over ninety-nine percent.

"This indicates that the record stored in Harrington's brain does not match the crime scene and does match his alibi," Farwell said.

Judge Timothy O'Grady of the Iowa District Court held a one-day hearing on the brain fingerprinting evidence presented by Dr. Farwell, on November 14, 2000.

"At the November 14 session, I testified and was cross-examined on the basis of my test reports. After the briefs were submitted and other unrelated grounds for post-conviction relief were tried, District Judge Timothy O'Grady issued his ruling on March 5, 2001, the court determined that brain fingerprinting was new evidence not available at the original trial and that it was sufficiently reliable to merit admission of the evidence. However, the court did not regard its weight as sufficiently compelling, in light of the record as a whole, as meeting its exacting standard, and thus it denied a new trial on this and the other grounds asserted by Harrington."

On the other spectrum, Dr. Farwell was involved in a 1999 brain fingerprinting experiment on James Grinder in Missouri.

"A Brain Fingerprinting test I conducted in 1999 showed that Grinder had the record of the 1984 murder of Julie Helton stored in his brain. Grinder and other alleged witnesses and suspects had previously given several contradictory accounts, some involving his participation and some not. The Brain Fingerprinting test showed that the account that matched the record in his brain was the one in which Grinder perpetrated the crime," Farwell said. "One week later, faced with a certain conviction and almost certain death sentence, Grinder pled guilty in exchange for a sentence of life without parole."

On May 2, 2016, Dr. Farwell performed his patented court-approved brain fingerprinting test on the man condemned to life imprisonment for Teresa's brutal killing in Manitowoc County, Wisconsin.

"The data analysis program that I applied ... in the Avery case was more sophisticated than the previously available analysis methods," Dr. Farwell said. "As in every crime, the brain of the perpetrator was central to the phenomenon revealed by the newly discovered blood-spatter evidence in the Avery case. The perpetrator's feet stood behind the car. The perpetrator's hands wielded the object and struck Teresa. The perpetrator's feet and hands, however, cannot operate independently. The perpetrator's brain controlled the actions of his hands and feet.

"The perpetrator's brain is different from the brain of an innocent person. The perpetrator's brain processed the information that, one, Teresa was behind the car and, two, the cargo door was open when the perpetrator attacked and struck Teresa."

Farwell noted his brain fingerprinting test would detect the difference between the brain of the perpetrator and an innocent person.

Obviously, Avery already knew lots of information about Teresa's murder case, based on his interactions with her on the day of her disappearance, from his interviews and interrogations with police, and from sitting through a five-week jury trial in 2007.

"Mr. Avery acknowledges knowing all of this. He claims that he knows information about surrounding events only through innocent participation in these events and not through participation in the murder itself," Farwell said.

"Prior to the Brain Fingerprinting test, Mr. Avery explicitly stated that he did not commit the attack on Teresa, nor did he witness the crime. He explicitly stated that no one had told him the specific details of the perpetrator's initial attack on the victim."

Here are some of the key questions that arose during Dr. Farwell's interview.

"Do you know where the victim was in relation to her vehicle when the perpetrator attacked and wounded her?

"Do you know if she was behind the car, in the driver's seat, or on the passenger side?"

"Such questions obtained a denial from Mr. Avery that he knew the relevant information, without revealing the correct information about the crime. If Mr. Avery did not commit the crime, he would have no way of knowing that the perpetrator attacked when, one, she was behind the car and two, the cargo door was open. He explicitly denied knowing these details about the crime on the basis of his contention that he did not commit or otherwise participate in the crime," Dr. Farwell said.

"This test was structured to determine definitively and scientifically whether or not two specific salient features of the murder of Teresa Halbach were stored in Mr. Avery's brain: A) where the victim was in relation to her vehicle when the perpetrator attacked and wounded her: **behind car.** B) The configuration of the victim's vehicle when the perpetrator attacked the victim: **cargo door open.**"

According to Dr. Farwell, the probe stimuli for brain fingerprinting test he conducted on Avery were "behind car" and "cargo door open."

"I told Mr. Avery that he would see a phrase correctly specifying where the victim was in relation to her vehicle when the perpetrator attacked and wounded her but did not inform Mr. Avery that the correct information probe stimulus was 'behind car.' I told Mr. Avery that he would see a phrase correctly specifying the 'configuration of the victim's vehicle when the perpetrator attacked the victim' but I did not inform Mr. Avery that the correct information probe stimulus was 'cargo door open,'" Dr. Farwell said.

Also, a number of irrelevant stimuli were developed for the test such as the victim having had a Saab 9 5 and Volvo S40. The irrelevant stimuli regarding Teresa's death were a deep stream and a golf club.

"For Mr. Avery or anyone else with a basic knowledge of the crime, clearly the target stimuli were correct, crime-relevant information and the corresponding irrelevant stimuli were irrelevant and had nothing to do with the crime."

Here's what Dr. Farwell told Avery prior to giving the test.

"The perpetrator attacked the victim, wounded her, and ultimately killed her. At trial, one specific attack with one specific weapon was extensively discussed, so everyone knows about that attack, including you. Just because you know about it, does not mean you did it, only that you heard about it at the trial.

"There was another attack with another method that was not mentioned at the trial. The perpetrator knows about that other attack, where it took place, and what happened, but an innocent suspect does not know these things.

"If you are innocent, you do not know anything about the other attack that took place because you were not there. If you are guilty, you know details about the other attack because you did it. This Brain Fingerprinting test will determine whether or not you know specific details about this other attack that was never mentioned at the trial; that no one ever told you about."

Farwell's experiments don't make determinations based on a visual inspection of the brainwave data, he emphasized. Instead, he uses mathematics to compute whether the "information present" or "information absent" is stored in the person's brain.

So what did he find for Avery?

"These results mean that scientific testing has determined with a 99.9 percent statistical confidence that Mr. Avery does not know certain specific details about the attack on Teresa Halbach," Farwell concluded. "This salient, crime-relevant information, which was experienced by the perpetrator when he committed the crime, is not stored in Mr. Avery's brain. Specifically, this information comprises the details that were revealed by the newly discovered blood-spatter evidence and embodied in the probe stimuli.

"This provides scientific evidence that Mr. Avery does not know specific critical, salient crime-relevant information regarding what actually took place at the time that the perpetrator attacked Teresa Halbach."

In the case of the condemned Omaha man, Terry Harrington, an Iowa judge allowed the experiments performed by Dr. Farwell that revealed his client was not involved in the murder of the retired Council Bluffs, Iowa police captain, but in the end, District Judge O'Grady rejected Harrington's post-conviction appeal and chose to keep Harrington incarcerated for the late 1970s murder that Harrington did not commit.

In 2003, Harrington's long fight to bring his injustice to an end came to a successful resolution when his case went before the Iowa Supreme Court. In April 2003, the Iowa Supreme Court ordered Harrington get a new trial. That October, Harrington was finally freed and prosecutors announced they would not retry the murder case against Harrington, who lost about twenty-five years of his life to a shotgun murder committed by somebody else.

Harrington and his codefendant, McGhee, were both exonerated and their case is now featured on the National Registry of Exonerations. Harrington and McGhee later obtained settlements from the cops in Iowa who were responsible for pinning the retired cop's murder on them, allowing the real killer, believed to be a white person, to walk free.

In 2013, the Omaha newspaper reported "Council Bluffs To Pay $6.2 Million To Settle Lawsuit with Wrongfully Convicted Omaha Men."

The article indicated Harrington and McGhee would be paid $2.3 million immediately and the rest would come in six annual payments of more than $528,500. A final payment of $728,500 would come in July 2020.

"The two were freed in 2003 when the Iowa Supreme Court determined that prosecutors committed misconduct by concealing reports about another man seen near the crime scene with a shotgun. The pair sued Pottawattamie County, eventually settling for $12 million," the article noted.

While housed in the Iowa Department of Corrections with his life wasting away, Harrington begged for the chance to take the brain fingerprinting test, insisting it would prove his innocence to the district court judge.

It eventually did.

As for Avery, his lawyer tells this author: "He was adamant about taking Dr. Farwell's brain fingerprinting test. Mr. Avery believed that the test was one hundred percent accurate in detecting if he was lying. Guilty people absolutely do not request new forensic testing or submit themselves to a test that could reveal their deceptions."

Zellner said there have been countless times during her representation of Steven Avery where he has made it clear to her that he is completely willing to undergo any kinds of testing and questioning if it helps prove his innocence.

"One of the biggest breakthrough moments was when Mr. Avery was so adamant about wanting all of the additional forensic testing done on the RAV4 and any other items we wanted to test," Zellner told the author.

For her, the recent scientific testing upon the bullet that was likely planted on the floor in Avery's garage in March 2006, was a huge deal for her side, and will be crucial as Avery's appeal moves forward. That item of trial evidence became known as Item FL.

"The second breakthrough moment was the discovery of the wood and paint on the bullet, but no bone," Zellner said. "I knew the State's entire theory about FL was false. The third breakthrough moment was the cumulative effect of not being able to replicate any of the State's forensic evidence.

"All of it was flawed."

But like she has had to do in many of her most high-profile wrongful convictions, Zellner will have to win Avery's innocence at the appellate level. Since she became involved in the case in 2016, following Judge Willis' retirement at the Manitowoc County Courthouse, the case got passed off to a judge from neighboring Sheboygan County, Angela Sutkiewicz.

She has a reputation for being a terrible judge and unfair judge. She was the subject of an unflattering investigative article produced by the USA TODAY NETWORK Wisconsin's investigative reporter Eric Litke, who is the state's leading reporter when it comes to analyzing Wisconsin's judicial system.

One of Litke's pieces revealed Sutkiewicz had an astonishing record that no judge should be proud of.

She was the fourth most substituted judge in the entire state of Wisconsin, an amazing feat because she isn't even in one of the state's most populated counties. Being the subject of repetitive substitution requests illustrates that the judge is not considered fair and not considered a knowledgeable person when it comes to interpreting the law. In other words, she's basically known as a hack judge, lazy and uninformed, not an exemplary member of Wisconsin's judiciary.

When it came to Avery's case, Sutkiewicz made it clear in her rulings that this was not a case to which she wanted to devote considerable time and attention. When she issued her first ruling on October 3, 2017, rejecting Avery's post-conviction appeal, her entire review of Zellner's motions and exhibits was less than six pages long.

"The reports submitted by the defendant are equivocal in their conclusions and do not establish an alternate interpretation of the evidence," Judge Sutkiewicz's ruling states. "Given the totality of the evidence submitted at trial and the ambiguous conclusions as stated in the experts' reports, it cannot be said that a reasonable probability exists that a different result would be reached at a new trial based on these reports. Finally, in light of the discussion of the evidence above and the conclusion with relation to the ability to appeal and venue for an appeal, the defendant has failed to establish any grounds that would trigger the right to a new trial in the interests of justice. As such, no further consideration will be given to this issue."

Wisconsin's Court of Appeals later kicked the case back to Judge Sutkiewicz after determining the lower court judge still needed to address an item Zellner had raised in her post-conviction motion regarding the computer disk Kratz had withheld from Buting and Strang regarding the violent pornography on Bobby Dassey's computer.

Realizing she got stuck with a stinker of an elected judge, Zellner filed a motion on June 14, 2018, asking Judge Sutkiewicz to step aside from the case.

"Moreover, for the convenience of the judiciary, the parties, and witnesses, Mr. Avery respectfully requests that his case be reassigned to a judge in Manitowoc County," Zellner said. "The record, evidence, and many of the witnesses in this matter are located in Manitowoc. All pleadings are filed with the clerk of the circuit court of Manitowoc. In short, at this juncture holding further proceedings in Manitowoc before a Manitowoc judge would be the most efficient use of judicial resources. At this juncture in Mr. Avery's case, all of the prior reasons for holding the legal proceedings outside of Manitowoc no longer exist ... Mr. Avery respectfully requests a substitution of judge in accordance with Wisconsin Statute 801.58." (115)

Judge Sutkiewicz ruled the motion before her was "premature."

She explained the Court of Appeals had kicked the case back to her to make a decision in regard to the new evidence, namely the CD. However, it was clear that under no circumstances did Judge Sutkiewicz want to allow Zellner's side to present evidence and call witnesses in her courtroom.

---

115. Defendant's Motion for Substitution of Judge, filed June 14, 2018

Instead, the Sheboygan judge had two objectives: one, being to prolong Avery's case on her court docket as long as practical and, secondly, to ensure that the state of Wisconsin, namely the Office of Attorney General Brad Schimel, did not, under any circumstances, lose the case.

Finally, on September 6, 2018, Judge Sutkiewicz issued an eleven-page ruling, again rejecting Zellner's bid for a new trial related to the Brady violation allegation surrounding the violent pornography computer disk Fassbender and Kratz chose to withhold from Buting and Strang as they prepared for trial, and were trying to build a strong case for a third-party alternative suspect defense.

"This matter is back before this court for a limited review pursuant to an order from the Court of Appeals," the judge wrote. "The defendant alleges that the prosecution withheld a CD created from a seized computer drive and that the failure to turn over this item of discovery directly impacted the defense in both the trial and appellate courts."

In her final analysis, Judge Sutkiewicz concluded, "In order for the defendant to establish that there was a Brady violation in a criminal prosecution, the defendant must prove that evidence was suppressed by the State. In this case, the defendant fails on this first burden."

In embarrassing fashion, the judge's written ruling showed her true colors and how little she even knew about Teresa's murder case. In her September 8, 2018 ruling, Judge Angie Sutkiewicz referred to the seized computer in question as being the computer of "**Brandon**" Dassey. As everyone familiar with the case knows, the 16-year-old nephew's name is Brendon Dassey, not **Brandon Dassey**.

"I believe we have an excellent chance of getting Mr. Avery's case reversed on appeal," Zellner assured this author. "It is much easier to get a case reversed for a hearing than to get a reversal of an adverse ruling after an evidentiary hearing."

In Avery's case, Judge Sutkiewicz staunchly refused to grant Zellner a chance to present evidence to show why the defendant should be granted a second trial.

For that reason, Zellner is upbeat and positive.

On September 8, 2018, Zellner proclaimed on her Twitter account: "So far only 1 Judge has ruled on Avery. At least 10 more will review before a final decision is made – on this evidence. If he is not freed we will file again. Never going to end until he is free."

At one point in time, before Zellner's involvement on Avery's case, Judge Sutkiewicz was simultaneously handling Mr. Avery's post-conviction motion in 2013 and the Halbach family's wrongful death lawsuit against Mr. Avery.

"Judge Willis immediately recused himself from the wrongful death lawsuit when he was given these dual assignments. Judge Sutkiewicz kept both cases and then delayed the voluntary dismissal on the wrongful death case of the Halbach's until Mr. Avery finally filed a motion complaining about her failure to dismiss, despite the Halbach's request to do so. She quickly granted the voluntary dismissal after Mr. Avery's motion to the appellate court was filed," Zellner said.

But it's also Judge Sutkiewicz's ties to Kratz that has Zellner concerned about justice and fairness for her client. Even though Kratz became an outcast in Wisconsin's legal community, there are still a number of lawyers and judges who worked with him over the years who don't want to rock the boat or say anything disparaging about Kratz.

"We are aware that Judge Sutkiewicz sat on the Wisconsin Crime Victim's Rights Board, as a private citizen, with former prosecutor Ken Kratz," Zellner said. "We attempted to have another judge substituted for her but she denied our motion as being 'premature.'

"We will re-file that motion if the appellate court reverses her dismissal of the Avery post-conviction motion. Her dismissal orders fail to address the vast majority of issues we raised."

In preparation for this book's publication, Zellner told this true-crime author "it is impossible to predict how long it will take to get the conviction reversed. The case was dead in the water for eleven years when I came on board. I think it is remarkable all of the evidence we have uncovered despite this significant lapse of time."

Overall, Zellner is very proud of what her team has accomplished in less than three full years on Avery's case, starting on it from scratch.

Sooner or later, other courts, other more sophisticated judges, other more experienced judges, will take notice.

"We have demonstrated that all of the State's forensic evidence used to convict Mr. Avery is flawed because none of this evidence can be replicated," she said. "By that I mean the blood was selectively dripped in the RAV4. Neither the quantity or location of the blood came from an actively bleeding finger."

The bullet used to persuade jurors of Avery's guilt is another major component of Zellner's quest to prove her client got convicted on manufactured evidence.

"The bullet with Teresa's DNA on it did not go through her head or any other part of her body," Zellner says convincingly.

"The quantity of DNA on the key and hood latch shows it was planted. No human body was ever burned in Mr. Avery's burn pit. The license plates and electronic devices were easy to plant. If the results of a scientific study cannot be duplicated, the results are considered invalid. The same principle applies here to the State's forensic evidence. It cannot be replicated."

CHAPTER TWENTY-NINE

BOBBY'S GARAGE

When Strang and Buting were preparing for trial, they had retained the services of Pete Baetz, the retired Illinois police detective whose claim to fame was that he was involved in the congressional investigation of James Earl Ray surrounding the 1968 assassination of Martin Luther King Jr. After retiring from law enforcement, Baetz moved back to his native Manitowoc County. However, the defense was handicapped at trial because Kratz had failed to turn over the computer disk with the violent pornography on Bobby Dassey's computer. As a result, Strang and Buting were unable to aggressively present a convincing case pointing the finger at Bobby Dassey as the more likely killer of Teresa Halbach.

Baetz has remained unwavering in his belief that the most likely people involved in Teresa's murder and dismemberment were Bobby Dassey and Scott Tadych. In 2016, he reached out and spoke with Kathleen T. Zellner about his suspicions and never heard back from the firm. Then, in 2018, he got a call out of the blue. It was Zellner.

Baetz told the author that Tadych had apparently become paranoid since Zellner has aggressively put him and Bobby under the microscope. Baetz said he learned from Zellner that Tadych is making sure he picks up all of his cigarette butts for fear that somebody would retrieve them since he could leave his DNA on them.

"The background we had done on him is that we had an individual who had no respect for women and he was aggressive with them," Baetz said. "He is what we cops would call an asshole."

Baetz said the story presented at trial suggesting that Teresa's body was burned in Avery's outdoor burn pile pit was preposterous. Baetz said the burn pit was almost on top of the garage and if the flames got as high as Tadych testified at trial, the entire garage would have gone up in flames and the propane gas tank that was also nearby likely would have caught fire and caused a great explosion.

Baetz said that any old-school detective, someone familiar with flames and burning trash, would have realized Teresa's body was incinerated inside of a fifty-gallon steel drum. Nobody in their right mind would have taken the chance of simply tossing the body outside because the weather elements are too unpredictable.

The use of a burn barrel would allow the killer to conceal the crime because nobody would see there was a body inside unless they physically walked to the barrel and peered inside.

And, the fact remains, several of Teresa's bones were recovered from the bottom of Bobby's burn barrel and nobody else's, Baetz said.

Although Baetz suspects the police from Manitowoc County were involved in rampant evidence planting and manufacturing during the case against Avery, he always doubted the notion that the scattered bones found at Avery's burn pile pit were put there by the cops. For starters, two of the biggest bones that were found turned up on the edge, not within the burn pit itself. Another reason why Baetz didn't think the police put the bones there was because of Bear, Avery's mean and vicious junkyard dog. Baetz said he had a chance to encounter Bear during his time working as the criminal investigator for Strang and Buting.

Bear was the type of dog that would attack and constantly bark if a stranger or prowler ever set foot on Avery's trailer property. The dog was on a metal chain and kept outside. The fact that the dog never went berserk leads Baetz to believe that Teresa's bones were transported under the cloak of darkness from Bobby's yard to the burn pile pit, where the barrel was spilled, but unknown to Bobby at the time, he failed to remove all of the bones, and that's why some of the bones remained at the bottom of his barrel when it was confiscated by the Manitowoc County Sheriff's Office on Sunday, November 6.

Baetz said there were two dubious actions taken by Tadych and Bobby around the time of the crime that also factored into his suspicions that both men had something to do with the killing.

The first was Bobby's first statement to the police, on November 6. That was when Bobby told Dedering he and Tadych both passed each other traveling on State Highway 147 but that the investigator should interview Tadych because Tadych would remember the area where they passed each other going in opposite directions on the two-lane state highway.

"It was very valuable for them to have a mutual alibi," Baetz said. "Again, that was so self-serving."

Whoever killed Teresa also dismembered her body, removing her arms, her legs, her torso, Baetz said. Most people don't realize that dismembering a body is an extremely messy and nasty job, Baetz said. Unlike most of his family, Steven Avery was not an avid hunter, Baetz added, but on the other hand, Bobby and Tadych were both avid hunters and both men had substantial experience at dismembering the carcass of a dead deer.

Both men claimed they were out deer hunting at separate locations around the time of Teresa's murder. However, in the aftermath of Teresa's disappearance, after the Manitowoc County Sheriff's Office was becoming a regular presence on Avery Road investigating Teresa's disappearance, it seems Bobby took the initiative to scour the country roads and find a dead deer carcass, throw it into the back of his truck, and bring it home.

In addition, he also made it a point to visit one of the local convenience stores to make them aware of the deer carcass he retrieved. He obtained a deer tag, which also generated a paper trail, which was handy to have when the police arrived and sought to question him about the blood spatter in his garage.

In the days after the Manitowoc County police began poking around Avery Road following Teresa's disappearance, Bobby Dassey scoured the countryside to retrieve a dead deer. He then kept the butchered deer carcass and hung it inside his garage for many days while the homicide investigation was still ongoing.

At 7:33 p.m. on Friday, November 4, authorities were notified that a deer was struck by a car just east of Larabee.

The following morning, the RAV 4 was identified on the Avery property. A massive police presence took over Avery Road for the next eight consecutive days and when the police opened Bobby's garage to look around, a dead deer carcass was strung up in the air.

The deer, Baetz said, was another perfect diversion to fool the police.

When the police arrived, it appeared as if Bobby was skinning a deer. "It was BS," Baetz said. "And if they dismembered the victim there, the police never did any forensic examination of that spot itself."

Baetz suspects Bobby either saw the deer or heard it on the police scanner and ran out to get it as soon as he could. "It would have been great for covering up the blood," Baetz said.

During the murder investigation, the Dasseys made the police aware they had lawfully taken the deer off the road, furnishing a tag they got at the local store to allow them to keep it.

"I think the deer being hit was a propitious incident. The deer gets hit and they take advantage of a situation that would help. They're always thinking of how can we cover up? There's a backup plan, and that's why they got it certified with a tag through the Department of Natural Resources," Baetz said. "Everything is covered."

Baetz said that dismembering the body inside the garage would be the perfect place to do the dastardly act. The garage would be closed, and it offered the comfort of privacy, unlike taking apart the body out in the woods, for example.

"You do it in your garage. You will be able to control it. That's when it was done and it was done in those burn barrels," he said.

Josh Radandt's affidavit indicates he saw a fire reminiscent of a burning barrel, in the area of where Bobby Dassey lived. "The electronic components of Ms. Halbach were burned in the Dassey burn barrel behind the residence at approximately 4:30 to 5 p.m. That fire was observed in the Dassey burn barrel by Josh Radandt," Zellner's filing states.

Baetz said he's also pretty sure what was used to take apart Teresa's body.

"I think they used a meat saw," he said. "Actually, dismembering a human body is not an easy task. It's extremely difficult. And if you get to take off the limbs, it's a nasty job. But if you've done this to deer before, you're comfortable."

Here are some of the key events of October 31, 2005, concerning Bobby Dassey's behavior, as outlined by Zellner, on August 9, 2018.

"Bobby had developed an obsession with Ms. Halbach and on a number of occasions watched her from his residence and commented on her visits the next day."

"Mr. Avery did not leave the Dassey phone number with Auto Trader because he was waiting for a return call on his cell phone or landline to confirm the appointment. Because Bobby was awake, he would have heard the voice mail message left by Ms. Halbach on the Dassey answering machine at 11:43 a.m. ... Bobby was the only person who could have listened to Ms. Halbach's voice message to the Dassey residence at 11:43 a.m. and known that Ms. Halbach did not have an address for the appointment."

"Bobby lied to the police when he denied knowing that on October 31, 2005, Ms. Halbach was coming to the property."

"Bobby told police that he saw Ms. Halbach by her vehicle for approximately 10 seconds. However, Bobby was able to describe Ms. Halbach's clothing, physique and hair style, indicating that he had more direct contact with Ms. Halbach than simply seeing her out of his window for 10 seconds."

"The Dassey computer Internet browsing data indicates that 22 pornographic searches were made on October 31, 2005. Bobby's computer was in use on October 31, 2005, which impeaches his trial testimony that he was asleep from 6:30 a.m. to 2 p.m. The computer was used to access the Internet on October 31, 2005, at 6:05 a.m., 6:28 a.m., 6:31 a.m., 7:00 a.m., 9:33 a.m., 10:09 a.m., 1:08 p.m., and 1:51 p.m."

"As Ms. Halbach left the property, Bobby followed her in his Blazer."

"Ms. Halbach's cell phone records indicate that she had left the Avery property by 2:41 p.m. and headed west on

State Highway 147 and south on County Highway Q. It was established at trial that Ms. Halbach frequently did hustle shots. Because Bobby lied about following Ms. Halbach from the Avery property, he most likely is the person who waved her down for a hustle shot. Ms. Halbach was in the area of Kuss Road, so it is a reasonable inference that she stopped her vehicle for the hustle shot at the Kuss Road cul-de-sac."

"The blood spatter on the inside of the RAV4 cargo door demonstrates that a struggle ensued between Ms. Halbach and her attacker."

"The dog alerts indicate that Ms. Halbach was in the area of the suspected burial site for a period of time where she may have been assaulted."

The scientific testing by Zellner's crew of world-renowned experts validates her position that the killer put Teresa's unconscious body into the back of Teresa's vehicle and drove the sports utility vehicle back to Avery Road near 4 p.m.

"The hair bloodstain patterns ... were created by Ms. Halbach being placed in the rear cargo area of the RAV4 and her injured head bouncing on the inside panel as the RAV4 was moving. It is a reasonable inference that Ms. Halbach and her vehicle were brought back to the Avery Salvage Yard after she left the property the first time."

There are two supporting eyewitnesses who back up her theory. One individual is John Leurquin, who was a propane truck driver for Valders Co-Op who spent time on Avery's property on Halloween.

He was called as a defense team witness by Strang and Buting. He testified matter-of-factly that "a vehicle similar to Ms. Halbach's drove past him at 3:45 to 3:50 p.m. Mr. Leurquin was uncertain whether the driver was male or female or which direction the vehicle turned as it exited the Avery property."

During the trial, Leurquin testified he loaded his propane truck for commercial and residential customer deliveries "on the southeast corner of Avery Road and 147."(116)

His work schedule was 7:30 a.m. to 4 p.m.

Buting: "Now on October 31, 2005, do you recall seeing any particular vehicle that later it became of interest to you?"

"Uh, yes. I recall seeing a green SUV. Uh, midsize SUV. Not the large size. It was smaller."

"OK. So tell us what you saw?"

"I seen a vehicle pass by the front of my truck, and I just glanced up, and it was a green SUV and that's all."

"Well, which direction was it going?"

"Back towards Avery Road. So that would be to the north. I mean, towards 147. It was leaving."

When asked on the witness stand if he was "a friend of the Avery's" the witness testified, "No."

"Did you happen to see which direction that green SUV went when it got to the intersection of Highway 147?"

"No, I didn't pay attention."

That same afternoon sixteen-year-old Brendan Dassey and older brother Blaine arrived home on their yellow school bus.

"I do not have any personal knowledge of who made the appointment with Auto Trader to have my mother's van photographed but I did help clean the van so that it could be sold," Blaine Dassey said.

"On October 31, 2005, when the school bus driver brought Brendan and me home as we traveled west on State Highway 147, I saw Bobby on State Highway 147 in a bluish or greenish vehicle heading towards Mishicot. Bobby was not driving his black Blazer. Bobby was not home the rest of the evening while I was home." (117)

---

116. John Leurquin, direct testimony March 8, 2007, Avery trial

117. Affidavit of Blaine Dassey, June 25, 2018

Blaine's affidavit also addressed the dark Internet searches made from the Dassey personal computer, the one that his mother hired someone to reformat as the murder case was widening in early 2006.

"There was only one computer at the residence and it was always in Bobby's room sitting near a desk. The computer had a password. The computer had an AOL dial-up Internet connection. Bobby was the primary user of the computer.

"At no time did I ever do searches for pornographic images or words related to pornography, words related to violence, words related to death, words related to mutilations, words related to torture, words related to guns or knives, words related to Teresa Halbach, words related to Steven Avery, words related to DNA, or words related to dead, mutilated, or dismembered female bodies."

Blaine Dassey's sworn statement indicates the only time he used the computer was for homework and occasionally to send instant messages to people.

"At no time did I ever create a folder for Teresa Halbach, my Uncle Steven, DNA, or news stories on the murder."

***

On August 9, 2018, in her thirty-second month representing Avery, Zellner unveiled to Wisconsin's criminal justice system how she suspects the murder was orchestrated and why the property next to Avery was the real site of suspicion.

"It is a reasonable inference that Ms. Halbach was shot by Bobby's .22 LR because Scott Tadych attempted to sell Bobby's .22 LR the next week to a fellow employee at the Wisconsin Aluminum Foundry. The Dassey garage was never luminoled or checked for forensic evidence of any type; however, blood, which was never tested, was found between the Dassey garage and residence."

As far as the victim's vehicle, Zellner argues it was backed into Bobby's garage and then it was dumped by a tree near the Mishicot dam. On Halloween, before sunset, eyewitness Paul Burdick remembers he saw the vehicle on Halloween. Witness Kevin Rahmlow saw the RAV4 in the same spot over the next few days, including November 2 and 3.

The distance to the old dam is 1.7 miles, a twenty to thirty minute walk, according to Zellner.

Zellner has submitted to the court the police statement of Bobby's mother, who was questioned about the deer carcass back on November 6, 2005, which was two days after the deer was killed. However, her statement gave the police the impression the deer was hit on November 3, when that was clearly not the case.

"Barbara Janda told the agents that her son, Bobby, had gotten a deer and that a deer carcass was hanging in Janda's garage. Barbara stated that the deer was gutted out and skinned. Barbara told agents that the deer hanging in her garage had been road kill, which Bobby had received Thursday evening, November 3, 2005."

The statement goes on to explain that mother and son gutted the deer at the site where it was killed. "After Bobby gutted the deer, Barbara and Bobby went to 310 Mobil located between Mishicot and Manitowoc on Highway 310 in order to register the deer … After they hung the deer up, Barbara and Bobby skinned the deer the same night … Barbara told the agents that the deer has not moved from where they had hung it since that time. Barbara told the agents that they only took the inner tenderloins out while the deer was hanging in Barbara's garage."

"It is a reasonable inference that Ms. Halbach was dismembered in the Dassey garage because of Bobby's attempt to conceal evidence by hanging a deer in the Dassey garage and lying about the time frame of when that happened."

On Halloween, the victim's body was put into one of the Dassey family burn barrels and taken over to the Manitowoc County Gravel Pit after dark, Zellner believes. The gravel pit is massive and it's bordered by other gravel pits.

Zellner said that her client asserts that Bobby was the only one in the family who regularly hunted inside the county-owned gravel pit, that Bobby knew the terrain and topography and that he often burned his deer carcass inside a burn barrel.

"Ms. Halbach's body was burned in the Dassey burn barrel and the odor was detected by Travis Groelle as he was working on County Highway Q after sunset. On October 31, Bobby was two hours late leaving for work from the Avery property. He did not leave for work until 11:30 p.m.

"Once the burning of the body finished at the gravel pit, somewhere in the neighborhood of 60 percent of the bones and most of the teeth got taken elsewhere for burning," Zellner maintains. "Some of her bones were inadvertently dropped on the ground in three locations in the Manitowoc gravel pit."

From her review of the Calumet County evidence tag numbers, Zellner realized there were actually three separate locations in the county gravel pit where piles of human bones were recovered by the police. Pile 1 was where the charred pelvic bones were found. However, there was a great distance within the quarry from Pile 1 to Piles 2 and 3. Pile 1 was 474 yards away from Pile 2. The distance from Pile 1 to Pile 3 was 518 yards. On the other hand, the human bones found in Piles 2 and 3 were much closer to each other, a distance of only 48 yards apart.

Zellner said she discovered the existence of the two other human bone piles, in addition to the one with the pelvic bones, after analyzing the evidence tags. The tags contained identifiers for where the bones were found as part of the DCI's investigative police report that was reviewed by Dr. Leslie Eisenberg, the state's forensic anthropologist, who testified for the prosecution at Avery's trial.

The realization that there were multiple sites within the quarry with charred human bones has Zellner convinced that someone was attempting to scatter the bones there by dumping them out of a burn barrel under the cover of darkness.

However, the barrel was put back on Bobby's property still containing a number of charred human bones of Teresa.

On November 3, news broke about Teresa's disappearance and Avery told Bobby and others about Sgt. Colborn's visit to Avery Road to question Avery. At that time, Avery's middle finger injury from two weeks earlier had busted open.

"When Mr. Avery left the property to go to Menard's, Bobby entered Mr. Avery's trailer and wiped up blood from Mr. Avery's sink. He transported the blood to the RAV4 and selectively dripped the blood into Ms. Halbach's vehicle in order to frame Mr. Avery for the murder. Bobby was the only one who could have planted Mr. Avery's blood in the sink during the crucial time period before the blood complexly coagulated."(118)

It's an undeniable fact that Avery saw tail lights by his trailer shortly after he and his brother Chuck headed over to Menard's. "It could only have been the taillights from Bobby's vehicle that Mr. Avery saw by his trailer because no one else could have driven to Mr. Avery's trailer in that time frame. Bobby is the only family member on the Avery property who was present and had access to the blood dripped in Mr. Avery's sink on November 3, 2005."

There were also the physical injuries to Bobby's body.

---

118.   Defendant's Reply to State's Response to Motion to Compel Production Of Recent Re-Examination of the Dassey Computer, August 9, 2018

"Bobby had scratches on his upper back in close proximity to the time of the murder, that were consistent with human fingernails," Zellner argues.

She provided the police photographs that were taken the medical examination room of Bobby's back the week after Teresa disappeared.

In November 2017, Dedering was brought out of retirement and made a special investigator on the case to help the state of Wisconsin which remains in a win-at-all-cost mode in regard to keeping their convictions of Avery and Brendan intact.

When Dedering questioned Bobby during an interview about the computer and the violent pornography, Bobby claimed it wasn't him. He also told Dedering the personal computer was not even kept inside his bedroom.

"In Bobby's 2017 re-interview by the police, he denied that the computer was in his bedroom even though the crime scene video shows the computer in his bedroom," Zellner found.

Zellner said the computer forensic evidence shows in convincing fashion that Bobby gave false testimony during the trial claiming he was still sound asleep until 2 p.m. and woke up shortly after Teresa rolled up to photograph his mom's van.

She said her investigator Steve Kirby interviewed Bobby in 2017 and confronted him about all of the violent pornography on the computer.

She also said he remained steadfast to his story that he was watching from the distance, inside his kitchen window, as Teresa walked over to Steven Avery's red trailer and that he never saw her again.

"He stuck with his story. He was given a chance to admit he was pressured by the cops and he would not," Zellner said. "That's because the lie is his. It isn't a cop lie. It's his lie. He made it up on November 5 (2005) and he's stuck with it ever since."

When asked about the hard-core violent pornography, "my investigator confronted him and he looked ill. He looked like he wanted to throw up," Zellner said. "It's the only thing they talked to him about that elicited some display of emotion."

Zellner said she has been recognized by other lawyers, including prosecutors, for her credibility and willingness to work hand in hand with the other side.

She said she has had a long-standing policy and made it clear to the prosecution side that they can interview her client in the post-conviction process, with the only stipulation being that she can be present during the line of questioning.

She said that many prosecutors have taken her up on her offer because she realized they were interested in fairness and justice, however, in Avery's case, she has always gotten the cold shoulder treatment from the police involved in the Avery case. She said nobody from the state of Wisconsin team of the Attorney General has reached out to her in hopes of re-interviewing Avery about the case or the other people she has identified as the more likely culprits, Bobby Dassey and Scott Tadych.

"We have recently Luminoled the Dassey garage and collected buccal swabs for DNA testing because the police failed to do this," Zellner told the author on October 4, 2018. "There was a blood drop collected between the Dassey garage and house which was never tested. The most damning evidence linking Bobby Dassey to the crime, in addition to the multiple lies he has told, is the presence of Halbach's bones in the Dassey burn barrel which Bobby used frequently to burn deer remains.

"Ms. Halbach was dismembered and burned in a burn barrel according to Dr. John DeHaan and Dr. Steven Symes. The timing of the crime makes the Dassey garage a place of interest that has to be considered as the site of the murder and mutilation of Ms. Halbach."

***

In 2017, authorities in Wisconsin started to become jittery about the prospect of having their murder conviction against Avery fall apart. In other states, such as Nebraska, it's quite common for the Attorney General to call upon an outside police agency to conduct an independent and impartial re-investigation of the entire case, starting from scratch. That's how the Beatrice 6 case came to fruition. The Nebraska Attorney General, a Republican conservative, called for a task force to examine the case. The end result was that six people convicted of the 1985 rape and murder of Helen Wilson, a small-town widow, were ultimately freed and pardoned by the governor of Nebraska. The attorney general, despite backlash from the local sheriff's office, announced in 2008 that the wrong people had been put in prison and that a different person, through DNA, was the real killer.

But with Zellner making the waves rise in Wisconsin, the State's response was to bring John Dedering of the Calumet County Sheriff's Office out of retirement and appoint him to be a special investigator. It seems clear that his role on the case was to maintain the status quo, to make sure Avery and his nephew remain vilified, and that suspicions swirling toward Bobby Dassey and Scott Tadych are minimized or downplayed. In other words, Dedering's task wasn't to reexamine the case with a critical eye, to investigate allegations of evidence planting against some of his long-time work colleagues, such as Mark Wiegert.

Dedering knew what he needed to do. Report back to Wiegert and the Wisconsin Attorney General Brad Schimel with words and written reports of reassurance.

But reading between the lines, Dedering's sixty-two-page report makes it obvious which items he and the others who are interested in the preservation of their cases against Avery and Brendan Dassey are deeply concerned about regarding Zellner's probe into the crucial pieces of overlooked evidence from their investigation in 2005.

"Radandt was asked about the lights that he mentioned in the Manitowoc County pit. Radandt stated they were large search lights. Radandt was asked about the pelvic bones. Radandt stated that attorney Kathleen Zellner's team or the media mentioned the pelvic bones. Radandt stated he was never made aware of any pelvic bones by law enforcement." (119)

Dedering also interviewed Ryan Hillegas, the ex-boyfriend of Teresa, who has also been mentioned at times as a possible suspect in her death.

"I asked Ryan about the damage to the left front directional assembly of Teresa's RAV4. Ryan indicated he could not recall who he had spoken with or where he had gotten the information he relayed to Special Agent Tom Fassbender in 2005 regarding the damage and the insurance claim. Ryan stated it was unknown to him who told him about the damage or the claim. I then displayed photographs of the damaged area and the damaged directional to him, but the photographs did not jog his memory." (120)

Another interview involved Bryan Dassey, the older brother of Bobby Dassey and the other Dassey boys. He was twenty at the time of the killing. "Bryan indicated that the reason he did not spend any time around his mother Barbara Janda's residence was that he could not stand Scott Tadych and was not happy with his mother's conduct of still being married while being involved with Scott. Bryan stated he spent enough time at his mother's residence to clean up and then leave on the majority of the days. I asked

119. Interview of Josh Radandt, October 4, 2017, special investigator John Dedering

120. Interview of Ryan Hillegas, October 23, 2017, spec. inv. Dedering

Bryan if he could remember what day the deer carcass was placed in the Dassey garage and he indicated he could not remember."(121)

Finally, it was time to question Scott Tadych. Dedering teamed up with Wisconsin DCI special agent Jeff Wisch and they decided to interview Tadych in a laid back environment to make Tadych feel at ease and not under pressure. The Subway restaurant on Main Street in Mishicot was chosen as the location.

"Scott was asked if he was in any way involved in the homicide of Teresa Halbach and he indicated, 'No, not at all.' Scott was specifically asked if he killed anyone, including Teresa Halbach, and his answer was 'No.'"

At the time of the killing, Tadych lived at a mobile home on State Highway 147, the property was about five hundred yards from where Teresa's SUV was believed to have been put for several days after her disappearance.

Here's what Tadych told the two investigators he was doing on Teresa's last day of life:

"Scott stated his mother had back surgery at Aurora Bay Care in Green Bay on that date. Scott was unsure if the surgery was in the late or early morning. Scott stated that after visiting his mother, he came back to his residence ... in Mishicot between 2:30 and 3:30 p.m. but thought closer to 3:30 p.m. Scott then changed into his hunting clothes and went hunting ... Scott stated after hunting he changed out of his hunting clothes and went to pick up his girlfriend at the time, who is now his wife, Barbara. Scott stated he and Barbara then went back to the hospital in Green Bay to visit his mother some more ..."

As the interview dragged on, another question came up regarding Teresa.

---

121. Interview of Bryan Dassey, November 3, 2017, spec, inv. Dedering

"Scott was asked if he knew or ever met Teresa Halbach and he denied knowing or having ever met her."

It became apparent Dedering's interview had less to do with questioning Tadych about whether he helped conceal Teresa's bones or conspired with Bobby Dassey. The only question concerned their relationship. "Scott stated he gets along OK with Bobby Dassey."

Dedering mostly wanted to talk about Avery, to help reinforce his side's justification for keeping Avery locked away from the outside world.

"Scott went on to indicate that Steven controlled and ruined the Avery family life in the two years that Steven was out of prison."

"Scott was asked if he had done anything that would minimize Steven's involvement such as 'fudging' statements and he indicated he had not."

Curiously, Dedering and his tag along did not ask Tadych the very same question about Bobby Dassey. (122)

The interview took a weird twist when Tadych, at the request of the two police, summoned his wife to the Subway to speak with them as well.

Their questions to her concerned the desktop computer inside her home.

"Barbara was asked about files on the computer titled, 'Teresa Halbach' and 'DNA.' Barbara stated she knew nothing about the files. Barbara stated she had never seen them and had no idea who would have created the files. Barbara denied seeing the page that showed Steven and Teresa together."

Dedering sought to pepper her with a barrage of questions about Zellner.

"Barbara was asked how many times attorney Zellner has been out to the Avery property. Barbara stated she was

122. Contact with Scott Tadych and Barbara Tadych, November 10, 2017, spec. inv. Dedering

unsure of how many times attorney Zellner had been at the property, and, at this point, Scott indicated this is pretty 'hush hush.'"

Minutes later, with her husband sitting with her at the Subway, she was asked why the country's foremost leading expert in exposing wrongful convictions, would be focusing so much attention on people close to her.

"Barbara was asked why she thinks Attorney Zellner is pointing the finger at Bobby and Scott and she indicated she did not know why. Barbara indicated that she never actually provided any evidence to Attorney Zellner concerning this matter."

Back in 2005, Dedering didn't bother to take steps to corroborate Tadych's alibi claiming he had spent much of the day at the hospital in Green Bay. Now, with Zellner lighting fire on the case, twelve years later, Dedering realized he needed to follow up on some of his shortcomings. On November 14, 2017, he contacted Aurora Bay Care Security in Green Bay. "I asked the representative whether there would be any existing video of the parking area or any other video from 2005. The representative indicated no videos exist from 2005 as their hard drive records override existing video every couple of months."

Zellner spent nearly three entire years dissecting the murder investigation before introducing evidence showing why she believes Bobby Dassey and Scott Tadych were involved in the murder and or dismemberment of the body.

Twelve years after conducting his first interview of Bobby Dassey, Dedering went back to question Bobby, now thirty-one. But this was hardly an interrogation. The interview took place on Bobby's terms, in a friendly setting, at his house on Horse Road in Mishicot. In fact, Dedering finished in only fifty minutes.

Zellner's filings to the Wisconsin's courts have made repeated assertions that Bobby has lied repeatedly to the police and during his trial testimony. When Dedering re-interviewed him with Jeff Wisch of the DCI on November 17, 2017, "we asked Bobby if he would be honest and truthful with us." (123)

In 2005, just five days after Teresa vanished, Bobby claimed remembering passing Tadych on the highway, which would have been around the time of Teresa's violent attack, but he urged them to interview Tadych because he would be able to remember exactly where the two passed each other and waved.

Now, with Zellner hot on his tail, the same question came up again, a dozen years later. Bobby, who was foggy before, now had a clear response.

"Bobby stated he saw Scott Tadych on State Highway 147 in the area of Jambo Creek Road. Bobby stated there is a large gravel pit in that area. Bobby stated he met Scott at approximately 3 p.m."

Questions turned to the sequence of events involving Teresa's visit to Avery Road, the last place she was seen alive.

"Bobby stated after he had awoken to go deer hunting, he looked out the front window of his mother's ... residence and saw Teresa's vehicle parked opposite to a van that his mother was going to sell ... Bobby stated the lady got out, started taking pictures and at this point, he got ready to take a shower before hunting. Bobby stated the lady was alone. Bobby stated he spent a couple of minutes in the shower and then got dressed and looked out of his window, again, and saw the lady walking toward Steven's trailer.

"Bobby stated he did not see Steven during this encounter. Bobby stated he spent maybe a couple of seconds looking out the window and during this time she was halfway to Steven's trailer ... Bobby stated he then went out to his vehicle and he did not see her when he got into his vehicle.

123. Interview of Bobby Dassey, Nov. 17, 2017 spec. inv. Dedering

Bobby stated he had no idea who she was so he really did not pay a lot of attention."

He was also questioned about his prior contacts and observations of Teresa, after all, she was a regular at Avery Salvage, having been there about a half dozen times during the previous year or so to photograph various vehicles the family wanted to sell through Auto Trader.

The question was posed if he had ever met or knew Teresa?

"Never."

Another question was asked if he knew Teresa was arriving on October 31?

"Nope."

Bobby didn't have a compelling answer when reminded that Bryan Dassey, his older brother, had given a statement to police back in November 2005, suggesting Bobby saw Teresa leave on Avery Road.

"Bobby was asked why Bryan would say something like this and Bobby responded, 'Your guess is as good as mine.'"

At this point, Dedering was obviously aware that Zellner was poking holes in the State's case concerning the dark secrets hidden on the Dassey computer, the one that was the subject of morbid, sadistic violent pornography searches only at times of the day when Bobby was home alone.

Had Bobby used the Internet and the computer, they asked him?

"If I did, it wasn't often," he answered.

"Bobby stated he thought the computer was on a desk in the living room at the time."

A police video captured by Dedering's colleague, Sgt. Bill Tyson, after Teresa vanished, conclusively showed the tower computer stationed at a desk in Bobby's own bedroom.

"Bobby stated he never downloaded any pornography. Bobby stated he may have watched porn at some point on it, but 'I don't know.'

"Bobby stated there were five guys with access to the computer and he doesn't know if they would have downloaded or viewed pornography ... Bobby identified his brothers, Blaine, Brendan, Bryan, himself, and Tom Janda as being the individuals with access to the computer.

"Bobby stated he did not use the computer much as he was working third shift at the time."

At that point in time, Bryan had a room in the basement, Blaine and Brendan shared a room and Bobby had his own room. (124)

Regarding the computer, the questions persisted.

"Bobby was asked if he knew who created the folder with the page depicting Steven and Teresa's photographs. Bobby indicated he knew how to create folders, but he had no idea as to who created those folders."

Questions about three specific computer folders then arose.

There was a 'Teresa' folder, a 'Halbach' folder, and a 'DNA' folder.

"Bobby was specifically asked who created 'Teresa' and 'Halbach' and 'DNA' folders that were on the computer and he stated he had no idea who did this. Bobby was asked if he did it and he indicated 'No.'"(125)

Finally, the topic of Kuss Road, which was about a half mile away from Avery Salvage, also came up during Bobby's follow-up interview in 2017.

This was the spot where, back in 2005, several cadaver and scent-tracking dogs were all led by their noses to this desolate seldom-traveled road, that was just over the other side of the Radandt gravel pits behind Avery Salvage.

---

124. Telephone contact with Barbara Tadych, Feb. 28, 2018, spec. inv. Dedering

125. Bobby Dassey interview with Dedering, November 17, 2017

"Bobby was unfamiliar with where I was talking about when I mentioned Kuss Road," Dedering's report states. "I then produced a map I had from the Josh Radandt interview and showed him where Kuss Road was located. Bobby indicated he had never hunted on the Radandt property or in the gravel pit. Bobby stated he had never hunted on the area off of Kuss Road."

At no point during the short interview that lasted less than an hour did Dedering and Wisch ask Bobby about why Teresa's bones were inside of his burn barrel, the one he used to slice up and burn his dead animal parts that were part of his hunting escapades. They also did not ask him if he had removed the missing blood taken out of his uncle's sink on the night of November 3.

"Bobby was asked why he and Scott Tadych were being singled out as suspects and he indicated, 'I don't know.'"

"Bobby was asked if he had any involvement in the death of Teresa Halbach and he indicated 'No.'"

Dedering touched on Bobby's testimony against his uncle at the trial, but it was only brief. "I asked Bobby if he had made anything up or had lied during his testimony. Bobby stated everything he said was true and he had no reason to lie during the trial."

Of course, on the other hand, if Bobby Dassey had culpability in the killing and the gross dismemberment of Teresa's body, he would have every reason under the sun to lie.

In 2005, Teresa Halbach had made at least six confirmed visits to Avery Salvage to photograph cars being sold. She was there June 20, August 22, August 29, September 19, October 10, and lastly October 31.

***

Curiously, the Subway restaurant interview of Barbara and Scott Tadych did not bring an end to Wisconsin's re-investigation of the case.

There was still something within Barb's home that Dedering, Wiegert, and others at the Wisconsin Attorney General's Office of Brad Schimel were deeply concerned about. It was a piece of evidence they had scrutinized back in 2006. Now eleven years later, they didn't know whether it might jeopardize their murder convictions.

"After the interview, I returned home to my residence ... in Mishicot. At this time, the investigators requested I turn over my computer tower, which was the same one that was in my home in 2005 and had been examined before. I agreed to turn the computer tower over to the investigators."(126)

On November 10, 2017, the state of Wisconsin law enforcement authorities seized the Hewlett Packard Pavilion computer of Barbara Tadych for the second time. The computer was first seized as evidence in 2006.

This time, something happened. Something was said that gave Barb pause.

"I distinctly remember at the time I turned over the computer tower to the investigators saying, 'I'm thinking of getting rid of this computer.' After I made the comment, Investigator John Dedering replied, 'That would be a good idea and you should not give the computer to Kathleen Zellner.'"

Actually, Zellner has undergone a remarkable transformation herself since she received a handwritten letter addressed to her, dated September 26, 2011. The letter was brief, only four lines long. It was written on a sheet of notepad.

"Ms. Zellner, I saw you on a case on TV. I need you to help me on my case, I'm innocent please let me know. Thank you! Steven Avery."

---

126. Affidavit of Barbara Tadych, August 2, 2018

Seven years later, in September 2018, Zellner was being honored by Maryville University in Missouri with the distinguished Sister Mary Byles Peace and Justice Prize. Sister Byles had served on the Maryville faculty as a professor from 1972 until 1990. The honor bestowed on Zellner was given for her achievements in fighting for civil justice on behalf of people of all walks of life.

"He had written to us and we had looked at it from just what the courts had filed and I saw there was all this forensic science against him," Zellner remarked. "His blood was in the car. His DNA was on her car key in his bedroom. Her bones were in his burn pit. The bullet in his garage had her DNA on it. It's like "Whoa, we were like 'No way. We don't want to take this case.' Then I watched the documentary and I thought, 'Oh, wait a minute. This forensic stuff is bogus. I can tell by watching it how unbelievably superficial it is. No photographs are even taken when they find the bones. They keep the county pathologist from coming on the property."

And that's essentially how Zellner became involved in Avery's crusade to overturn his murder conviction.

"So I thought, I'm going to take and I'm going to hire world renowned experts. I'm going to do ballistics, blood, and if I dump a ton of money in it, I'm going to do it. Because I think this guy is innocent. I'm even going to do brain fingerprinting, that the CIA does, on him."

One of the biggest revelations, according to Zellner, concerns Dr. John DeHaan's analysis of the bones found in Avery's backyard burn pit.

"So I hired John DeHaan, probably the leading fire forensic expert in the world, and he said, 'There wasn't a body burned in that burn pit. He said there's absolutely no evidence.' And he's actually burned human bodies more than anybody in the world, which is a weird occupation. But this is the guy that knows ... He said a barrel was used and forty percent of the bones were tipped into the burn pit. So someone poured bones into the burn pit. He said 'The teeth are missing.' He said, 'The teeth never melt.' And he said if you had burned at a crematorium level of heat at this burn pit, outdoors, you would have burned down the garage and blown up the propane tank. He said you could not sustain the temperature degree for the bones. He said it's totally fabricated. No body burned in there." (127)

And then there was the DNA on the hood latch. Her client's DNA was on the hood latch. "Guess what we found out, we found out that the amount of DNA on the hood latch is ninety, nine-zero, times the quantity that would have been left if a person had just opened a hood latch."

And that led to the quest to track down the elusive swab that had to be taken from Avery and substituted in as the hood latch swab.

"And we found it. They took two groin swabs from him when they had arrested him for a gun charge. So we're like what are you doin' doing groin swabs when somebody's arrested for a gun charge? They pocketed the two groin swabs, because we knew they would be epithelial DNA, and they turned those into the crime lab."

But Zellner's favorite find, she said, was dismantling the prosecution's theory that Teresa was shot in the head with a .22 caliber bullet, which was laying in Avery's garage, but they had just missed finding it the first six times they searched the garage for hard evidence.

"They couldn't find it, couldn't find it, couldn't find it, couldn't find it, then they found it. And they said. 'Whoa, it's got her DNA on it.'"

And then, with the state's permission, Zellner got to bring the bullet to the Microtrace laboratory, which solved the Unabomber case and numerous airline crashes. "It's probably the best forensic trace laboratory in the world. And they looked at it under a microscope, very advanced

---

127. Zellner presentation at Maryville University, September 2018

sophisticated microscope, 'Oh, that bullet, that bullet's got red paint on it and wood. So, wait a minute! Where's the bone. If you shoot a .22 through somebody's head, I don't care how many times you shoot it, the lead is so soft it's like a sponge. It's going to have bone on there. So then I flew to Arizona. I hired Luke Haag. We shot out in the desert .22s through bovine bone and every single one of them was embedded with bone. So what do we know? We know that .22 was stuck in the Avery wood in the garage and they just pried that thing out of there. Again, we found her DNA that traced back to what DNA of hers they used to put on there. Because it also had wax on it and they just happened to have her Chapstick."

Zellner's message to her legions of supporters all around the world is this: don't lose faith in her. Her quest to undo Avery's murder conviction and regain his freedom still remains in the early steps of the post-conviction appeals process.

"It's just staying on it, that's what we did. We're going to be like a wrecking crew with this evidence, and we're going to expose what they thought was a dunk-shot case."

On Nov. 6, 2018, Zellner posted the following statement to her Twitter account, which had ballooned to more than 459,700 followers: "It would be so much easier to walk away, close the door, not spend another dime, believe all the unproven allegations IF we could have just duplicated the State's forensic evidence but neither we nor anyone else can do so.

"Why? Because he is INNOCENT."

Pete Baetz maintains that Avery's vicious junkyard dog Bear would have growled and barked like crazy if a nighttime stranger tried to dump Teresa's bones out of a burn barrel into Avery's backyard. But if the person was someone familiar, Bear would not have barked.

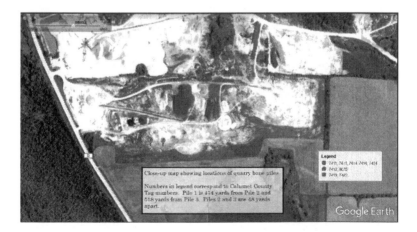

This geographic map shows the terrain for the Manitowoc County Gravel Pits where three different piles of human bones were discovered by authorities.

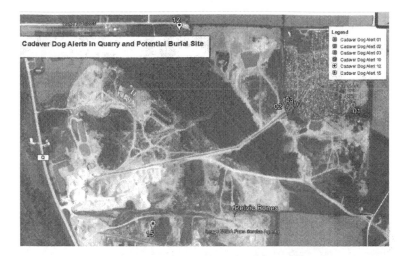

This map shows the areas where the police cadaver dogs picked up Teresa Halbach's scent; notice these are all areas far away from Steven Avery's trailer including near Kuss Road.

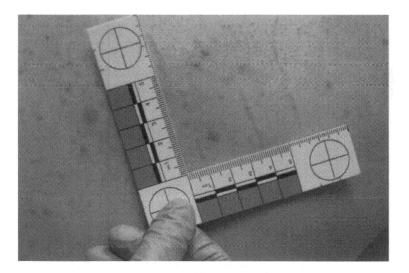

Bobby Dassey claimed these scratch marks on his back were caused by his Labrador puppy jumping on him earlier that same morning, just hours before he was interviewed by two police investigators on the afternoon of Nov. 7, 2005.

*Mark Wiegert, at right, with Jerry Pagel, who was the Calumet
County's Sheriff at the time of Halbach's murder. In 2018, Wiegert
won a close election to become the new sheriff. Meanwhile,
Attorney Kathleen Zellner has uncovered strong evidence
indicating that Wiegert was perhaps intimately involved in
fabricating DNA evidence later used to convict Avery.*

For More News About John Ferak,
Signup For Our Newsletter:

http://wbp.bz/newsletter

Word-of-mouth is critical to an author's long-term success. If you appreciated this book please leave a review on the Amazon sales page:

http://wbp.bz/wca

OTHER WILDBLUE PRESS BOOKS BY JOHN FERAK

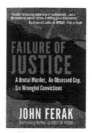

FAILURE OF JUSTICE: *A Brutal Murder, An Obsessed Cop, Six Wrongful Convictions*
http://wbp.bz/foja

DIXIE'S LAST STAND: *Was It Murder Or Self-Defense?*
http://wbp.bz/dixiea

BODY OF PROOF: *Tainted Evidence In The Murder Of Jessica O'Grady*
http://wbp.bz/bopa

THE BIGGEST WRONGFUL CONVICTION CASE IN HISTORY FROM JOHN FERAK AND WILDBLUE PRESS

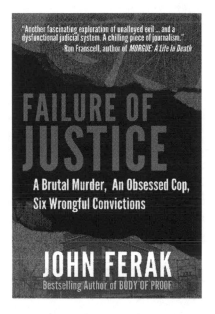

FAILURE OF JUSTICE by JOHN FERAK

http://wbp.bz/foja

Read A Sample Next

CHAPTER 1

THE PROWLER

Tucked away in America's Heartland along the Big Blue River sits an aging blue-collar community accustomed to hearing its name, Beatrice, mispronounced as an old-fashioned name for a woman. Properly addressed as Bee-AT-triss, this small city is nestled in deep southeastern Nebraska, bordering Kansas, a couple of counties over from the murky waters of the Missouri River. The region is dominated by livestock and farming. Summers are hot. Winters on the Great Plains can be downright wicked. Landowners since the first pioneers have faced howling winds and bitter cold.

Beatrice's claim to fame is the Homestead National Monument of America, marking the area's role in the settlement of the American West. Since the mid-1800s, settlers passed through the area on the famous Oregon Trail, many on their way to stake a claim in the federal government's land giveaway. After Congress passed the Homestead Act of 1862, the first application filed was for a piece of land west of Beatrice that is now part of the national monument.

During the last half of the twentieth century, Beatrice fought hard to retain its small-town charm. The population remained relatively stable, hovering around 12,000. Industries such as a dairy plant and windmill and metal manufacturers were longtime employers, but for decades the backbone of the local economy was a state-run institution for persons diagnosed with profound and severe mental retardation. The care facility first opened in the late 1880s as the Institution for Feeble Minded Youth. The forty-acre tract later became known as the Beatrice State Home. Today, it's called the Nebraska State Development Center.

A fascinating footnote about Beatrice: The community is the self-proclaimed "lawn mower capital of the world." Several companies that make lawn mowing equipment are clustered near the city's industrial park. If Beatrice residents don't work at the state mental institution, chances are they or someone they know work in the lawn mower industry.

Beatrice has long been regarded as a pleasant place to call home and, overall, a safe community with very few incidents of violent crime. During the 1980s, a stable city police force consisting of twenty to twenty-five officers provided round the clock courteous service for the citizens.

But even this quaint city forty miles south of Lincoln, Nebraska's capital, was not immune from the stain of the occasional undesirable element. Downtown Beatrice saw its share of riffraff and aimless drifters who patronized the local watering holes and occasionally caused mayhem. Civic leaders and the local churches decried a certain element of the bar culture. Some taverns were a haven for attracting troublemakers, alcoholics, drifters, and dopers. Such customers generally consisted of the uneducated, the poor, unskilled laborers, people with no sense of meaning or purpose in life. Some authority figures loathed the so-called dregs of society who tended to be frequent visitors to the local jail and kept the city's cops constantly busy, being at the forefront of many of the community's crimes.

In 1983, a series of frightening late-night home invasions put residents of Beatrice on edge. The targets of these crimes were all older women who lived alone. That June, a seventy-three-year-old was sitting in her living room, knitting and watching television just before going to bed. Suddenly her life flashed before her eyes as she found herself face-to-face with a young man wearing a full-length stocking cap, with tiny holes cut out for his eyes. He brushed a twelve-inch knife against the older woman's neck, holding the weapon just below her ear. This parasite of a human being was sexually aroused. He clasped his hand over the older woman's mouth to keep her from screaming.

He moved in for the attack, the zipper on his pants wide open. As the attacker tried to pull up her nightgown, the woman bravely fought back. She brushed away his knife. Then she kicked him in the groin. The man felt immediate, intense pain. He tumbled backward and fell on the living room floor. When he got off the floor, he whimpered and tucked the knife back into his belt. He no longer lusted for rape. Instead, he bolted straight for the door and ran out into the night. Thanks to the cloak of darkness, the prowler managed to get away, police reports show.

Obviously, this particular woman was lucky. She escaped with only small minor cuts to her thumb. Flustered, she told Beatrice police officers that her attacker appeared tall and thin. He wore a dark shirt and khaki pants, she thought. Over the course of several days, detectives aggressively investigated the attempted sexual assault, but police had little else to go on. These were the days before cellphones and video surveillance cameras were everywhere.

No one was immediately arrested for the attack. Six weeks passed before another horrifying incident.

Around 10:00 p.m. that night, a woman in her seventies who lived on Ella Street suddenly heard a strange noise. Curious, she wandered through her house to investigate. When she flipped on the light switch, there was a prowler creeping around her garage. The light startled him, and he made a mad dash into the night, police reports show.

Later that night, another elderly woman was in a chair minding her business inside her house on Bell Street. She was caught in total shock when a masked intruder appeared at her side. He clutched her throat. He wedged his knees between hers. This was life or death, she sensed. The eighty-two-year-old screamed loudly. Her shrieks of panic startled the would-be rapist, whom the woman described to police as being about twenty years old with straight blond hair parted down the middle. He jumped off her and darted for the door.

Yet another violent rape was averted in Beatrice. The distressing news, of course, was that it seemed the late-night prowler who pulled a knife on one of his victims that night was not finished terrorizing elderly Beatrice women. By August, this so-far frustrated predator was growing more brazen. He seemed fearless about being caught. He decided to return to the residence on Elk Street where he had hidden inside a woman's garage, only to be scared off when she turned on the light. This time, the seventy-one-year-old was fast asleep when he made his move. At 12:40 a.m. a sudden and jarring noise awoke her. She lifted her head, but quickly dismissed the sound. She turned over and fell back asleep not knowing the attacker had cut a hole through her back screen door. Once inside the dark house, he sneaked into her kitchen. He was careful not to make any loud commotion. There in her kitchen, he pulled a long steak knife from one of the drawers. He tiptoed through the darkened home until he came to her bedroom door. He flipped on the light switch. The woman awoke. She saw the stranger towering over her bed, his face concealed with a rag he stole from her garage. The predator lunged at her. He brushed the knife against her throat.

"If you scream, I'll kill you," he growled.

Even faced with grave danger, she screamed her lungs out anyway. She hoped everyone in Beatrice would hear her. As she tried pushing her attacker away, he punched one of her eyes. Luckily, she freed herself from his grip and fended him off. She escaped from her bedroom and hustled outside. Dazed, the rapist ran out the door, turned away again.

The victim suffered minor cuts to her neck, left thumb and right little finger, but luckily she was not seriously harmed. Another courageous and determined older woman had managed to escape the grip of this young attacker. But no matter how many times he was turned away that summer, there seemed to be no stopping his behavior.

***

All four of those incidents transpired within a six-week period. It was a tough ordeal for the city's police force, who didn't know when the serial predator would strike next. The police did not want fear and paranoia to rule their normally safe and peaceful town. Above all, the cops did not want every elderly woman in town to be consumed with fear as they went to bed every night.

Officers knew they were trying to nab an abnormal perpetrator. It was uncharacteristic for the small-town force to be challenged by a sexual deviant with an appetite for older ladies. Perhaps he was a troubled teenager who attended the local high school, some officers suggested. Whoever he was, the police suspected he was sure to try to invade the home of another woman when she least expected.

But then … that did not happen.

No more older women were victimized inside their residences that fall and winter. Then Beatrice made it through all of 1984 without a single such home invasion. Some officers thought the predator skipped town. Others figured he landed in jail or ended up in prison for an unrelated crime such as a residential burglary. In fact, if a different town's cops had arrested him, the chances would be good that those officers had no knowledge of the rape attempts in Beatrice.

In any event, all remained nice and quiet in Beatrice as the city celebrated the Christmas holidays and welcomed New Year's Day 1985. Snowplows kept the paved streets easily passable for travelers that winter. Children loved the cold weather because it meant snowball fights and snow angels. Overall, residents in the Heartland were resilient as always -- not just in braving the cold, but embracing the chill with mittens, insulated jackets and warm stocking hats as a part of life in the cold-weather region.

As the winter dragged along, February 5, 1985, would mark one of its coldest nights on record. But it wasn't the extreme chill that would burn that date into the community's consciousness and bring Beatrice widespread infamy some years later. It was the traumatic violence that night that visited Unit 4 of an unassuming apartment building on the town's main thoroughfare.

***

Mrs. Helen Wilson had dark gray hair. She stood about five feet tall, weighed about 110 pounds, and was regarded as a fiercely independent woman. She was also a longtime widow. Her husband, Ray, died of a heart attack during the 1960s, when he was only fifty-four. After burying her husband, Helen Wilson never remarried. In fact, her close friends and family were absolutely sure that she never had any male suitors or romantic acquaintances in the years after her husband's untimely death. Helen Wilson was known as a dignified, helpful lady around Beatrice. She had a sharp mind and liked to stay active. On Sundays, she volunteered in the children's nursery at her Methodist church. For leisure, she played bingo several nights each week at the local church halls. She usually bounced between the local Catholic Church and the Fraternal Order of Eagles Club.

Two of Wilson's three grown children still remained in Beatrice, but one of her sons lived far away, at the other end of the state. Regardless of distance, the Wilsons stayed a close-knit family. In January 1985, as Helen Wilson was approaching her sixty-ninth birthday, she boarded a bus to visit her son Larry, who lived in Scottsbluff, near the Wyoming border. The Beatrice woman was excited to spend time with family. "When we picked her up, she was wearing this little crocheted beret type hat with a plastic lining she had made," recalled Wilson's daughter-in-law Edith "Edie" Wilson of Scottsbluff.

"Come to find out she had washed her hair that morning and it was in rollers. She wore the hat to cover the rollers. When she took off the hat, her hair was still wet from wearing the plastic. Later she became very sick from this."

Still, the visit was a great time to bond with her faraway family. While in western Nebraska, her grandson Mark graduated from a welding technical school out in Casper, Wyoming. Wanting to savor the memories, Helen snapped numerous keepsake photographs of her smiling grandson posing with his diploma. That would also be one of the last times Helen Wilson was happy.

Unfortunately, Helen developed a terrible, nagging cough during her two-week stay in western Nebraska. As her cold persisted, Helen contemplated seeing a doctor. "I didn't want to call him on the weekend so I kind of talked her out of it … At one point she said, 'I wish someone would just shoot me,'" Edie Wilson recalled years later.

The next day, Saturday, was crazily busy around the Wilson household in Scottsbluff. Two of Helen's teenage grandsons, Shane and Tadd, competed in a wrestling tournament, and both earned their win into the championship finals for their respective weight divisions. Larry Wilson knew this was an extraordinary accomplishment so during a break in the matches he rushed back home to pick up his mother. They made it back to the high school just in the nick of time so she could cheer on both of her grandsons from the bleachers. Both of the Wilson boys won their wrestling weight classes that day and the family was in a joyous mood. "I can still hear her laughing proudly as they won," Edie Wilson said. "Again, out came the camera and a lot of pictures were taken with the boys and their medals. These were to be the last pictures she took and were taken of her."

The next day Helen Wilson decided to return to Beatrice.

"On Sunday morning, she wanted to go home and see her own doctor and sleep in her own bed," her daughter-in-law said. "We took her back to the bus station. She slipped Larry twenty dollars just like she always did when she left."

Several hours later, the large Greyhound bus rolled into the depot in Lincoln, Nebraska. Wilson wore her beret and clutched her suitcase as she saw her relatives there to welcome her. She was relieved to get a ride back to Beatrice, the final leg of her long journey.

Wilson lived at 212 N. Sixth St., a three-level brick apartment building near the heart of downtown Beatrice. Most people around the community knew the structure as the former Lincoln Telephone & Telegraph Co. building. Beatrice's Sixth Street is otherwise known as U.S. Highway 77, the main thoroughfare for motorists heading into and out of town. The apartment building made of high-quality masonry brick was built around 1900. During the 1980s, the complex was bordered by the green space of Charles Park, Beatrice Public Middle School, professional offices, a funeral home and a few smaller apartments. A church sat across the street.

Wilson had lived in the building since the mid- to late 1970s, and it served her needs. Her apartment was within walking distance of numerous downtown retail stores and shops. She grew comfortable living here. It was home. In addition, her sister, Florence, and Florence's husband, Ivan "Red" Arnst, lived right next door, in Unit 5, also on the second-floor level. When you entered the unlocked building and scampered up a short flight of carpeted stairs, Wilson's apartment was the very first door in the second-floor hallway. The names of the tenants were etched on their doors and also on the building's mailbox for postal deliveries.

Wilson's apartment was a simple and economical four-room unit. In her small kitchen had a stove, a refrigerator, cabinets, and her trusty coffeepot. A large bay window in her living room overlooked the sometimes busy traffic passing along U.S. 77 in the distance. She kept her apartment immaculate and decorative. However, one of the drawbacks of living even on the second and third floors was the potential loss of personal privacy. If residents failed to shut their drapes or blinds at night, people walking along Sixth Street could peer into those units and view a tenant's activities, especially if the unsuspecting renter had his or her lights on.

Less than two blocks south of the old telephone building was Court Street, otherwise known as State Highway 136, and the handful of drinking establishments that operated in the vicinity of Sixth and Court Streets. A place known as the R&S Bar was about four blocks southwest of Wilson's apartment building. A friendly watering hole known as The Little Bar was just two blocks away. Wilson did not frequent the local drinking establishments, but the local riffraff who did would pass by her apartment building as they headed to and from the bars, day and night.

That first Sunday night in February 1985, Wilson towed her suitcase in hand into her apartment building. She trudged up the brief flight of stairs. Finally, she stared down the narrow illuminated hallway. At long last, it was a relief to be home, though she knew she was very sick.

***

Two days later, it was February 5, and Wilson's nagging cough had not let up. In fact her health was becoming progressively worse. At about 6:00 p.m. that Tuesday, her sister Florence cooked up some hamburgers next door and brought them over for Helen's supper. Florence and her husband regularly cooked Helen's meals. They also ran errands and fetched her groceries, reports show. After Wilson ate her burger, her son Darrell, who lived in Beatrice, paid her a visit. While there, he drank two cans of Miller beer that he found in his mother's refrigerator. Mother and son sat with the television on in the living room, where Helen also kept a bowl of fruit and another with baked cookies. Later on, Darrell's wife, Katie, came over after she finished her regular Tuesday night bowling league. Darrell and his wife both expressed deep concern about Helen's poor health. Since they knew she was stubborn, they promised to call her around midnight to make sure she took her daily dose of medicine. They didn't want her to end up in a hospital bed. Wilson gave them a warm smile as her son and her daughter-in-law left her apartment at approximately 9:45 p.m. They shuffled down the short flight of stairs and drove home. Outside, it was unbearably cold. Temperatures had plunged below zero. Practically nobody was out wandering the streets of Beatrice that awfully frigid Tuesday night.

With her family gone, Wilson retreated to her back bedroom. She slipped off her clothes and put on a blue nightgown. She wore a pair of calf-length nylons and booties to keep her legs and feet warm. Before going to bed, she removed her dentures. She put her false teeth on her bedside table. The cluttered table also contained a washcloth, a handkerchief, an empty glass, a piece of fruit, and a Kmart-brand tissue box. The weary widow with the nagging cough turned off her bedroom light. She snuggled into her cozy warm blankets and drifted off to sleep.

As the night wore on, Wilson's sleep was likely disrupted by her severe, persistent cold. A sea of white tissues would be found uncharacteristically littering the floor around her bed. But the rest of her apartment remained immaculate, just the way Wilson always tried to keep her place.

***

As far as the other tenants were concerned, that Tuesday night was uneventful in the three-story apartment building. Of course, this was not a fraternity house. Renters were not accustomed to keg parties, stereos blaring rock 'n' roll music or obnoxious noise complaints. The tenants who resided in the old Lincoln Telephone & Telegraph building were typically the elderly or younger single working women. People who lived there minded their own business. Night after night, residents slept soundly and comfortably, and February 5, 1985, didn't seem any different, except for the blistering cold winds howling outside the sturdy brick building as the temperature plunged to minus 7 degrees.

Then, without warning, a strange sequence of events struck the normally well-maintained apartment building. The hallways on all three levels suddenly grew dark as a cave. For reasons unknown at the time, the power went out. The abrupt, middle of the night mechanical failure also left tenants without precious heat, though most didn't immediately notice because they were already sound asleep. However, when they awoke the next morning, February 6, they knew something was amiss because their apartments felt cold as a meat locker.

***

Before most of Beatrice woke up that Wednesday, a young aimless drifter with pock holes or some other kind of marks on his face wandered into the Gas 'N Shop around 6:00 a.m. The gas station was a short distance from the old telephone building. The twenty-one-year-old clerk behind the counter, Jerry Rowden, was alone when he spotted the unfamiliar customer with shaggy, dark brown hair dangling past his ears. The young man, about the same age as the clerk, approached the front counter to pay for one bag of Doritos. To his embarrassment, two more bags of Doritos concealed in the customer's long, tan-colored Army bomber jacket fell to the floor. The clerk glared and asked if he intended to pay for them. Yes, the man who looked like a drifter meekly replied. He reached into his pockets and scrounged together enough money to pay for all three Doritos bags. Afterward, the young man walked out the Gas 'N Shop and headed west.

A few weeks later, the store clerk was asked for his best recollection about the suspicious snack-food thief. During that interview with Beatrice police, the Gas 'N Shop clerk remembered something else that stood out, something dark and eerie. The employee thought he saw stains of blood on the young man, police records state. However, these were the days before retail stores had nonstop video surveillance cameras recording. The police had to rely upon the clerk's memory. Unfortunately, too much time had elapsed for the clerk to remember any more specific details about the young man's appearance. Not helping matters, the police furnished Rowden with a woefully outdated photo of a young man they were seeking, from when he was fourteen or fifteen. The gas station clerk studied the photo and told them that "the facial features were familiar but the hair was not, and he was then advised that the photo was approximately seven to eight years old," police reports state.

***

At the apartment building in Beatrice on that frigid morning, Florence Arnst hadn't heard a peep from her ailing sister next door. She knew Helen's lingering cold showed no improvement.

Shortly after 9:00 a.m. on Wednesday, February 6, Florence told her husband, Ivan, that she was going next door to check on Helen. At the door, Florence called for her sister. Her beckoning call drew no response. Fortunately, Florence had a spare key. She reached into her pocket and opened the door. When she walked into the unit, Florence did not notice anything out of the ordinary. However, the elderly woman's eyesight was failing miserably. As she walked through the apartment, Florence overlooked the fresh bloodstains on her sister's bedroom walls and the bedsheets that were in disarray. When she checked the bathroom, Florence didn't find her sister there, either. Eventually, she walked past the living room a second time and realized to her surprise that her sister was lying on the floor. Helen appeared to be sleeping, she thought. But something did not seem right. Florence summoned her husband to check on her sister's well-being. His eyesight was far better.

Right away, he saw that his sister-in-law was nude from the waist down and lying stretched out on her living room carpet, her face completely concealed. Towels covered her head. A thick, winter scarf was tightly wrapped around her eyes and face and used to gag her mouth. Ivan "Red" Arnst bent down. He touched her body, trying to determine if his sister-in-law, who brought so much warmth into the world, was still alive.

http://wbp.bz/foja

WRONGFULLY CONVICTED OF OLDEST COLD CASE FROM ALAN R. WARREN AND WILDBLUE PRESS

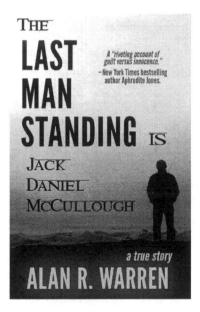

THE LAST MAN STANDING by ALAN R. WARREN

http://wbp.bz/tlmsa

Read A Sample Next

CHAPTER 1 — INMATE #M33566

I love meeting new people. I think everyone has a story to tell. We should all listen sometimes. – Kim Smith

I am reminded every day by things around me of just how easy it is to be fooled by appearances. This came to mind the first time I met Jack McCullough. In my mind, I was about to meet a man who was convicted of kidnapping and murdering a 7-year-old girl by the name of Maria Ridulph back in 1957 in Sycamore, Illinois.

After all, what could a man like this be like? What perception of that kind of man would you have if you knew nothing about him other than the reason he was convicted and put into prison? With this alone, I would think of a rough, heartless, maybe even sociopathic character.

After reviewing the interrogation tapes of Jack during the investigation of Maria's murder and finding as many pictures as I could, I thought that I was ready. I saw Jack as a large, mechanic-like figure, not easily swayed, and one who had no problem looking the detectives directly in their eyes during the questioning. He was obviously a smart man and knew how to talk with most anybody. Remember, this was before prison, so add a lot more aggression and anger along with the strength to survive prison with murderers, rapists, and men with absolutely nothing to lose as they were incarcerated for life.

It was a bright spring day in 2017 when I headed to the place I would meet with Jack. It was at a restaurant located in Edmonds, Washington, on the bay looking out on Puget Sound. It had a beautiful view of the Olympic Mountains and sandy beaches, with quite a few families out enjoying one of the first warm days in the Northwest.

When I arrived and parked, I started running through many of the questions that I wanted to ask Jack, trying to make sure that they sounded polite and respectful, but still invasive enough to explain the events in a logical way.

I looked out of my car window and noticed the back of a man's head wearing a cowboy hat. This was how I was to recognize Jack. I couldn't see his face, only his back, as he walked through the restaurant door and up the stairs to the dining room.

I quickly got out of my car, entered the restaurant, and ran up the stairs, not wanting to keep Jack waiting. As I reached the top step, I looked around the host area and noticed a gray-haired man with a cowboy hat standing patiently. He seemed small, much smaller than I expected. Could this be Jack?

I walked across the lobby to him, introduced myself, and asked if he was Jack. He smiled, said yes, and quickly excused himself as he had to use the washroom. When he got out, we were seated at a table that had an incredible view of Puget Sound. It was just then that a large man came up behind us, and Jack looked at him and said, "Hi, yes, this is okay. I'm okay with him, this is going to be fine."

I didn't realize that there would be someone else there, and why would there be?

Jack looked at me and said, "Yeah, he's just there to make sure that I'm okay, no problem." The first thing I asked Jack was if he got a lot of threats or had problems with people. "Oh, sometimes. There's still a lot of people that think I did it, you know? Even after they proved I didn't and let me go. I know how to read people; that's something I learned to do."

Jack then had a large smile as the waitress approached our table to take our drink orders. He was very polite and seemed really happy to be out having lunch. "I love it here," he said as he looked out over the bay. "When I first came here, I saw the ocean and knew I'd live here. I mean, who wouldn't fall in love?"

Just then, Casey Porter, Jack's son-in-law, came and sat down beside me. Jack asked Casey if he wanted lunch, but Casey said he just wanted to say hi and he had to go to work. "Well, okay," Jack responded, and then looked at me and said, "I couldn't make it without him. He's been great," referring to Casey, "but he thinks I'm a racist. Have you seen my book?" Jack asked me. I replied I hadn't. "Here," he said as he handed me a small, 60-page self-published book called "You Don't Know Jack." He explained that it was his memoir from his time in prison. Jack had kept a diary of sorts and after he got out of prison he decided to self-publish it. I was excited to read it, as it would give me a window into his thoughts during the time he had been incarcerated.

After Jack handed me the book, Casey got up and smiled, said his goodbyes to both of us, and left for his work. Jack stood up and shook his hand, and then returned to his seat and continued on about how Casey thought he was racist because of his book.

Jack's book has a section that talks about American society and how it tore apart the family by allowing women to work rather than stay home and care for the family. I could understand why people could jump to the judgment of it being misogynistic, but after taking a closer look at what Jack wrote and talking with him, I understand what it is that he was trying to get across to people.

Jack has a good memory of life with his mother running the household—not just cooking dinners, washing the clothes, and cleaning the house, but actually taking the time to care for the members of the household, solving their problems, and discussing events in life and their problems at school. Looking back, I think it was more about having someone to guide the children in their early life, and I can agree that it's more helpful to have that than not.

I'm not exactly sure why Jack brought that particular subject up. Maybe to try and clear the way or maybe to see how I felt about that kind of subject. Either way, I moved right on and asked him how his relationship with his mother was. Jack started to tell me how much he loved his mother before the waitress approached the table with our drinks and took our lunch order.

Jack, who was holding a copy of his book, then asked the waitress if she would like a copy. The waitress smiled and you could tell she was surprised, but she took it from him anyways. Jack is a very charismatic talker and always holds a smile, and it's a real smile. He is very genuine and really appears to love talking with people. He was so excited that the waitress was really interested in his book and story. Jack's expression reminded me of a man who just watched his favorite sports team win the big game.

As soon as the waitress walked away, Jack started to tell me about his life in England with his mother, and how during the war she met the man who would soon become his stepfather, and they moved to Sycamore, Illinois, in America to start a new life.

Jack would then proudly tell me about how while he was in prison he had learned four other languages. Not only did he learn to speak them, but he also learned to write them. Jack would jump around from subject to subject in his conversation. It almost seemed like he had so much to tell me, but not enough time to tell it.

Jack learned some of the toughest languages around, such as Chinese, Japanese, and Arabic, especially at an adult age. He told me that there were some really smart people in prison he had met who constantly worked on improving their minds. Jack would spend as much time as possible in the library trying to find out information about all sorts of things, including history. He told me that he had a lot of time to waste and wanted to put it to good use and learn something.

Jack told me he could have easily spent his time doing nothing or doing something useless, such as gambling. Jack then brought up how whenever somebody asked him when he would be getting out of prison, he would tell them that it would be the day he died. In his mind, he was never getting out of prison. This stuck in the back of my mind, and I wondered why a man who was sentenced to prison and thought he would never be getting out would spend so much time and effort on studying four languages and trying to gain so much knowledge about history?

The waitress brought our lunch to the table and after a quick exchange with her, we both began to eat. Jack had ordered a seafood pasta and I had a salad. I didn't say much while we were eating, and Jack mainly commented on the view while looking out the window at our table. You could see the love he had for the ocean and beach surroundings that Edmonds offered. It was the look of having seen the eyes of a long-lost love on his face.

It was after the waitress had cleared away our finished plates that Jack first looked me directly in the eyes with a more serious demeanor and told me that he didn't want any dirt in the story. He told me the minute I asked anything about sex, he would stop talking to me. I was taken aback for a second, but I really didn't have that thought in my mind, so I assured him that was not what I wanted in the story either. He finished by telling me not to ask about his sister.

After all of the pain and struggle Jack had been through in the last years, he was still protecting his sister. I found this to be admirable, and I think it also shows the kind of character that Jack possessed, even after his sister betrayed him. Jack then told me that as long as I told the truth and didn't print any dirt, I wouldn't have a problem with him.

"Did you know Maria Ridulph?" I asked directly.

"I only remember her when she was about 3 years old. Maria was walking down the street one day, as I was going to the store. This was only about 50 yards from her house, but very near a very busy street, where my dog got killed." Thinking about his dog being killed by a car, he decided to warn Maria. He told her she shouldn't be there, and to go home. Jack said Maria turned around and headed toward her home, and that was the last time that he saw Maria.

Jack described Maria as "so lovely," dressed like she was going to church. Jack had used that description before in other interviews he had done, and it created some back talk because of his use of the term "lovely." Jack would answer that by saying that it wasn't the correct term, that Maria was precious, and that all children that age were precious. We also have to remember that Jack was only a young teenager at the time that he reports this event happened with Maria.

Jack then went on, saying, "I'm a protector. I'm a born protector. I'm from a long line of military people."

Jack then started telling me about the corruption and injustice, and that the most important thing I could know was that what had happened to him could happen to anybody. Anybody could be convicted and sent to prison, even if they were innocent. Jack then went into his conviction and how the whole courtroom let out a loud cheer, and everybody was hugging each other, smiling, and even laughing.

Jack's first thought was that this was real; he was a convicted child killer. Jack was also a former police officer, and those were the biggest two things you did not want to be in prison.

After the conviction, they removed Jack from the courthouse under heavy guard and took him to jail. One of the most important things to Jack was to contact his wife once he got there to make sure she knew that he was okay. But the guards withheld Jack's code so that he was unable to call anybody, which left his wife to think that he didn't want to talk with her. Jack brought up the point that his wife had not been found guilty of anything, so why did they treat her so badly? It would be two months before Jack was finally able to call her.

Jack then told me how he had chosen well when he married her, as she stuck by him the whole time.

Eventually, Jack was taken to the maximum-security prison at Menard in Southern Illinois. Menard Correctional Center was officially opened in 1878 and was originally used as a military prison during the civil war. This was also the prison where executions were held by the state.

Jack told me that after you arrive at the prison, the guards make you get naked. They tell you to move your private parts, bend over, spread your cheeks, and cough. After your shower, they give you your clothing and bedding. He then told me that the cells were like dungeons, very cold and damp, and most times you would sleep with your clothes on to keep warm.

The first three months Jack was in Menard, he said there were three inmates who were killed as well as a pastor and two guards who were beaten badly in the church.

Jack then went on to talk about his experience when he arrived at Pontiac Correctional Center in Illinois. Because of Jack's heart condition and age, they gave him the bottom bunk in his cell. The bottom bunk in prison is always given to the toughest or meanest guy, and that just happened to be the guy who lost his bottom bunk to Jack! The guy was a Texan mechanic who had murdered somebody, and when he returned to his cell to find Jack was in his bed, he was livid. To top things off, he found out that Jack was an ex-cop and child kidnapper and murderer; all the more reason to kill him. It would not even take two days for the Texan to threaten to slaughter Jack. Jack reported it to the guards, and soon after he was moved to another cell with a different cellmate. Jack said that the new cellmate was short and he didn't consider him much of a threat, which he later found out was a mistake.

The day after he had been placed in his new cell, Jack took his afternoon shower and went back to his cell to take a nap. Shortly after he fell asleep, he thought he was dreaming and something kept hitting his head. Before opening his eyes, Jack brushed his face with his hands to try and stop the feeling of whatever was hitting him. He then felt something long and pen-shaped slip through his fingers. He opened his eyes quickly and saw his cellmate viciously stabbing at his face with what appeared to be a toothbrush.

The toothbrush penetrated through to the back of Jack's eye socket twice. His eye filled with blood and popped out of the socket by about half an inch. Jack quickly sat up and pushed his eye back into the socket, which forced a large squirt of blood to fly out about six feet. The cellmate attempted to keep on stabbing Jack with his toothbrush, but now he was only able to reach Jack's back and the side of his head and was able to cut Jack's ear. Soon, the guards came, stopped the attack and eventually took Jack to the hospital, where the doctors were able to help Jack regain his eyesight.

Jack then told me how corrupt things were, and his message was to tell people to do something about it before they, too, became a victim like he was.

"These folks tried to destroy me; they found people to lie about me," Jack firmly stated. "They have manufactured evidence and gave false testimony to the grand jury," he continued. "They all profited and enjoyed some fame, and some have retired with good retirement. Some still have their jobs, so we are all in danger from these corrupt officials who neither know nor care about the Constitution. This story is bigger than me; it's about what they can do to you."

The waitress brought over the bill for lunch and Jack refused to let me pay. He grabbed it and paid for lunch. He stood up and suggested we go to a park down the road and talk more. I agreed and followed Jack into the parking lot. He turned around and asked if I wanted to ride with him. I declined. I didn't want to leave my car in the parking lot, as it was a foreign car I had driven down from Canada and I didn't feel comfortable leaving it alone there. Jack smiled and said that he knew I wouldn't, because I didn't trust him, and he laughed. "You see? I do know how to read people."

We both got into our cars and I followed Jack to a park that was located only a few miles away from the restaurant. We parked. Jack walked to a picnic table located up on a hill in the park that overlooked the beach and Puget Sound and sat down. I followed him over to the table and sat across from him. He looked up and asked me what I wanted to know.

For some reason, I was at a loss for what to ask. I was still thinking about how I could find out more about Jack's relationship with his sisters. I wanted to know why his sister would lie about Jack in the way she did. I was still thinking about the family dynamic and trying to figure out what could have happened in the past between the family members. Now, I look back at my train of thought, see how wrong it was and what the real story was surrounding the events that happened to Jack, exposing the reasons it happened and that it wasn't really about his family relationships. After all, the injustice that happened to Jack could happen to anybody; it wasn't about the breakdown in his family, but the breakdown in the justice system and the members behind the corruption who run the legal system now.

Quite often throughout the day, Jack would stop talking, or just after he'd ask a question, he would look me dead in the eyes, smile, and sing "O Canada." This was one of those moments. Even though he had done this several times already, it would make me stop thinking about the case and return his smile.

Jack then asked me if I had ever met Jeff Doty, the man who wrote the book about him called "Piggyback." I told Jack that I had interviewed Jeff, he seemed like a real nice guy, and that I had also interviewed Charles Lachman, the author of "Footsteps in the Snow," which was also turned into a Lifetime movie. He then sneered and told me that Lachman wouldn't know anything about the truth. I could tell that he was upset by Lachman because of his work on the story.

Lachman, to me, seemed like a nice guy both times I had interviewed him years earlier, but I do question his motives in not only writing his book the way he did, with Jack being guilty with absolutely no doubt, but also making a movie out of the script at a time when we all knew Jack was to be released from prison with his conviction overturned.

Not wanting to have the rest of the afternoon focused on Lachman and his work, I steered the discussion toward how he was treated by people now that he had been released from prison. He answered me by saying that people will believe what they want to, but he also didn't care. "I am not important, so they can say what they want. Most people were told lies about me, and the liars will be exposed, and that will make my time spent in prison count for something."

I thought that we had spent enough time together by now to follow up on the question of Jack being a racist at the very beginning of our meeting. I asked Jack why Casey considered him a racist; after all, thinking that the mother of a family should stay home to take care of the home rather than go out and work a job is hardly what I would consider racist.

Jack responded by telling me the story of when one of the judge's employees asked Jack what caused him stress, and Jack had answered, "Blacks, Muslims, and Democrats." Even though he was halfway joking with her, he blamed that slip of the lip on the fact that all of his cellmates fit at least one, and sometimes all three, of those labels.

http://wbp.bz/tlmsa

**COMING IN FEBRUARY FROM STEVE JACKSON
AND WILDBLUE PRESS! PREORDER NOW!**

SAVING ANNIE: A TRUE STORY by STEVE JACKSON
http://wbp.bz/savinganniea

Read A Sample Next

CHAPTER ONE-*The 911 Call*

March 16, 2009
Hood River County, Oregon
6:09 p.m.

When the 911 call came into the Hood River Sheriff's Office, it wasn't so much what the caller said, but how he said it. His voice neither rose nor fell as he phlegmatically relayed the information.

911 OPERATOR: *"911, where is your emergency?*

CALLER: *"Hello. I need help. I'm at, uh, Eagle Creek."*

911 OPERATOR: *"Okay, and what's going on there?"*

CALLER: *"My girlfriend fell off the cliff. I hiked back. And I'm in my car."*

911 OPERATOR: *"Okay. You're at the Eagle Creek Trailhead right now?"*

CALLER: *"Yeah."*

911 OPERATOR: *"Okay, and where on the trail did she fall?"*

CALLER: *"I don't know. I think about a mile up."*

911 OPERATOR: *"Okay."*

The 911 operator thought it was odd. That he was odd. Normally people calling 911 to report a traumatic event are in an agitated state with an emotional element in their speech ranging from weeping to a rapid-fire data dump to shouting or screaming. This guy might as well have been reading a manual on how to change a sparkplug.

CALLER: *"I hiked down and got her, uh, and I'm in my car now, and I don't know if I ...* (unintelligible)"

911 OPERATOR: *"Okay."*

CALLER: *"... suffering from hypothermia. I don't think it's that cold but ..."*

911 OPERATOR: *"Okay, so she fell off the trail down a cliff, and then you went down the cliff and pulled her, brought her back up onto the trail?"*

CALLER: *"No she's dead."*

There was a stunned pause as the operator absorbed his last statement; 911 callers in emergency situations tend to get to the point right away and gush with information. But this was more worried about telling her in his flat, monotone voice that he was cold than that his girlfriend had just died.

And every time the operator tried to get more details about the victim, he turned the conversation back to his needs.

CALLER: *"I went down to get her. I went to the bottom. Then in the river (unintelligible) took me about an hour to get to her. I finally go over to her, then I was startin' to shake. I got too cold, so I'm, uh, now, I just got to my car, and I need someone to come and help me ... Please send someone I'm at, uh ..."*

911 OPERATOR: *"Okay, hang on just a minute ..."*

CALLER: *"... Eagle Creek."*

911 OPERATOR: *"... one second."*

CALLER: *"Okay."*

911 OPERATOR: *"And what's, what's your name, sir?"*

CALLER: *"Steve."*

911 OPERATOR: *"Okay Steve, what is, um ..."*

CALLER: *"I'm freezing. Will you please send someone?"*

911 OPERATOR: *"Um, hang on just one second for me, okay?"*

CALLER: *"All right."*

911 OPERATOR: *"Steve, what is your last name?"*

CALLER: *"Nichols."*

911 OPERATOR: *"And what's her name, Steve?"*

CALLER: *"Rhonda."*

911 OPERATOR: *"Rhonda's last name?"*

CALLER: *"Casto."*

911 OPERATOR: *"Could you spell that for me please?"*

CALLER: *"R-H-O-N-D-A ... C-A-S-T-O."*

911 OPERATOR: *"Do you need an ambulance? Do you feel like you might need medical attention?"*

CALLER: *"I don't know if I'm shaking from, I don't know ... I'm really cold."*

911 OPERATOR: *"Okay, okay, Steve."*

CALLER: *"I'm just really cold."*

911 OPERATOR: *"Are you able to start the car and get warm?"*

CALLER: *"Yeah, the ..."*

911 OPERATOR: *"Blankets?"*

CALLER: *"... car is running."*

911 OPERATOR: *"And now Steve, I know this is a difficult question for you to answer for me, but what makes you think she was deceased?"*

CALLER: *"I don't know it for sure. I stayed with her for about an hour and a half, and I gave her mouth-to-mouth, and I tried covering up her leg. There was blood coming out of her leg, and I just sat and helped her, and then I started shaking uncontrollably, so ...* (unintelligible)*"*

911 OPERATOR: *"Okay."*

CALLER: *"Had to go back, and ..."*

911 OPERATOR: *"Was she breathing when you left her?"*

CALLER: *"No."*

911 OPERATOR: *"Do you know if she had a pulse?"*

CALLER: *"Uh, no, I don't think so."*

911 OPERATOR: *"Okay, Steve, we have an officer who's on his way."*

CALLER: *"All right. How long ... how long will it take an ambulance to get here?"*

911 OPERATOR: *"It'll take just a minute. Would you like an ambulance for you?"*

CALLER: *"Uh, uh ..."*

911 OPERATOR: *"If there's a question, I can send them, and, um, then you can decide not to go with them if that's what you choose to do."*

CALLER: *"Just so cold. That's the thing, I'm cold. ... How long will it take to the police car to get here?"*

911 OPERATOR: *"They're on their way, okay? Hang on just a second. How far down the trail, how far over the cliff is she?"*

CALLER: *"Uh, I don't know, like a hundred feet ..."*

911 OPERATOR: *"A hundred feet, okay."*

CALLER: *"I don't know."*

911 OPERATOR: *"Steve, how old are you?"*

CALLER: *"Uh, 34."*

911 OPERATOR: *"I'm going to send the ambulance for you, okay?"*

CALLER: *"All right."*

911 OPERATOR: *"Hang on just a second for me. You're going to hear some silence, okay?"*

CALLER: *"Okay."*

The caller waited patiently and quietly for the 911 operator to get back on the line. When she did, she assured him that the ambulance was on its way and she would stay on the line with him until somebody got there.

CALLER: *" 'kay."*

911 OPERATOR: *"And we have an officer on his way from Hood River."*

CALLER: *"Where's that?"*

911 OPERATOR: *"Hood River? Um, it's about twenty minutes away, but he's on his way, about seven minutes ago, okay, and we have an officer coming from Corbett. Do you know where that's at?"*

CALLER: *"No I don't."*

911 OPERATOR: *"He's a little closer so he'll be there shortly."*

CALLER: *"Okay."*

911 OPERATOR: *"So I'm going to stay on the phone with you. Are you getting any warmer in the vehicle with the heat on, Steve?"*

CALLER: *"No but I have it on full so that should heat up."*

911 OPERATOR: *"Are you in wet clothes at all?"*

CALLER: *"Tried to ... (unintelligible) ... up river. Uh, was too strong, so ..."*

911 OPERATOR: *"Are you able to get your wet clothes off and put something else warmer on?"*

CALLER: *"Yeah ... (unintelligible) ... shirt off."*

911 OPERATOR: *"You what? You have warmer clothes to put on or dry clothes at least?"*

The caller was silent.

911 CALLER: *"Steve?"*

Still no answer.

911 OPERATOR: *"... Steve? ... Steve?"*

CALLER: *"Yeah, that helps. ... How far away is he?"*

911 OPERATOR: *"He said just a few minutes."*

CALLER: *"Okay."*

911 OPERATOR: *"Are you there?"*

CALLER: *"Yeah."*

911 OPERATOR: *"Hang on just a second for me, okay?"*

There were several more pauses over the next couple of minutes as the operator checked with law enforcement and the ambulance crew. Again, the caller patiently waited for her return and would then inquire as to when someone would be there to help him. He never once said anything about his girlfriend without being asked a direct question.

CALLER: *"What time is it?"*

911 OPERATOR: *"It's 6:18. They're going to be there in a few minutes, okay?"*

CALLER: *"Okay."*

911 OPERATOR: *"So Steve, how far up the trail did you say she is?"*

CALLER: *"I don't know. I think a mile."*

911 OPERATOR: *"Okay. What was she wearing?"*

CALLER: *"Uh, jeans. ... I don't know the top. ... She put on my shirt, but I think she put one over ..."*

911 OPERATOR: *"Okay. They're on their way, okay?"*

CALLER: *"Yeah."*

911 OPERATOR: *"Hang on one second for me, Steve, okay?"*

CALLER: *"Mm hmm."*

The 911 OPERATOR spoke to one of the responding officers: *"Brandon ... (unintelligible) ... responding? I have a hypothermic guy sitting in his car."*

The 911 OPERATOR then addressed the caller. *"They're on their way, okay."*

THE CALLER: *"Uh huh."*

911 OPERATOR: *"They're on their way. They said less than five minutes, okay? He'll be there in just a couple of minutes."*

THE CALLER: *"All right."*

The operator asked a few more perfunctory questions, such as date of birth for both the caller, January 4, 1975, and his girlfriend, July 2, 1985. The operator then attempted to gather more details about the "accident."

911 OPERATOR: *"Do you know what made her fall, Steve? Did she lose her footing, or did she get hurt? ... Do you know why she fell?"*

CALLER: *"I think she's high on something."*

911 OPERATOR: *"Have you done any drugs or alcohol today?"*

CALLER: *"No."*

911 OPERATOR: *"What do you think she's high on?"*

CALLER: *"I don't know. She always hides that stuff from me."*

911 OPERATOR: *"Okay. Are you doing okay?"*

CALLER: *"Yeah, I'm warming up a little."*

911 OPERATOR: *"Oh, you're ..."*

CALLER: *"Shaking. ... I can't stop shaking."*

911 OPERATOR: *"The ambulance is on its way. It will be there in a few minutes."*

CALLER: *"Uh huh."*

Again the 911 OPERATOR broke to speak to the responding officers: *"Are you guys aware of what's going on?"* After speaking to them, she returned to the CALLER: *"Did you leave anything on the trail showing where she went down over the cliff? ... Did you leave a backpack or anything there?"*

CALLER: *"No, I left my backpack ...* (unintelligible) *... farther down, so I could go down. But then when I made my way back up, I got it. ... Only thing I left was my sweatshirt."*

911 OPERATOR: *"You left your sweatshirt there on the trail?"*

CALLER: *"No that was down by the river. ... It's close to where she is, but that's where I went in the river. ... The policeman's here."*

911 OPERATOR: *"Okay. I'll go ahead and let you go."*

CALLER: *"Okay."*

911 OPERATOR: *"Okay."*

CALLER: *"Thank you very much."*

911 OPERATOR: *"You're welcome."*

CALLER: *"Bye."*

911 OPERATOR: *"Bye bye."*

With that exchange of pleasantries, the call ended. A young mother was dead. But the important thing, at least according to the 911 call, was that her boyfriend was cold.

http://wbp.bz/savinganniea

AVAILABLE FROM HENRY J. CORDES AND WILDBLUE PRESS!

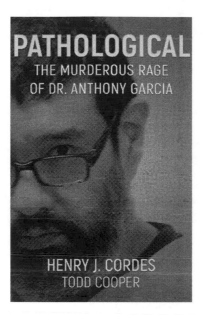

PATHOLOGICAL by HENRY J. CORDES and TODD COOPER

http://wbp.bz/pathologicala

Read A Sample Next

CHAPTER 1: 'WHAT THE HELL IS THIS?'

When police detective Derek Mois stepped over the threshold of the stately red brick home, he was immediately struck by the contrast between the everyday and the horrifying.

First to catch his eye were the cleaning supplies. A blue plastic bucket. A mop. A bright yellow bottle of Lysol. All casually set down in the middle of the entryway. And then just to the left, on the floor of an adjoining room, a waif of a boy with a knife through his neck.

It was the body of 11-year-old Tom Hunter, the gifted young son of the two doctors whose home Mois had just entered. Tom was splayed face-down on the blood-splattered dining room carpet. His spindly arms were straight as pins by his side, his bookish, wire-rimmed eyeglasses just above his head. Mois could see the knife's stainless steel handle protruding from the right side of the boy's neck, surrounded by an angry cluster of crimson stab wounds, both deep and superficial.

Mois' jaw tightened. A driven detective with short-cropped hair and sleeves of elaborate tattoos — still works in progress — going down both arms, the two-year veteran of Omaha's homicide unit had, unfortunately, seen dead kids before. And his experience confronting the handiwork of society's worst had long ago taught him to check his emotions as soon as he came through that front door.

But as a father with two young sons of his own, this sight was a punch in the gut, a memory that would never leave him. Who could do this? How cold, how callous, how depraved did someone have to be to stab a little boy until his life, future and promise drain away? This was about as ugly and evil as another human being could get.

Steeling himself, Mois walked through a set of French doors into a freshly cleaned kitchen. He right away spied on the immaculate counter a Farberware knife block, the knives' stainless steel handles matching what he'd just seen sticking from the boy's neck. Whoever killed the boy had drawn the murder weapon from right here in the kitchen.

Mois carefully stepped through the dinette, spotting Tom's shoes, backpack and hooded sweatshirt, all on the floor where he'd cast them off hours earlier. Mois heard an eerie sound coming from the basement stairwell, the theme music of the video game Tom had abandoned just before he died.

Following that sound, Mois turned the corner into a hallway and was confronted by a large pool of blood and the second body he'd been told about. This was Shirlee Sherman, the Hunter family's 57-year-old house cleaner. Mois could see Shirlee likewise had a steel kitchen knife protruding from her neck — clearly the killer's calling card.

The blue paisley scarf Sherman had donned for her cleaning that day still covered her head. As with Tom, she'd suffered numerous stab wounds, all concentrated along the right side of her neck.

Mois could already see this grim scene was an extreme departure from the gang- or drug-related shootings that were the staple of homicide work in Omaha, both the victims and perpetrators usually no strangers to law enforcement. Almost everything about these murders was different.

A grandmother and a young boy as victims.

Killed with knives left impaled in their necks.

In a gorgeous home filled with valuables — all completely undisturbed.

And perhaps most troubling, no obvious suspect or motive.

Later as Mois worked into the gray hours just before dawn documenting the crime scene, he held an aside with his sergeant, speaking just out of the earshot of the crime lab technicians working nearby.

"Holy shit," Mois told his supervisor. "What the hell is this?"

It was a question Mois would spend more than five years trying to answer.

CHAPTER 2: TOM AND SHIRLEE

It was a brilliant March 13, the radiant sunshine and balmy air a reminder that while winter on the Great Plains wasn't officially over yet, it was losing its icy grip.

A school bus lurched to a halt in front of a home on North 54th Street in Dundee, one of the most desirable streets in one of Omaha's most distinctive old neighborhoods. Tom Hunter popped up like a gopher from his seat in the very back, glided down the aisle and bounded down to the street. Dressed for the mild weather in a lightweight, striped blue hoodie, Tom walked past the last surviving patch of snow melting in the sloped front yard and entered his house around the back.

Elsewhere around Dundee, an affluent neighborhood known throughout Omaha for its old-fashioned globe-style street lights, life on this Thursday in 2008 was moving to a familiar mid-afternoon rhythm.

Dana Boyle watched Tom's 3:18 p.m. return through her living room window across the street. Five months pregnant and feeling every bit of it, she was grabbing some much-needed rest on the couch. Not for long, though, she now knew. For the sight and sound of Tom's bus served as a daily touchstone for the full-time mom, a reminder it was almost time to meet her own 7-year-old son after school.

Just down the street, Katie Swanson also prepared for her kids' imminent return from school. Deciding this would be a great day to shake off winter, she pulled out of storage her "Slow Children at Play" signs. She later placed the unofficial traffic signs down at "the Pie," a wedge-shaped, grassy median where 54th Street kids had gathered to play for generations.

This was Omaha circa 2008, a thriving Midwest metropolis of some 850,000 people that was little like anything imagined by those who saw the state of Nebraska as rural flyover country. The former cow town actually boasted the headquarters of five Fortune 500 companies — for its size, more than New York, Los Angeles or Chicago. It was probably best known, though, as home to famed investment wizard Warren Buffett, one of the wealthiest men on the planet. The Oracle of Omaha, in fact, lived in a relatively modest Dundee home just blocks from where Tom Hunter hopped off his bus.

Not far removed from his own pre-adolescent play dates at the Pie, this street and this spacious home were the only ones Tom had known in his life. Now just three months shy of his 12th birthday, Tom had grown into a bright and worldly kid who seemed destined for big things.

Tom was the youngest of four children — all boys — of Drs. William and Claire Hunter. Both parents worked as practicing and teaching physicians at Omaha's Creighton University School of Medicine. Befitting his parents' professional status, Tom enjoyed a privileged, idyllic childhood on 54th Street. Eight years younger than his next closest brother, Tom had always been a delightfully precocious child. He interacted easily with those much older, possessed a mischievous grin and always had something to say.

At nearby Dundee Elementary, Tom proved an academic prodigy, something that for his parents came to be both a blessing and curse. Tending to pick things up quickly, Tom found homework rote and boring. He put it off. He rebelled. Why should I have to do all this stuff when I already know it? The Hunters had to hound him daily, his father often sitting down with him in the living room to force him to fill out his math tables or diagram his sentences for English.

Such battles waned when Tom left local Dundee Elementary School after fourth grade and transferred to King Science and Technology Center. In that inner-city magnet school, Tom found a true home for his intellectual gifts. At King, Tom was able to indulge his fascination for all things scientific and technical. The school even had its own planetarium. Tom seemed poised to shoot for the stars himself. His teachers could easily see the well-liked kid who smiled through silver braces following his parents into medicine or some branch of the sciences.

Outside of school, Tom loved to read, getting his hands on the latest Harry Potter tome as soon as it hit the bookstore shelf and devouring it in hours. Tom even looked a bit like the young wizard Harry, with his roundish eyeglasses and mop of brown hair.

Books aside, Tom really wanted to play football, a sport his slight build — not to mention his parents — wouldn't allow him to play. Instead, he competed for years in the local YMCA basketball league. A regular ritual for father and son was a Saturday morning game at the Y followed by lunch at one of Tom's favorite fast-food restaurants. The boy enjoyed close relationships with both of his parents.

Tom also had lots of neighborhood friends, and they tended to travel in a pack. They'd play basketball in the school yard or go buy candy in Dundee's quaint old business district. He and his friends would also often beat paths to each other's homes to play video games. Favorites included various violent shoot-'em-ups and Madden football, where Tom competed as his beloved Green Bay Packers. As Tom roamed the quiet and safe streets of his neighborhood, his parents' rule was simple: Be home by 6 for dinner.

Treasured family snapshots from the time captured Tom just being Tom: intently at the controls of a video game; relishing a stimulating visit to the Smithsonian in Washington; suited up for basketball; at rest on the same couch where his dad once forced him do his math; patting the family cat outside on a brilliant day — a day much like this March day.

Now near the end of sixth grade, Tom was a latch-key kid, his parents trusting him to take care of himself in the two to three hours before they got home from Creighton. He entered the house just like the careless pre-teen he was, kicking off his black Adidas shoes and dumping his hoodie and backpack right on the floor.

This being Thursday, Tom also knew it was the one day each week he didn't arrive to a completely empty house. Thursday was cleaning day in the Hunter home, the day Shirlee Sherman came to scrub, dust and vacuum.

The 57-year-old Sherman was a resilient, no-nonsense woman who had endured some tough times — many of them traced to her unwavering willingness to put the happiness of others ahead of her own. As one of her brothers would later put it, "She got a raw deal in a lot of things in life."

The former Shirlee Waite grew up in a working-class neighborhood of Omaha with three siblings and four close cousins — all of them boys. So, during her early years, Shirlee turned her back on dolls in favor of baseball, basketball and box hockey, often besting the Waite boys in those pursuits. As the oldest, Shirlee stood up for her kin on the playground and helped care for them at home, a role that particularly grew after her parents divorced. She never argued or complained. She just did it. It was the beginning of a lifetime of Shirlee shouldering the burdens of family.

Her brothers considered Shirlee the smart one. But by the time she got to Omaha's Central High School, she didn't have much use for books. She followed a fairly traditional track at the time for a girl from a blue-collar family. Within six months of getting her diploma in 1968, she was married, and in short order she gave birth to a daughter.

Shirlee worked tending bar and at one point ran a tavern that her father owned. But that didn't last long. After her parents' divorce, the stubborn, opinionated Shirlee didn't always see eye to eye with her dad. Sherman's own marriage fell apart shortly after her second child, a son, was born in 1974. That's when she largely turned to cleaning houses. It gave the single mom the flexibility to work around her kids' schedules. And with her strong work ethic and barkeep's friendly demeanor, Sherman had no trouble landing jobs.

Many of her clients came to have ties to Creighton's medical school, her name passed around among doctors there. Sherman had come highly recommended to the Hunters and had now cleaned their home for almost two years.

By this point, Shirlee's children had grown and long since left the house. She had bad knees, a smoker's wheeze and lines in her face carved by the tough times. She'd reached a point in life when she should have been able to give more time to herself. But true to her nature, she remained the Waite family caretaker and glue, her days still revolving around the wellbeing of others.

She talked to her elderly mother every day and visited a few times a week. Often she would bring fresh-cut flowers or vegetables from the big garden she tended every summer. In fact, anyone visiting the generous Shirlee would inevitably leave with a bag of whatever was in season.

One of her greatest joys in life was spending time with her five grandchildren. Shirlee had a huge capacity for kids. Any extra money she saved would inevitably go to make sure they had what they needed.

Daughter Kelly, herself now a single mom, lived in the house right next door to Shirlee. That certainly had its benefits. Shirlee cherished her time with 6-year-old granddaughter Madison. Shirlee would often see Madison in the morning and then care for her after school until her mom got home.

But that living arrangement had also recently been a source of tension and conflict between Shirlee and her daughter. Shirlee had big problems with the latest man in

Kelly's life. For one, he was married. Most alarming to Shirlee, though, was his violent temper. Several times he'd lashed out in her daughter's home, kicking in the front door or punching a hole in the wall. Shirlee had warned Kelly, "It's going to be you next."

It was of course no surprise to Shirlee when in March 2007, the boyfriend broke Kelly's jaw in three places. Police arrested him for felony assault. But like so many women caught up in abusive relationships, Kelly refused to swear off the creep. Even after he broke her jaw, she'd try to sneak around to see him behind Shirlee's back. It drove Shirlee bat crazy. She knew men like this from her bartender days. He wouldn't change. So she vowed to do everything possible to keep them apart.

Since Shirlee held the deed to Kelly's house, she tried to legally keep the boyfriend away. She called the cops on him for property damage. She had his car towed. Though of medium build, Shirlee proved fearless as a wildcat in confronting the boyfriend. "She would literally get right in his face," Shirlee's brother, Brad Waite, would recall years later. " 'Go ahead and hit me.' "

Shirlee also told the Hunters of the abusive boyfriend, the subject coming up after she failed to show up to clean one day. "I'm going to get the SOB if it's the last thing I do," she said. The nurturing Shirlee was concerned for more than just Kelly's safety. Shirlee didn't want Madison exposed to the violence. "I need to protect my granddaughter," she'd written in a court affidavit.

As Shirlee cleaned that day in March 2008, those concerns for Madison had not diminished. In fact, it's very likely Shirlee had thoughts of Madison as she room-by-room worked her way through the Hunter house. She was due to pick her grandchild up from daycare as soon as she was done.

It's unknown whether Sherman greeted the young Tom Hunter when he came home from school that day — they typically tried to stay out of each other's way — but it seems possible she did. Because at some point, Tom went upstairs where Shirlee was cleaning to change into a favorite pair of long black basketball shorts. He left piles of clothes all over the floor as he dug the shorts from the bottom of the drawer.

Tom's parents would have preferred he at that point launch right into his homework. But as was often the case, Tom figured homework could wait. He popped open a can of Dr. Pepper, foraged a bag of SunChips from the pantry and headed to the basement to play his Xbox 360.

That's how he would spend the final carefree minutes of his life.

http://wbp.bz/pathologicala

 **WILDBLUE**
P R E S S

See even more at:
http://wbp.bz/tc

More True Crime You'll Love From WildBlue Press

 A MURDER IN MY HOMETOWN by Rebecca Morris
Nearly 50 years after the murder of seventeen year old Dick Kitchel, Rebecca Morris returned to her hometown to write about how the murder changed a town, a school, and the lives of his friends.

wbp.bz/hometowna

 **THE BEAST I LOVED** by Robert Davidson
Robert Davidson again demonstrates that he is a master of psychological horror in this riveting and hypnotic story ... I was so enthralled that I finished the book in a single sitting. "—James Byron Huggins, International Bestselling Author of The Reckoning

wbp.bz/tbila

 **BULLIED TO DEATH** by Judith A. Yates
On September 5, 2015, in a public park in LaVergne, Tennessee, fourteen-year-old Sherokee Harriman drove a kitchen knife into her stomach as other teens watched in horror. Despite attempts to save her, the girl died, and the coroner ruled it a "suicide." But was it? Or was it a crime perpetuated by other teens who had bullied her?

wbp.bz/btda

 **SUMMARY EXECUTION** by Michael Withey
"An incredible true story that reads like an international crime thriller peopled with assassins, political activists, shady FBI informants, murdered witnesses, a tenacious attorney, and a murderous foreign dictator."—Steve Jackson, New York Times bestselling author of NO STONE UNTURNED

wbp.bz/sea